Annapurna Devi

Annapurna Devi

The Untold Story
of a Reclusive Genius

ATUL MERCHANT JATAAYU

Foreword by
PT HARIPRASAD CHAURASIA

EBURY
PRESS

An imprint of Penguin Random House

EBURY PRESS

USA | Canada | UK | Ireland | Australia
New Zealand | India | South Africa | China | Singapore

Ebury Press is part of the Penguin Random House group of companies
whose addresses can be found at global.penguinrandomhouse.com

Published by Penguin Random House India Pvt. Ltd
4th Floor, Capital Tower 1, MG Road,
Gurugram 122 002, Haryana, India

Penguin
Random House
India

First published in Ebury Press by Penguin Random House India 2021

10 9 8 7 6 5 4 3

The views and opinions expressed in this book are the author's own and the facts
are as reported by him which have been verified to the extent possible, and the
publishers are not in any way liable for the same.

ISBN 9780670095339

Typeset in Minion Pro by Manipal Technologies Limited, Manipal
Printed at Replika Press Pvt. Ltd, India

www.penguin.co.in

This is a legitimate digitally printed version of the book and therefore might not
have certain extra finishing on the cover.

To
Shārdā Ma, the goddess of wisdom, learning, art and music,
Her prodigious son, Baba Allauddin Khansaheb, and
his daughter and our revered Guru Ma, Annapurna Devi

सर्वेषां वेदानाम रसों यत्साम
—शतपथ (शुक्ल यजुर्वेद)

'Music has the essence of all Vedas'
—*Shatpath (Shukla Yajurveda)*

Contents

Foreword

My first reaction when asked to write the foreword for a book on Guru Ma was: What would be a novel thing to say about an illuminated soul that has not already been said? Whatever one said would only come across as basking in one's own futility. Those of us who have experienced Guru Ma Annapurna Devi's spirit and soul in the time she gave us in our lives would have to take a deep breath and compose their thoughts meticulously in order to describe the layers of a complex phenomenon such as her.

I laud the efforts and rigour of the author, Shri Atul Merchant, and his 'gurubhais' to lace together such a well-researched series of chapters that evoke raw emotion, narrate unheard facets of her life, and throw light on the spiritual side of a decorated soul.

Maa was not just a mother, but a supreme mother, and an embodiment of knowledge, compassion and abundance. In Hindu mythology, Annapurna is the goddess of food and nourishment, and to a lot of struggling souls like me, she provided nourishment for the body and soul. She was the mother I never had. She gave me unconditional care and love in return for my sincerity and dedication to art. Just like the Annapurna massif in the Himalayas, the journey to seek my guru was steep and arduous, almost three years of my life, to convince her that I was worthy of being her student. My first step of initiation with my guru was to undo everything I had known and done until that point in time. It was to break my ego and surrender myself completely to an illuminated master.

People might wonder why a *bansuri* player would go to a *surbahār* player for training. I learnt the tenets of music from her; the instrument was just a medium. I met her at a time when I was already a successful professional musician, running from one music studio to another, often clocking twenty hours of work daily and earning a handsome amount, fulfilling the ambition that my wife, Anuradha, and I had of leading a good life in Mumbai. Yet, there was a void within that required a guiding light. I needed a guru to emancipate my soul, to give wings to my music, to calm me down and make me look deeper into my music.

Maa devoted herself exclusively to teaching, and excelled especially in the knowledge of raga, in the development of the prelude, in the repertoire of old compositions and mastery of certain improvisation techniques. She would say, 'Improvise the *ālaap* as long as you like without any repetition and make it so beautiful, enchanting, musical that it touches your soul, not just your body.'

I learnt from her about the 'Dhrupad' style of rendition, the 'Khayāl', 'Alankaar', 'Thumri', 'Chaiti', 'Kajri', etc.—all signature styles of the Seniya–Maihar Gharana, I began the art of experimentation, which this gharana encourages openly, to play 'jod' and 'jhala' on a wind instrument even though these techniques are traditionally associated with string instruments. Guru Ma taught me to make my music richer and fuller, allowing me to expand my repertoire on the bansuri. This great initiation into the world of music seems like such a plunge into a deep, unfathomable ocean.

Instead of a certificate she gave me her blessings to go out and show the world what it means to be made of sterner stuff, which I try to do till this day.

'The heights by great men reached and kept
were not attained by sudden flight;
they while their companions slept,
were toiling upward in the night.'

Poet Henry Wadsworth Longfellow must have had the likes of Guru Ma in his sights when he penned the above lines.[1]

Maa has taught me everything I know, nurtured me with selfless care and affection, without expecting anything in return except hard work, to be the best I could be. No one can do more, and no one can ask for more. I certainly blossomed under her tutelage, a fact that I never forget to teach my students as well.

I want to follow in the footsteps of my Guru Ma and give back to future generations of aspiring musicians and bansuri players what Guru Ma has given me. The idea of starting a gurukul (the guru's family) along the lines of our age-old gurukul system of education took root in my mind after I saw what Baba and Maa had created in Maihar, and when I leave this place, the legacy of my guru will remain.

This book gives us a glimpse of a part of her which none of us will ever decipher and be able to resolve. Some riddles stay unsolved, and that is why they remain an enigma. Through this book, certain aspects of her life have been revealed, but only to create more questions, and more riddles about her. For me, it is a sincere attempt to unravel the mystique of a great spiritual and musical genius that touches human lives once in several centuries.

Musically yours,
Hariprasad Chaurasia

Preface

Except for a brief few years after the birth of her son Shubho, Guru Ma (Annapurna Devi) spent her life as a recluse, confined within the four walls of her home. Until the age of sixteen, she was confined to Madina Bhavan, the family home at Maihar. During that time, she devoted herself exclusively to the deepest study and practice of Indian classical music, under the strict tutelage of her father, Baba Allauddin Khan. She rarely ventured outdoors.

By nature, Guru Ma was an extremely introverted person. Since the year of her estrangement from Panditji (Pt Ravi Shankar)—that is, from 1956 onwards—Guru Ma went ever deeper into self-imposed seclusion. Even while she was with Panditji in Mumbai and Delhi, she hardly left her house or socialized or interacted with others. Obviously, the life of a recluse like her is bound to be shrouded in mystery. Even for us, her disciples, she always remained an enigma, an unsolved riddle.

It was a ritual for us, the disciples of Annapurna Devi, to gather every Saturday evening at her residence in Akashganga building (Akashganga is the Indian name for the Milky Way galaxy). We did this to be in her proximity and to experience her effortless grace. In Hindu mythology, Annapurna Devi is the goddess of food and nutrition. True to that name, Guru Ma had excellent culinary skills, and on Saturday evenings we would feast on her cooking. The other agendas of our gathering were to create a laughter riot, and listen to Ma's (Annapurna Devi) captivating stories and discover a thing or two about her, Baba (Acharya Allauddin Khan), Pannalal Ghosh, Ali Akbar Khansaheb, Ravi Shankar, Nikhil Banerjee, Timirbaran, Bahadur Khan, Aashish Khan, Sharan Rani, Hariprasad Chaurasia, etc. These stories and anecdotes were so fascinating, enlightening and precious for us that we decided to write them down. As the proverb says: 'The faintest ink is better than the sharpest memory.'

The writing of this book started as what we used to call 'The Saturday Diary'. Our original thought was to create a written record to assist future generations in solving the 'Socratic Problem'. There are already too many bizarre stories about Annapurna Devi in print. For instance, one journalist published in his article that Annapurna Devi and Ravi Shankar were both dancers who met at a discotheque in Paris and fell in love. When we read this out to Ma, she laughed, stating she had never been outside India and had never danced in her entire life. Another journalist wrote that when Shubho was on his deathbed, Annapurna Devi rushed to the USA with her surbahār and tried healing Shubhoda with her music. Many tablā players have claimed that they heard Ma's playing when they visited her home to accompany her in *riyaaz*. Ma asserted that no tablā player ever accompanied her while she played the surbahār. In her childhood, while learning the sitār, either Baba or her brother (the revered Ali Akbar Khansaheb) would accompany her, but never anyone outside the immediate family. There are many such imaginary stories in circulation; we are therefore compelled to put Ma's version in print.

For us, this exercise proved to be like solving a giant jigsaw puzzle, gathering random pieces over weeks and months, hoping to create a larger picture. Numerous valuable pieces may have been lost forever due to our inertia and indolence.

Obviously, there can't be 100 per cent congruence in the way each of us are able to remember the finer details of what Ma spoke, what Ali Akbar Khansaheb told us during his brief visits here, what Aashish Khan (the eldest son of Ut. Ali Akbar Khansaheb) narrated about his childhood under Baba's harsh regime, and whatever little Dhyanesh Khan (the second son of Ut. Ali Akbar Khansaheb) shared with us.

While we were with Ma, there was no audio-recording or taking notes of what she spoke. This work is our collective effort in trying to reproduce the way we are able to recall things now. Though Ma was extremely kind and affectionate towards us all, each of us had a unique equation with her.

What was remarkable about my equation with her was that unlike the others, I had been granted a licence to speak freely and candidly to express my observations, the way a court jester was allowed by the monarchs during the medieval and Renaissance eras. My equation with Ma was in sharp contrast to most of the disciples, who either remained silent in front of her or spoke what they presumed would please her.

Among the disciples of Annapurna Devi, Prof. Rooshikumar Pandya, the most learned of us, had gathered a lot of information about Ma's life. With his linguistic prowess, he was the most capable for authoring this account. However, his sudden demise was so traumatic that none of us could contemplate resuming this project for an extended period. With his eloquence, Smarth Bali seemed the next logical choice for this undertaking, but he migrated to Chandigarh and got too busy with his profession. The project was shelved for a few years. Suresh Vyas has inherited linguistic and communication skills from his father, Shri Madanlal Vyas. Suresh is the most articulate of us, and can comfortably speak multiple languages, and therefore was the obvious choice. However, for reasons beyond my logic, he refused to write this book. Fortunately, he has been guiding me with the factuals in this endeavour.

After Guru Ma's demise, we, her disciples, have been receiving numerous requests from around the world to write about her. The task required a high degree of madness and a ridiculously high investment of time and effort. Yours truly, being the most dispensable, took the onus to assemble the abundance of stories, anecdotes and parables that each one of us could remember, and compiled it in the format of a book, albeit with the permission of Nityanand Haldipur, who is presently at the helm of the Annapurna Devi foundation.

Writing about music would have been a pointless exercise, and an absurdity in itself. This book is an attempt to present an insight into the personalities of some of the greatest musicians our century has seen. This is our humble attempt to share with you what for us, as Guru Ma's disciples, have been transforming experiences—our interactions with Guru Ma Annapurna Devi, her teachings and messages.

दिल से जो बात निकलती है असर रखती है
पर नहीं ताक़त-ए-परवाज़ मगर रखती है

[*The words springing from the heart surely carry weight,*
Though not endowed with wings, they are able to scale heights]
—*Allama Iqbal*[2]

As a disclaimer about the linguistic drawback of this book, kindly note that the author had been dyslexic as a child. As I reached adulthood, the dyslexia receded. However, despite my best intentions and most serious attempts, I am not eligible enough to write a book of such great import. Another challenge for us has been that Ma spoke to us in Hindi. Ma's preferred language was Bengali, but in Mumbai, there were hardly a couple of us who knew the language. Ma, in fact, knew English as well. We were pleasantly shocked when we heard her speak in fluent English with some foreign pupils like Peter, James, etc.

When we asked Ma from where she learnt English, she said she owed it to a childhood gift of P.G. Wodehouse books. As we probed further, we discovered that in order to help Shubho in his studies, she would read all his school books. Gradually, she developed a liking for reading, and during Panditji's IPTA (Indian People's Theatre Association—a cultural wing of the Communist Party of India) days, Ma had read Tolstoy's *War and Peace*. None of us, not even Prof. Pandya, had attempted to read something as intimidating as *War and Peace*, which is a veritable tome, with 580 unique characters. Before discovering this, we were in the habit of speaking in English the phrases we wanted to filter out from Ma's very sensitive audio radar. On that day, each of us felt like it was the day of judgement as we recounted the sinful words we had spoken in English thinking that Ma wouldn't understand.

Another challenge was that Ma had a habit of speaking terse, aphoristic words like a Zen master. It was not easy to fully comprehend what she really meant as her words could be subjectively interpreted by each listener. Translating from an Indian language to English can be very tricky, since the essence is often lost in the process. Nonetheless, we have made our sincerest attempt of translating what we could best interpret of Ma's dialogues with us.

We were depending heavily on stalwarts like Aashish Khan and Hariprasad Chaurasia, but they narrated the same incidents a bit differently each time. So, we had to either let go or stick to the crux of the story and choose the version which sounded most logical. The greatest help came from what is recorded by Pt Jotin Bhattacharya in his books on Baba. Nobody else has written as extensively, in such detail, about Baba, simply because no other well-educated person was in such close proximity and intimacy with Baba as Jotinda was.

As we compiled the segments, we realized to our dismay that there were too many grey areas, and most of them pertained to the calendar. For instance, there was a big controversy about Baba's birth year, with at least three to four assumed years of his birth spanning from 1861 to 1881. It is impossible for any child to remember the time and date of his birth unless told by his parents. Baba related his age by an event he remembered as per the Bangla calendar. When asked about his age, Baba used to say, 'There were incessant rains in Cumilla in the Bangla year 1293. I was six at that time. Now do the math and figure it out yourself.'

The zero year in the Bangladeshi calendar era is April 593 CE. Therefore, the year 1293 of the Bangla calendar was 1886 CE. It is extremely difficult to relate it to the event of floods, as East Bengal has a long history of destructive floods. In the nineteenth century, six major floods were recorded in 1842, 1858, 1871, 1875, 1885 and 1892. Therefore, the closest event of a major flood as described by Baba was in the year 1885. According to this theory, it could be concluded that Baba was born in the year 1879 or 1880. Again, the problem is Baba didn't say 'floods', he said 'incessant rains'. Well, regardless of the calendar, Baba's achievements remain monumental.

There is also speculation about the birth years of Madina Begum (Baba's wife), Zubeida Begum and Guru Ma. Some say Ma was born in 1927, some say 1926, and some say 1925. However, we, the disciples of Annapurna Devi, are unanimous that she was born on the full moon day of the Indian festival Chaiti Purnima in 1926, which fell on 27 April that year.

Therefore, our collective decision is to refrain from including any incident or anecdote where we are not confident of the authenticity. As a result, many dramatic incidences, juicy stories and anecdotes have been left out. However, whatever we have heard from Ma herself, in person, is the truth for us.

Readers will find an excessive mention of Baba Allauddin Khan in this book. Just like it is not possible to understand Beethoven without understanding Mozart, and it is not possible to understand Mozart without understanding Bach, it is impossible to understand Annapurna Devi, Ali Akbar Khansaheb, Ravi Shankar,

Nikhil Banerjee, Pannalal Ghosh, etc., without understanding their guru, Baba Allauddin Khan.

The story of Baba and his disciples (in this case, Annapurna Devi in the thematic centre) spans over 140 years (1879 to 2018). There are numerous characters in these stories about whom we have heard primarily from Ma, Jotin Bhattacharya, Ali Akbar Khansaheb, Hariprasad Chaurasia and Aashish Khan. None except Aashishda and Hariji are alive today to endorse what we have written in this book. Even we, the gurubhais who have heard the anecdotes at the same time and place from the same person, were not unanimous on each and every point written in this book. Every story has a *Rashomon* effect. Obviously, there are bound to be several angles and several versions of what we have heard and what we have written. What we have written is what we think is true without entering into any form of debate or challenge with anyone.

Prologue

In August 1982, I was attending Parvez Mistry's karate camp at Khandala. I deliberately chose to be in the team that had Dr Neville Bengali, the magnet therapist, in it. Since neither of us had much interest in the fun and frolic around the bonfire, I requested Dr Bengali to educate me about magnet therapy. Soon, the discussion digressed to parapsychology, and subsequently to telepathy, telekinesis and hypnotism.

In those days, hypnotherapy was a new fad for enhancing performance in sports. The Soviet Olympic team, a number of famous boxers, and some cricketers like Vivian Richards were reported to have benefited from hypnotherapists. Dr Bengali recommended that I attend hypnotherapy training seminars held by the Canadian visiting professor Rooshikumar Pandya under the banner of the Indo-American Society. However, I had to wait until the month of December of that year as Prof. Pandya visited India only during the winter months. He was professor of behavioural science at St Abbots College in Montreal, Canada. Thanks to Werner Erhard, seminar training had become a new fad in India.

On Saturday, 11 December 1982, just a few days after my twenty-fourth birthday, I attended Prof. Pandya's two-day seminar at the Oberoi Towers hotel at Nariman Point. I was so intrigued by the subject of behavioural science that I became his committed pupil. That was the time when Rooshiji had announced that he had migrated back to India for good and was going to devote the rest of his life learning the sitār. When I asked, 'From whom are you going to learn the sitār?' he said, 'From my wife.' He didn't tell me the name of his wife and I didn't bother to ask.

While having lunch, I noticed that a meendhal—a dried fruit—was tied to Prof. Pandya's wrist. As per the Hindu marriage ritual, the meendhal is tied on the wrists of the bride and the groom.

'Is this a meendhal?' I asked.

'That's right,' he replied with a smile. 'I got married yesterday.'

Prof. Pandya was in his mid-forties at that point in time. I found it a little strange that a newly married man in his mid-forties was holding a seminar the day after his wedding instead of going for his honeymoon.

After the seminar, I went along with him to his place to borrow some books that he had recommended me to read. That was my first visit to 6A Akashganga. The house was in a run-down condition. The walls seemed as if they had not been painted for decades. They were also spattered with carbon monoxide stains, as if the house had had a fire.

I was chatting with Prof. Pandya in his room when the doorbell rang. A gentleman and his son had come to meet him. It wasn't difficult to guess that the son was intellectually disabled.

Rooshiji requested me to wait in the living room until they left. As soon as I went into the living room, a middle-aged woman with a broom and dustpan came in and started sweeping the floor. The only thing remarkable about her was her exceptionally high focus on doing something as mundane as sweeping the floor.

She was wearing a Bengali-style cotton saree that had lost its sheen from overuse, and which she had not bothered to iron. She wore it an inch or two a bit too high above her ankle. Her hair was tied behind her head in a bun. She was wearing no make-up whatsoever, nor was there a single piece of jewellery on her.

She approached the corner I was standing at, and without eye contact politely requested me in a very soft voice, 'आप ज़रा उस तरफ़ चले जाईए ना [Could you please move to that side.]'

The quality of her voice amazed me. Thanks to my maternal cousins living in the Prabhu Kunj building at Peddar Road, as a child, I had become friendly with Asha Bhosle's son, Anand Bhosle. I often visited their house, with Lata Mangeshkar and Usha Mangeshkar living in the adjoining flat. This woman's voice had a striking resemblance to the voice of Lataji and Ushaji, whom I had heard conversing. Most singers speak steadily in a consistent pitch (frequency), and their intonation too sounds remarkably rhythmic.

After she was done sweeping, she returned with a bucket of water and started mopping the floor. When she came to the corner where I was standing, she again said, 'आप वापिस उस तरफ़ चले जाईए ना [Could you please again move back to that side?]' Once again, the quality of her voice fascinated me.

Done with the sweeping and mopping, she went near the northern balcony and opened two gunny sacks, one filled with millet and the other with wheat. With the help of an aluminium vessel, she kept pouring ridiculously large quantities of grains to feed the pigeons. In no time at all, the balcony was filled with about a hundred pigeons dashing towards the feast.

Remarkably, during this entire time, the woman didn't once make eye contact with me. The moment the patient left, I heard Rooshiji calling me back to his room.

'You know,' I said. 'Your maidservant has an amazing voice quality.'

'Maidservant?' Rooshiji was surprised. 'I have no maidservant.'

'Arrey!' I said, 'The one who was sweeping and mopping your living room a few minutes ago.'

With a surprised look, he asked, 'Did you talk to her?'

'No, I didn't talk to her, but twice she asked me to shift from one spot to another, I heard her amazing voice that resembles Lata and Usha Mangeshkar. Ashaji has a little more bass in her voice. If this woman was trained in music, she would have been a star playback singer.'

'How do you know she didn't get music training?'

'Rooshiji! If it were so, instead of her sweeping and mopping your house, you and I would be sweeping and mopping her house.'

Rooshiji kept staring at me in amazement.

'Can you come here tomorrow after 4.30 p.m.?'

'For what?'

'A sarodist named Basant Kabra is coming to learn.'

'From whom?'

'Annapurna Devi.'

'Which Annapurna Devi? Hariprasad Chaurasia's guru? Ali Akbar Khansaheb's sister? Ravi Shankar's wife?'

'Yes, the same. What do you know about her?'

'What an irony!' I exclaimed. 'In December 1978, my father was making a documentary film for the Chinmaya Mission. The background music was being recorded at the Western Outdoor Studio. Zarine Daruwala was playing the sarod and Hariprasad Chaurasia the bansuri. I went to Zarineji and pleaded with her to teach me the sarod, but she said she was too busy with recordings and had no time. I was rather disappointed. Hariji, who was overhearing the conversation, said, "Young man, don't be disheartened. I'll request my Guru Ma to teach you. She won't refuse."

'As I was leaving the recording room, Zarineji said, "Remember, listen only to Ali Akbar Khansaheb and no one else, not even me. Just by listening to him you'll learn the *swars*."

'I came out and asked the music director Jayesh Gujarati, "Who is Hariprasad Chaurasia's Guru Ma?"

'"Annapurna Devi," replied Jayesh Gujarati.

'"Who is Annapurna Devi?" I asked in bewilderment.

'"Haven't you seen the film *Abhimaan*? It was based on Annapurna Devi's story."

'A week after this conversation, calamity struck my family. My father died a sudden mysterious death and the surviving partner inherited the firm with no share for us. Learning music was too luxurious a proposition.'

Rooshiji kept listening to me with rapt attention, but he didn't react.

The next day, I left my business early and reached Akashganga at about 5 p.m. Rooshiji opened the door. The house was filled with the sound of the sarod. Though an amateur, I was not uninitiated in classical music. I vividly remember that Raag Bihāg was being played. When I walked down the passage and reached the living room, I was shocked to see the same lady I had thought to be a maidservant was teaching Basant Kabra. I ran back to Rooshiji, who was right behind me. Rooshiji laughed and said, 'Yes, she is Annapurna Devi.'

When there was a pause in the lesson, I paid my obeisance by touching her feet. Rooshiji introduced me by saying, 'He is the one who thought you were the maidservant.' She recognized me and laughed. It was the same priceless childlike laughter which I would see on her face for the next many years to come. Obviously, Rooshiji had told her about my foolishness in mistaking her for a maidservant, which made me feel like jumping out of the window, although it made no difference to her whether I called her a maidservant or the numero uno of Indian classical music.

As Ma got up from her seat and went to the kitchen, she told Basant Kabra, 'इतना ठीक से बजाओ फिर मैं आगे सिखाऊँगी [Get this right, then I'll teach you more.]'

Basant kept playing that long and complicated piece repeatedly while Ma was busy cooking. The kitchen was quite noisy with a pressure cooker whistling away and the sputtering sound of Ma's pan-frying. Despite the noise, Ma suddenly came rushing out of the kitchen and yelled at Basant: 'निषाद का तरब का तार उतर गया है, सुनाई नहीं पड़ता? [Can't you hear that the *tarab* (sympathetic) string of *nishad* (the leading note B) is out of pitch?]'

Basant immediately checked the nishad tarab. Needless to mention, it was indeed out of tune.

Untrained though I was, I had learnt elementary sarod and was well aware of the fact that tarab—sympathetic strings—are not actively played but resonate in response to the notes played on the main strings. How on earth could Ma, standing in the noisy kitchen, about 30 feet away from Basant Kabra's sarod, perceive that the tarab string was out of tune? This was surely a case of ultrasensitive auditory perception.

On a later date, when I told Ma that it was very kind of her to forgive me for calling her a maidservant on my first visit, Ma narrated an anecdote:

'Baba loved gardening. Once, while he was at it, a suited-booted man came to meet him and mistook him to be the gardener. "Is Allauddin Khan home?" he asked in an arrogant tone. Baba nodded in affirmation. The man gave his visiting card to Baba and said, "Go and tell your master that I have come to meet him." As Baba kept staring at him, the visitor said, "Hurry up, I don't have time." Baba ushered him into the living room. Baba then went in, washed his hands and feet, came out and greeted the guest with folded hands, saying, "This *naacheez* [cipher] is called Allauddin. Tell me, what can I do for you?"'

We were subsequently told that the visitor was a prince of an annexed kingdom in the southern part of the country, and he had come to Baba to be his disciple and learn music. Baba politely refused him saying, 'Those who don't have time, can't learn music.'

Later on, we learnt from Ali Akbar Khansaheb that Baba was training Ma to be a singer. However, Ma developed severe tonsillitis and had to get her tonsils surgically removed. The doctors advised Baba not to make her sing for some time. Baba didn't clarify the duration of the term 'some time'. Someone had told Baba that Ma's voice would be spoilt after surgery and she wouldn't be able to sing. Baba therefore got a small-sized sitār from Lucknow and started teaching Ma on it. Her extraordinary dexterity pleasantly surprised Baba. With time, Ma kept gaining proficiency in the sitār. Baba, incidentally, was also surprised to realize that Ma's voice was not affected and it was as good as it was before surgery. The dilemma now was whether Ma should continue learning the sitār or resume singing. Baba decided to continue with the sitār.

Throughout her life, Guru Ma dressed and groomed in this way.

Flashback

In 1934, Uday Shankar was planning a tour of eighty-four cities in Europe and America with his ballet troupe. Timirbaran, who had been in charge of the music, expressed his inability to join them on this tour as he had signed a contract with New Theatres that made him music director for the film *Devdas*, starring K.L. Saigal.

'Could you suggest a suitable substitute for you?' a worried Uday Shankar asked.

'I can't think of anyone who could substitute me in Indian orchestral music,' replied Timir. 'But I know someone who is far superior to me. That is my guru, Baba Allauddin Khan.'

'I have heard of the great ustad, but tell me more,' Uday Shankar asked curiously.

'Baba is a disciple of Ut. Wazir Khan, one of the last direct descendants of the legendary Mian Tansen. Baba is not only a maestro of Indian music, but he is highly proficient in Western music as well, having learnt Western classical violin and Western staff notations from Robert Lobo, a band conductor from Goa, the seat of Western music in India. Baba can play more than thirty musical instruments.'

'Sounds too good to be true. Will he agree to join our troupe?' Uday Shankar eagerly asked.

'It may be difficult to convince him, but if he does join you, your orchestra will be unmatched.'

'Where is he now?'

'Presently, he is the court musician of Maihar, a princely state in the Bundelkhand Agency.'

'How can we persuade him to join us on this tour?'

'The easiest path would be to convince HH Brijnathsingh, the maharaja of Maihar, who is also Baba's disciple.'

Shortly after securing an appointment with Maharaja Brijnathsingh, Uday Shankar arrived at the ornate palace.

'*Saadar pranam* to Maharaj.'

'Welcome, Udayji, my Gurubhai Timirbaran has told me many good things about your acclaimed ballets. Your adaptation of European theatrical techniques to Indian dance is pathbreaking. You are a true ambassador of the Indian culture.'

'With your blessings, the going has been good so far.'

'Tell me, what brings you to Maihar?'

'Maharaj! We have planned a performance tour of eighty-four cities in Europe and America. I am seeking your help for the finest music for my ballets.'

'And how may I be of help to you?'

'Actually, I have come to seek your permission to borrow your court musician and guru, Acharya Allauddin Khan. If he takes charge of the music, our performances can scale trailblazing heights.'

'Oh! Then let me contribute my bit to your noble cause. I grant you permission to take Acharyaji with you to America.'

'I am truly honoured and grateful to Your Highness; my further plea is if Your Highness could be troubled to convey this idea to Acharyaji, he won't refuse.'

'Ha, ha! Very smart indeed, but please realize that he is my guru. I can only request him. It is up to him to accept or reject your proposal. Take this note imprinted with the royal seal, addressed to guruji. My car will take you to his house.'

Uday Shankar and Timirbaran arrived at Baba's house.

'I guess we will have to wait for an hour or two,' Timirbaran told Uday Shankar. 'This is the time for Baba's daily visit to Shārdā Ma's temple.'

'Why would a Muslim go to Shārdā Ma's temple?'

'He is as Muslim or Hindu as Saint Kabir was. His ancestors were Bengali Brahmins with their surname as Devsharman. In the Battle of Plassey, they fought on the side of Nawab Siraj-ud-Daulah against the British. Betrayed by Mir Jafar, the then commander of the Nawab's army, Siraj-ud-Daulah lost the battle on 23 June 1757. Baba's ancestors then joined Bhavani Pathak, the Robin Hood of Bengal, who was the leader of the Sanyasi Movement in Bengal. Bhavani Pathak along with Devi Chowdhurani had a large following in the downtrodden society. In 1787, Bhavani Pathak was killed in a skirmish with the Company's troops. Baba's ancestors had to flee and seek asylum in a native kingdom ruled by another nawab, who had a precondition that all the asylum seekers should convert to Islam. Baba's ancestors converted to Islam, but behind closed doors, they continued practising Hinduism. They eventually settled in Shivpur.'

'Does he visit the Shārdā Ma temple for two hours?'

'Yes, Maihar boasts of the world's only Goddess Shārdā temple. It is on top of Trikut hill. Every day, come rain or shine, Baba climbs 1063 steps, scaling the height of 600 feet, to pay his obeisance to Shārdā Ma. In the evenings, Baba visits the local mosque to offer namaaz.'

'But tell me, how do they allow a Muslim to enter the temple and perform pooja?'

'There is a dramatic story behind it.'

'Please tell me, we have enough time.'

'Baba was in Rampur under the tutelage of Ut. Wazir Khan. A time came when Wazir Khansaheb concluded his training, saying there was nothing more left with him to teach Baba. He advised Baba to become a court musician of a rich princely state. For a musician of Baba's calibre, there were numerous options available. However, when the name of Maihar came up, the only question Baba asked was, 'Maihar? The same place which has the famous Shārdā Ma temple?' When the answer was yes, Baba instantly opted for it, without caring that most of the other available options were states far richer than Maihar.'

'He must be either a simpleton or a saint to ignore the monetary considerations.'

'I guess he is both,' Timirbaran said with a smile. 'After arriving at Maihar, Baba's first agenda was to visit Shārdā Ma's temple. However, the priest in charge disallowed Baba from entering the temple. Baba paid his obeisance to Shārdā Ma without entering the temple and went away.

'The next day, the priest came to the maharaja's palace and said, 'Maharaj, yesterday, your newly appointed Muslim musician tried to enter the temple. As per our tradition, I disallowed him to enter. However, Shārdā Ma came in my dreams last night and scolded me for driving away Her *param bhakt* [supreme devotee].'

'Thenceforth, with the consent of His Highness, not only was Baba allowed to enter the temple, but he was also allowed to enter the *garbhagriha* [sanctum sanctorum] to perform pooja. Thus, it became Baba's daily ritual.'

Uday Shankar and Timirbaran reached Baba's home, and as they waited in the living room, they heard the sound of the sitār from the adjoining room.

'Beautiful! Who is playing?'

'Baba's eight-year-old daughter, Annapurna.'

'Unbelievable! How can such a young child play so well?'

Uday Shankar peeped through the door ajar, and indeed, a small girl was practising the sitār inside the room.

'Well,' Timirbaran said with a smile. 'She has truly inherited Baba's genes.'

'How did HH Brijnathsinghji become Baba's disciple?'

'HH Brijnathsingh was looking for someone who could play each instrument of his extensive collection. It was Jagatkishorji, zamindar of Muktagachha, who recommended Baba to Brijnathsinghji as Baba had a proficiency in playing more than thirty musical instruments. When Baba Allauddin Khan first arrived at the Maihar palace in 1918, he was escorted to the room containing all these instruments. The minister asked Baba to play as many of them as he could. One by one, Baba played them all. From the adjoining room, Brijnathsinghji was listening attentively. Impressed by his talent, Brijnathsinghji invited Baba to perform at the royal court the next evening.

'The court was filled with an audience when Baba started playing the ālaap of Raag Shree. Within about five minutes, HH Brijnathsinghji got up from his throne and walked away hurriedly. All including Baba were in shock. Despite the insult, Baba continued playing.

'When Baba concluded his rendition, HH Brijnathsinghji returned to the court with the paraphernalia of a pooja ritual, and pleaded with Baba to accept him as his disciple. Baba in his terse manner said, "In the middle of the rendition you walked away showing utter disrespect for music. How can I accept you as my disciple?"

'Brijnathsinghji, with folded hands, said, "I beg your pardon for my action. Within the first few minutes of your rendition, I became so emotional my tears betrayed me. No king sheds tears in front of his subjects; therefore, I had to walk away."

Baba Allauddin Khan.

Baba in the centre. Some say the two girls are
Annapurna Devi and her elder sister Jahanara.
The person sitting on the left of Baba is the
binkar Birendra Kishore Roy Chowdhury.

'I Don't Teach Sissified Dandies'

Ut. Allauddin Khan took charge of Uday Shankar's orchestra, and the music became a sensation. Between dance performances, when the curtains fell for a change of set and for dancers to change costumes, Baba filled the time with his solo sarod renditions, as well as his brief renditions of other instruments. These solos transfixed Western audiences, and Baba's playing soon became a bigger attraction to the audience than the dance performances.

From Baba's letters to his younger brother Aayatali Khan, and a few others, we get to know many details about Baba's tour with Uday Shankar's troupe. Baba was fascinated with European and Middle Eastern music and wrote some notations too in his letters to his nephew Mubarak. In these letters, he also mentioned the troupe's visits to Egypt, Jerusalem, Palestine (Israel was founded on 14 May 1948 and before that it was called Palestine), Greece, Austria, Switzerland, Budapest, Vienna, Prague, Germany, Paris and London. In his letters, Baba lamented about the food problems he faced as he didn't eat beef or pork. Baba began losing weight and became so weak that Uday Shankar thought about sending him back to India. However, it was a risk to send Baba all alone on such a long journey back. At Uday Shankar's insistence, Baba remained with them for the entire tour. In his letters, Baba wrote

Uday Shankar and Amala Shankar.

that during the tour his diet was limited to milk, bread, fruits and boiled vegetables. His earnings on the trip were all exhausted in his lodging and boarding expenses. The net savings from such a long and arduous tour finally amounted to zero. This was true for the other artists as well, including Uday Shankar. Therefore, financially, the tour was an ill-conceived venture.

Baba's letters speak of the music he listened to while on tour. Be it Egypt, Palestine or Jerusalem, he saw music and dance everywhere. Baba wrote, 'I had heard from our maulvis that music is forbidden in the Arab world but it is wrong. Muslims and non-Muslims all sing and play music. Baba said he heard wonderful music performed both by men and women even at the Bait al-Maqdis (House of the Holiness) Mosque, Jerusalem.

Readers ought to be reminded that Baba suffered the worst trauma of his life when his elder daughter Jahanara (married to a Muslim family from East Bengal), faced severe hostility from her in-laws. The conservative Muslim in-laws had forbidden her from practising music. However, because Jahanara was very fond of music and had learnt Dhrupad singing from Baba, she would do her *riyaaz* when she was alone at home.

One day, her mother-in-law, upon returning home, heard Jahanara's singing. What made things worse was that Jahanara was singing a Dhrupad composition of *Shiv Stuti*. All hell broke loose for Jahanara. Her tanpurā was burnt, she was declared a *kafir*, and she was forcibly made to eat beef to prove her fidelity to Islam. When Jahanara refused to eat beef, she was beaten up. Jahanara was pregnant at that time, and the beating caused a miscarriage. She was sent back to Maihar in poor health. After remaining bedridden for a few days, she died. The local doctors found her symptoms resembled that of arsenic poisoning, a mystery which remains unsolved, because no autopsy was performed.[3]

One of the members of the tour was Uday Shankar's youngest sibling, Ravi Shankar, who was around thirteen or fourteen years old at the time. In Baba's words, 'विदेश जाते जहाज़ में चढ़ते समय, उदय शंकर की माँ ने मुझसे कहा था, "रवि को मैं आपको सौंप रही हूँ। आज से आप ही उसके बाबा है।" यह सुनकर मैंने पुत्रवत भाव से विदेश में उसे थोड़ी बहुत शिक्षा दी और बाद में मैहर में सिखाया।' [While boarding the ship, Uday Shankar's mother told me, "I am entrusting Ravi to your guardianship. Henceforth, you are his father." Accordingly, I treated Ravi as my son, and during the long tour, I gave him some music lessons and later on taught him at Maihar.]'

It bears noting that Shyam Shankar Chowdhury, the father of the Shankar siblings, had been murdered in London in 1936. Shyam Shankar had abandoned his first wife, Hemangini Devi, the mother of Uday Shankar, Rajendra Shankar, Debendra Shankar, Bhupendra Shankar and Ravi Shankar. Bhupendra died young in 1926.

During this period, the young Ravi Shankar had been occasionally learning music; first from Timirbaran, Vishnudas Shiralee and Gokul Naag, and later from Baba. However, young

Ravi was not focused and he kept switching between the isrāj, sitār, jaltarang and vocal lessons. Baba, however, told him that music could not be learnt in such a sporadic manner.

Panditji in his salad days.

Quoting Baba, 'पहले रवु बिलकुल अनाड़ी था, भांड की तरह नाचता था। स्वभाव भी अच्छा नहीं था। लड़कियों के प्रति दुर्बलता थी। ठीक प्रजापति का स्वभाव था। [Earlier, Robu (Baba always addressed Ravi as Robu) was rather clumsy. He used to dance like a buffoon. His nature too was not good. Despite the young age, girls were his weakness. He had *rajasic* (highly self-centred and passionate in the gratification of sensory pleasures) tendencies.]'⁴

In order to understand Ravi Shankar, we need to understand the events of his formative years. His father, Shyam Shankar, abandoned his wife and children and migrated to London, where he married an English woman. Ravi Shankar saw his father very briefly once, for the first time when he was eight years old. Shyam Shankar, however, became the mentor of Ravi's eldest brother, Uday.

While in London, Shyam Shankar became an amateur impresario (a person who organizes and often finances concerts, plays or operas), introducing Indian music and dance to Britain, and Uday joined him there. Uday danced at a few charity performances his father had organized in London, and on one such occasion, the noted Russian ballerina Anna Pavlova happened to be present. Uday's encounter with Pavlova had a lasting impact on his career.

In 1938, Ravi's mother, Hemangini Devi, died after a prolonged illness. According to the psychologist Prof. Rooshikumar Pandya, the marital discord and estrangement of his parents followed by the traumatic news of his father's murder and mother's death, all in quick succession, deeply impacted Ravi Shankar's psyche and affected his personality and behaviour for the rest of his life. There were three father figures in Ravi Shankar's life. First was the elder brother, Uday Shankar, followed by Baba Allauddin Khan, and finally Tat Baba.

Pt Ravi Shankar once recalled an early experience with Baba, saying, 'Baba himself was a deeply spiritual person. Despite being a devout Muslim, he could be moved by any spiritual path. One morning, in Brussels, I brought him to a cathedral where the choir was singing. The moment we entered, I could see that he was in a strange mood. The cathedral had a huge statue of Virgin Mary. Baba went towards that statue and started howling like a child: "Ma, Ma" (Mother, Mother), with tears flowing freely. We had to drag him out.'[5]

In March 1938, Germany annexed Austria, followed by Czechoslovakia, and then the invasion of Poland led to the start of World War II. Touring Western countries was no longer possible. Uday Shankar's troupe was forced to cut short their tour and return to India. In 1938, Uday Shankar made India his base, establishing the Uday Shankar India Cultural Centre at Almora, with Baba Allauddin Khan as its music teacher. Many of Udayji's students later became celebrities, including stellar names like Guru Dutt, Shanti Bardhan, Simkie, Amala, Satyavati, Narendra Sharma,

Ruma Guha Thakurta (the first wife of the famous actor-singer Kishore Kumar), Prabhat Ganguly, Zohra Sehgal, Uzra, Lakshmi Shankar, Shanta Gandhi, as well as his own brothers Rajendra, Debendra and Ravi.

This was the time when Ravi Shankar shifted his focus from dancing to music. Baba told him that if he was serious about learning music, he had best come to Maihar and live with Baba's family in a traditional gurukul-like system in the ancient *guru– shishya paramparā* by renouncing his Western mindset. Ravi heeded this advice.

Upon reaching Maihar, the first test imposed on young Ravi was when Baba refused to teach him, saying, 'I don't teach sissified dandies.' Young Ravi returned to Baba after shaving his head, proving he was willing to lead the ascetic life of a disciple. Thus, he passed the first test with flying colours.

Ravi Shankar's lodging and accommodation was arranged by renting an adjoining house. 'After the life of luxury and glamour in the cities of Europe and America, rural Maihar was tough,' Ravi Shankar admits. His small, rented room was spartan. 'The doors and windows creaked with the passing wind, and scorpions and cockroaches abounded. Snakes were not rare and jackals howled all night.' There was no electricity or running water. All his meals were, of course, provided at Baba's house.

Young Ali Akbar and Ravi became the best of friends. After dinner, Ali would sneak out of his room, jump over the boundary wall, and go to Ravi's room to indulge in some juvenile mischief. Ravi was not only two years elder to Ali, but also much smarter, wiser, more educated, and with enormous international exposure due to his extensive travels with his brother's troupe. It was obvious that Ravi had tremendous influence over the unworldly Ali, who had never been out of rustic Maihar.

However, there was a trade-off here. Ravi would request Ali to share his notations in reciprocation for Ravi sharing the naughty magazines that he had acquired from Paris and Copenhagen. What was considered 'naughty' in the 1930s was quite chaste compared to what our children are exposed to these days, but for young Ali Akbar, those guilt-laden indulgences during his impressionable age had a profound influence on his psyche. Hence, a lifelong relationship of 'follower' and 'dominator' was formed—Ali Akbar being the former and Ravi Shankar the latter.

Ali Akbar was already a performing artiste at the age of fourteen, while Ravi Shankar was just a beginner at the age of eighteen. The notations and initial rehearsals with Ali Akbar were of tremendous help to the extremely intelligent and focused Ravi as it enabled him to be well prepared for his lessons from Baba. Needless to say, Ravi's progress was rapid.

> 'Genius is composed of 2 percent talent and 98 percent persevering application.'
>
> —Ludwig van Beethoven

Maihar Band

In 1918, the last year of World War I, the Spanish flu pandemic claimed 50 to 100 million lives worldwide, more than the death toll of both World Wars combined. An estimated 18 million Indians lost their lives to this mysterious flu between 1918 and 1920, making India the focal point of the pandemic.

Maihar, too, was a victim of this pandemic. Soon after Baba went there, too many people died because of the pandemic, leaving behind countless orphans. Baba gathered forty orphaned children and brought them to his house. He bathed them, fed them and gave them accommodation in his house. Baba's gesture became the talk of the town. When the news reached the surviving relatives of the orphans, they started coming to Baba to take away their children, but seventeen children remained with him forever.

Considering the fact that he himself was not too literate, Baba decided to make these children proficient in music to enable them to earn a livelihood. When Brijnathsinghji learnt of this, he allotted a building to be used both as an orphanage and a music school. The first batch of the Maihar Band consisted of twelve orphan boys and five orphan girls. Brijnathsinghji announced he would give an allowance of Rs 12 a month to each orphan child of the Maihar Band, thus saving Baba from spending from his own pocket.

Brijnathsinghji helped Baba in procuring and preparing the required instruments. Until the time a cello could be ordered and supplied, Baba got a sarangi made which measured twice the size of usual one and named it the 'sāraṅgā'. When played with a large bow, it would give out a rich, deep tone, like that of a cello.

Apart from the usual instruments like the tablā, dholak, harmonium and sitār, Baba used some special creations—the sāraṅgā and sitārbanjo. He trained some of the children to play Western instruments including the piano, violin and cello with equal ease. In the royal palace, arrangements were made for the band, and they played for visiting dignitaries from the gallery above the main hall. For the Maihar Band, Baba created several compositions based on Indian raags. He also taught them some Western tunes.

Sitārbanjo.   Sāraṅgā.

Teaching the orphans of the Maihar Band, however, became a big headache for Baba. The poor children were not only rustic and illiterate, they couldn't follow simple instructions or grasp elementary lessons. As a teacher, Baba's regime was so harsh that twelve of the children ran away to the neighbouring state of Nagod. After a month, with the intervention of Brijnathsinghji, they returned to Maihar to resume their training.

Baba achieved what seemed impossible. The children started performing well. When Brijnathsinghji heard about the progress of the Maihar Band children, he expressed his wish to listen to them. A time was set for them to go and perform in the palace.

The children were extremely excited to visit the grand venue. Baba gave them all a good bath and well-laundered uniforms, his wife Madina Ma groomed them the best she could. Baba took the children to the palace at 6.30 p.m. as the scheduled recital was at 7 p.m. However, to their dismay, Brijnathsinghji didn't turn up until 9.30 p.m. and nobody offered them food or even drinking water. Some of the children were so hungry and tired that they fell asleep. Baba was utterly disgusted. He took the children home, left them there and returned to the palace alone. Brijnathsinghji came to the court at 10 p.m. and asked where the children were.

Then and there, Baba submitted his resignation. A shocked Brijnathsinghji asked him the reason for such a drastic step. 'These little children may be rustic orphans, but they came to your palace as performing artistes. You not only insulted them but you have insulted the music itself. I can no longer be your guru, nor can I be your court musician.'

Brijnathsinghji caught Baba's feet and pleaded for forgiveness. He explained his predicament in detail—a major crisis as it was— which pacified Baba.

Baba again went to the children. Most of them had gone to sleep. Baba had to awaken them, dress them all up again, and bring them back to the palace. Despite the late hours and hardships, the children performed so well that Brijnathsinghji was enthralled.

Soon, the Maihar Band became very famous. It became a status symbol to call the band for marriage functions and other important events. Baba and the Maihar Band travelled to numerous places to perform.

Baba with his Maihar Band. He was too reluctant to wear the medals while posing for the photoshoot but HH Brijnathsinghji insisted.

Initially, one of the orphans in the band was a blind boy. Baba had trained him to play the jaltarang, a melodic percussion instrument that originated in India. The jaltarang consists of a set of ceramic or metal bowls filled with water. The bowls are played by striking the edge with beaters, one in each hand. The pitch is adjusted by varying the level of water in the bowls.

The blind boy often faltered while striking the bowls; tipping them over and spilling the water. The whole orchestra would then have to pause until Baba retuned it by refilling the bowl with the precise level of water that was previously in it to resume the playing.

Baba was on the lookout for a solution, and with extraordinary serendipity he found a terrific one.

Make Music, Not War

Military science developed rapidly during World War I. The smoothbore barrels of guns were replaced by rifled barrels. Since the princely state of Maihar was under the British Crown, and His Highness Brijnathsinghji was awarded the KCIE (Knight Commander of the Order of the Indian Empire), Maihar too followed suit and adopted the prescribed changes in its arsenal.

Once, Baba was taking a stroll with Brijnathsinghji outside the palace when he accidentally stepped on some discarded smoothbore barrels dumped there. The hollow barrels produced a sonorous sound which amused Baba. He inquired, 'What are these pipes for?'

'These are the discarded barrels of guns,' Brijnathsinghji explained.

'What are you going to do with them?'

'They will all be sold as scrap to a metal refinery.'

'Can I take some of them?'

'What are you going to do with them?'

'I want to make a musical instrument.'

Fascinated by the idea, Brijnathsinghji allowed him to take as many as he wanted. Baba collected the barrels, cut them into various lengths to match the notes of the standard musical scale, and arranged them in the format of piano keys. The instrument resembled a glockenspiel. The difference was that Baba used metal barrels instead of metal bars. Baba named the instrument 'nāltarang'. Nāl means barrel and tarang means waves, as in soundwaves.

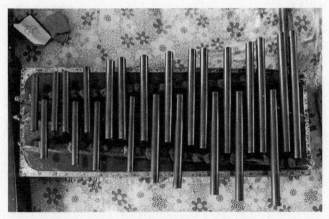

Nāltarang.

The Maihar Band with Indira Gandhi, the then prime minister.

The Kitten that Refused to Eat Grass

Here is a story Ma narrated to us about her childhood.

The garden within the compound walls was quite large and well taken care of by our gardener, who was under Baba's constant supervision. Baba also devoted an hour daily to gardening.

As a child, my geographical world was limited to the boundary walls of our house. Dozens of people would visit Baba every day, but they were all adults, and none of them ever interacted with us. It used to be just the two of us, Bhaiyā and me. We didn't have anyone else to play with. An exception was His Highness Brijnathsinghji's niece. She was my age and liked me. She would often send a horse cart to fetch me to the palace, and after a few hours of playing there, bring me back home. Those were the only times I went out of home by myself.

One day, Bhaiyā was all charged up after a lesson he must have learnt about importance of *shram* (labour), or perhaps he must have heard the catchy lines of Maithili Sharan Gupt, and got hooked on them:

कुछ काम करो, कुछ काम करो
जग में रह कर कुछ नाम करो

[*Work, work your way to acclaim
In this world, make your name*]

Once, when we went out to play in the garden, Bhaiyā saw that the lawn had not been mowed for several days. The gardener was on leave and Baba too was travelling. Bhaiyā started giving me a lecture about the importance of *shram*. 'We should not waste precious time by playing in the garden,' he preached. 'We ought to work.'

'But we are so small and don't know anything,' I argued. 'What work can we possibly do?'

Bhaiyā picked up the gardener's sickle and started cutting the grass. 'The gardener is absent, let's mow the lawn.'

The sight of Bhaiyā violently swinging the sharp sickle was scary for me. I retreated to a safe spot to witness his adventure.

'Don't just stand there like a mute spectator,' Bhaiyā commanded. 'Help me cut the grass.'

'But there is only one sickle and you are using it.'

'Stop making excuses and use your hands,' Bhaiyā commanded.

With my bare hands, I couldn't contribute much, but after about an hour of hard labour, we were able to gather a heap of grass.

'What are we going to do with this?' I asked.

'We will sell it in the market,' he replied.

Bhaiyā's entrepreneurial aspirations, however, vanished when I warned him that Baba would never approve of anything like that. As we were wondering what to do with the result of our hard work, we were joined by a little kitten, Billo.

Bhaiyā said, 'Let's feed the grass to Billo.'

A few days earlier, a stray cat had given birth to a few kittens. When they first entered our compound, we tried to shoo them away, but Baba asked us to let them be and told us not to bother them. Bhaiyā developed a liking for one of the kittens and tried to tame it by naming it Billo. Strangely enough, Billo's other siblings and the mother cat went away, and Billo was the only one left behind in our garden.

His heart overflowing with kindness, Bhaiyā tried to feed the kitten grass, which it refused to eat.

'Bhaiyā, cats don't eat grass,' I tried to enlighten him.

'Says who?' Bhaiyā argued. 'Cows, buffaloes, goats, sheep, horses all eat grass, so why not cats?'

We were too young and ignorant at that point in time to differentiate between herbivorous and carnivorous animals.

After repeated failed attempts to feed grass to the kitten, Bhaiyā got frustrated and angry with the kitten for rejecting his gesture of kindness. He gave it a tight slap. The kitten escaped, never to return again.

'When I was about four or five years old, Baba gifted me a doll. She would make a short babbling sound and open her eyes when you held her upright. It was quite a high-tech toy for the early 1930s. As every girl child, I too was instantly attached to this doll.

'Typically, as a boy, Bhaiyā never cared for dolls, but he was fascinated by the sound this doll made and wanted to figure out how. He asked me to give him the doll but I wouldn't. Bhaiyā tricked me by saying, "All your doll can do is make a short babbling sound. I can teach her to speak sentences." Fascinated by the idea, I gave him the doll.

'Bhaiyā took away the doll and dissected her. When I would ask him to return the doll, he would say, "Be patient, it takes time to teach a doll to talk." I soon lost patience and threatened to complain to Baba. Bhaiyā immediately gave me the dissected pieces of the doll. I cried a lot but didn't complain to Baba.'

—Annapurna Devi

Omnipresence

विभुर्व्याप्य सर्वत्र सर्वेन्द्रियाणाम्

[*God is omnipresent, in everyone, in everything*]
—*Atmashatkam*

Baba was free of materialistic desires. The only noteworthy materialistic asset he ever desired and acquired was a house of his own. For more than five decades, he had not lived in a house which he could call his own. Madina Bhavan was built while he was travelling abroad with Uday Shankar's troupe, and Baba spent his entire savings to build it. In the mid-1930s, it was an enormous undertaking.

Ma often narrated this anecdote, calling it the lesson of her life: 'I was very young, not more than ten. Once, a street sweeper woman, very ugly and rather dirty, fascinated by the grandeur of Madina Bhavan, entered our compound and kept peering at our house. As I glared at her in contempt, Baba intuitively read my mind.

'Baba went up to the woman, respectfully held her hand, and ushered her in, saying, "Ma [mother], why are you outside? Please come in." Baba not only welcomed her, but asked me, "माँ को प्रणाम करो [Pay your obeisance to Ma]." I obediently touched the sweeper woman's feet. Baba showed her the house and offered her some sweets as *prasād*.

'After the woman left, Baba said, "Never, look down upon any other human being. We are all part and parcel of the same. Every creation is a manifestation of the Supreme Self. This woman is a street sweeper, but her job too is as important as any other. We should be grateful for her keeping our town clean and ensuring us good hygiene."'

Advaita (non-dual) Vedanta (the essence of the Vedas) philosophy considers *ātmaa* as self-existent awareness, limitless and non-dual. It asserts that there is a 'soul' (*ātmaa*) within each living entity, which is the same as the universal, eternal Brahman. It is this 'oneness' which unifies all beings. The divine is in every being, and all existence is a single reality. Baba's compassion was universal and not limited to the human species.

The Maihar region was infested with snakes. There were numerous instances of cobra sightings in the garden of Madina Bhavan, and on a few occasions inside the house too. Perhaps there was a snake burrow in the huge property surrounding Baba's house. Baba had given a strict instruction to never harm any species, therefore killing a cobra was out of the question.

The children of the Maihar Band used to regularly come to Baba's house for their lessons, which took place in the garden, with Baba at the far end playing the violin and conducting the band, and all the children facing him.

The sound or vibrations produced by so many instruments playing together in the band attracted cobras, drawing them close to the direction of sound. On a few occasions, a cobra would come very close to Baba's feet, raising four quarters of its body above the ground in an erect stance, swinging along with Baba's movements. The terrified children looking at this would stop playing. When asked about the reason for the interruption, the children would simply point at the cobra at his feet. Baba would greet the cobra with a smile and say, 'Have you come to listen to our music?' Baba would then lift the cobra with the bow of his violin and put it a few metres away, saying, 'Please go away, let us practise.' The snake would then slither away.

There was not a single instance of a venomous cobra harming any human in or around Madina Bhavan. However, on one occasion, a human did kill a cobra; that too in Madina Bhavan.

Girdharilal was the harmonium player in the Maihar Band and had been very close to Baba since early childhood. Once, when he had come to meet Baba, Baba was not home. On seeing a cobra in the washroom, Zubeidaji (Ali Akbar Khansaheb's first wife) panicked and ran out, screaming. Girdharilal rushed there with a bamboo and killed the cobra. In the panic, he had forgotten Baba's cardinal rule of not harming any creature.

Just as he was taking away the dead cobra, Baba entered the gate of Madina Bhavan. He was furious to learn that Girdharilal had killed a cobra. Baba said, 'You've committed the sin of killing a Brahmin!' Baba took the dead cobra to the crematorium and cremated it in accordance with a Hindu last rites ceremony.

Ma also told us a story of a baby monkey. The rhesus monkey is one of the most common species of monkeys found in India, especially in villages and smaller towns.

Once, a baby monkey of this species touched an overhead power line and fell unconscious near Baba's house. Baba brought it home and administered first aid. The baby monkey regained consciousness, and eventually recovered fully, but became so attached to Baba that it just wouldn't leave him alone.

Baba too developed a fondness for the baby monkey and named it Hanuman (a Hindu god and the divine monkey companion and devotee of Lord Rama. Hanuman, a popular deity by himself, is well known as one of the central characters in the Ramayana, the famous Hindu epic).

The monkey later became so possessive of Baba that he wouldn't allow anyone to come near his master. When Baba would teach his disciples, or would himself do his sādhanā, Hanuman would quietly be seated beside him. Just for fun, if Baba pointed to a person and said, 'He is a bad man', Hanuman would show his canines and everyone would laugh.

Unfortunately, one day when Baba had gone out, Hanuman ventured out of the boundary walls of Madina Bhavan and fell prey to a bunch of ferocious stray dogs. Grief-stricken, Baba cremated Hanuman and performed the last rites, as he would for a dear relative.

सा विद्या या विमुक्तये।

[The teaching is what sets you free]
—Vishnu Purān (1.19.41)

Despite the strict regimen and spartan discipline, Baba's teaching was highly liberal. Baba allowed each disciple to manifest his inner self through his renditions. No spoon-feeding, no strict dos and don'ts, but a map would be given to the disciple allowing him to find his way. Guru Ma's aim was to perpetuate Baba's teaching in its purest form.

When Suresh Vyas was learning Raag Bihāg, Ma encouraged him to create his own ālaap phrases. Nervous though he was, Suresh tried his best. Ma patiently listened to his ālaap and said, 'साँप को पैर क्यों लगाते हो? [Let the serpent glide, no need to put legs on it.]'

With such one-liners and without getting into confusing theories, Ma would explain the entire chapters of legato, staccato, portago, glissando, portamento, slur, etc.

The Reluctant Genius

'Bhaiyā must be the most reluctant maestro in the history of music,' Guru Ma often told us when reminiscing about her childhood in Maihar. 'The greatest sarodist ever was not really interested in learning music during his childhood. If it wasn't for the fear of corporal punishment from Baba, Bhaiyā had no intention of learning music.'

Young Ali Akbar Khan.

Ut. Ali Akbar Khan (Khansaheb) and Pt Ravi Shankar were gurubhais, best lifelong friends and *jugalbandi* partners while being two highly contrasting personalities. Volumes can be written about them, but what follows captures their differences.

Panditji consciously chose the path of music. It was his thoughtful, deliberate decision to give up dancing and pursue music instead. However, for Khansaheb, music wasn't a matter of choice. Due to his past karma or some unknowable celestial design, he was born into a house where not pursuing music was not an option. As a guru, Baba was perhaps the best ever, but he belonged to an era which believed that corporal punishment was the best way to raise a child.

'भैया ने जितनी मार खाई उतनी तो शायद किसिने नहीं खाई होगी [Nobody must have got more beating than what Bhaiyā got],' Ma would tell us. 'At his core was a free spirited, careless, rebellious and spontaneous person. Extremely creative, a master of lateral thinking, full of original ideas, Bhaiyā was not very good at adhering to instructions, nor was he as serious towards his lessons as Panditji and I were.

'Learning music from Baba wasn't easy. We had to memorize whatever he taught us as he never dictated notes. After each lesson, we would rush to our rooms and note down whatever we had learnt during the training session. Training of rhythm and singing was compulsory for us despite our focus being on playing the instrument. Though Baba gave instrument lessons one to one, singing lessons were given together. Baba taught us numerous Dhrupad bandishes. We had to memorize not only the notations, but the lyrics too. Bhaiyā would invariably forget a few words in between and use my singing as a cue.

'Another problem with Bhaiyā was that compared to Panditji and me, he was very casual about his riyaaz. Within moments of Baba leaving the house, Bhaiyā would put down his sarod and go and sit on the windowsill. Panditji and I would warn him, "Baba will be very angry if he finds out that you were goofing off instead of practising." However, Bhaiyā would pay no heed to our warnings. "क्या आप लोग सुबह शाम जंत्र लेके बैठे रहते हो! संगीत के अलावा जिंदगी में और कुछ है ही नहीं क्या? [Don't you guys have any other interests in life other than playing music all day?]"

'But it wasn't easy to fool Baba, because he always kept track of who did what in his absence. During the early days of our training, apart from scolding and corporal punishment, Baba had another indirect technique of motivating us. He would bring *mithais*—sweets from the market. The sweets were a reward for the sibling who practised more, which was invariably me and never Bhaiyā. In front of him, Baba would give me the mithais, and exclude Bhaiyā from the treat, telling him, 'Mithais are a reward for the one who practises sincerely.' This was a potent technique as Bhaiyā was extremely fond of sweets.

'However, those rewards used to prove bitter for me. As Baba rewarded me all the time, Bhaiyā grew resentful. At that tender age, Bhaiyā felt angry towards me. In Baba's absence, Bhaiyā would beat me up in childish rage.

'For a while, we went to a nearby private school run by a widow. It wasn't that far, but Bhaiyā would go on a bicycle with me as a pillion rider. Often, during those rides, Bhaiyā would intentionally tilt the bicycle to make me fall. At that age, he was much taller than me—his feet reached the ground, he never fell, but I did, and often got hurt. Bhaiyā would then blame the potholes on the road.

'Psychologists say, "If the top dog is dominating, the underdog becomes cunning." And that was true in our case. As Bhaiyā was much bigger and stronger than me, I devised a little scheme to get even with him.

'During our singing lessons, when Baba made us both sing the bandishes, I knew that Bhaiyā wouldn't bother to memorize the lessons. Most of the Dhrupad compositions taught to us had four parts; स्थायी [Sthāyi], अंतरा [Antarā], संचारी [Sanchāri] and अभोग [Abhog]. We used to practise singing together so I knew where in the song Bhaiyā would struggle. Bhaiyā depended on my singing to remind him what to sing. When we reached the point which I knew Bhaiyā hadn't memorized, I would stop singing and pretend to cough. This would put Bhaiyā in a fix, as he could

neither remember the lyrics nor depend on my singing as a crutch.
I would then sneak away for a glass of water, which left Bhaiyā
with no choice but to stop singing. This infuriated Baba, who
would ask, "Why do you stop singing every time she coughs? You
keep singing without paying attention to her coughing." Because
Bhaiyā was unable to sing those parts he did not remember, Baba
would become angry and beat him. Standing behind Baba, I
would make faces at Bhaiyā as I savoured my victory over him,
but this only made him angrier, and he would pummel me even
more as soon as we were alone.

'During one of our singing lessons, I tried this same trick and
began coughing. Bhaiyā was cornered, but this time Baba turned
towards me, asking, "Is anything wrong with your health? For
quite some time, I've been observing your cough. Maybe we should
consult a doctor." Bhaiyā grabbed this golden opportunity to
turn the tables on me and complained, "Baba, she keeps plucking
guavas from our garden tree and eats too many of them."

'Now, this was a master stroke from Bhaiyā! I was very fond
of guavas, but Baba at once forbade me from eating them. This
is how Bhaiyā had the last laugh. This vicious circle went on for
some years, but as we advanced in age, our sibling rivalry and
hostility vanished.'

Years later, when Ali Akbar Khansaheb visited Ma at
Akashganga, I acted as an escort to Khansaheb during the trip.
In my presence, Ma intuitively felt that Khansaheb wanted to
tell her something but was unable to open up. 'आप कुछ कहना
चाहते हो? [You want to say something?]' Ma asked. Khansaheb
remorsefully remembered his childhood acts of beating her up
and apologized in front of me, saying, 'बचपन में मैं तुम्हें मारता था,
मुझे माफ़ कर देना [In childhood, I used to beat you, please forgive
me.]' Khansaheb's eyes welled up with tears as he momentarily
folded his palms in namaskar. Ma was tearful as well, and
responded, 'अरे भैया, आप भी क्या पुरानी बातों को निकाल कर दुःखी हो रहे

हो! मैं तो सब कुछ भूल चूकी हूँ [Why are you punishing yourself by
digging up the past? I have long forgotten everything!]' I too
was in tears as I witnessed this poignant moment between one
of the greatest pairs of siblings in musical history.

Like assembling a giant jigsaw puzzle, we keep gathering and
placing the pieces to create an image, however faint, of what life in
Maihar would have been in those days.

Maihar was such a small town that there used to be only one post
office, one primary school, a small public hospital, one pharmacy,
one police station with a jail, a goldsmith and two *tangaas* (horse
carriage taxis). Electricity was available only for a few hours a day.
The only industry was a lime factory and the wholesale trade of
tobacco and betel leaves. Of course, there was a small market with
various grocery shops, vegetable sellers, a *halwāi* (confectioner),
potters, cobblers, etc. The Shārdā Ma temple was a major tourist
attraction and tourism played a major role in supporting the local
economy.

There is the oft-told story of Ali Akbar Khansaheb which Ma
recited over the years. It was hilarious and tragic at the same time.
Here we try to reconstruct it as best we can.

'Once, Baba had gone on a very long tour,' Ma told us. 'Baba's
prolonged absence meant a grand vacation for Bhaiyā. Every day,
in the late afternoon, Bhaiyā would sneak out of the house to play
games and hang out with a group of local boys.

'One day, when Bhaiyā and his gang were rambling through
the Maihar market, they came across a halwāi's shop. The boys
were tempted by the sight of a variety of sweets, but none of them
had any money as most of them were from poor families.

'One boy requested Bhaiyā to buy them imarti. "I would surely
buy you sweets," Bhaiyā generously told him, "but I don't have
any money with me." The boy was very smart. He told Bhaiyā, "As
Baba's son, you don't need money. Just ask for whatever you want
and the shop owner will give it to you."

'As Baba was the court musician and the guru of the maharaja, he was held in the highest esteem and was highly regarded by all. Bhaiyā tried his luck. Lo and behold, the halwāi handed over a plateful of imarti without demanding any money.

'Bhaiyā realized that Baba Allauddin Khan's name in Maihar was like a miniature version of Aladdin's magic lamp. That day, the entire group of friends feasted on the sweets to their hearts' content.

'After this incident, Bhaiyā became an instant hero and the undisputed leader of the gang. He surely enjoyed the newfound power, respect and attention he now received from his peers. As the word spread, some more boys joined the gang, and it became a routine for them to visit the halwāi and feast on as many sweets as they desired. But Bhaiyā would soon realize that in life, there is no such thing as a free lunch.

'Upon his return to Maihar, as Baba was walking through the marketplace, the halwāi approached him and demanded an exorbitant amount of money. Baba was shocked and argued that he had been away for quite a few months, and he didn't remember owing him any money. The halwāi showed Baba an absurdly long list of all the sweetmeats Bhaiyā and his gang of friends had consumed in his absence. Baba was furious. He had no choice but to pay. As Baba was not carrying much money on him at the time, he brought the halwāi to his home so he could pay the full amount.

'Full of furore, Baba rushed home. He summoned Bhaiyā and showed him the bill. A shiver ran down Bhaiyā's spine when he saw the bill amount. He knew he had no defence. Baba was more concerned about Bhaiyā's goofing off than the money spent. "Instead of doing your riyaaz, you were loafing around with your friends! Do you want to be a music maestro or do you want to be a vagabond eating imarti with your friends?" Baba asked angrily.

'"I prefer eating imarti with my friends," was Bhaiyā's remorseless, rebellious reply. Baba was livid, and imposed an inhumane degree of corporal punishment to a minor. Bhaiyā was tied to a tree and caned. A crowd of onlookers gathered to witness the violent act, but Baba was so angry that none dared to intervene. Finally, my mother came to rescue Bhaiyā.'

Decades later, when Khansaheb graced my house for dinner, I made it a point to serve him imarti. The mere sight of imarti made Khansaheb fall into a reverie.

Padded Jacket in 40°C

सु:खार्थिन: कुतो विद्या विद्यार्थिन: कुतो सुखं ।
सुखार्थी वा त्यजेत विद्याम विद्यार्थी वा त्यजेत सुखं ।।

*[Those in pursuit of comforts should waive erudition,
Those in pursuit of learning should waive comforts]*
—*Chanakyaniti*

When Suresh's father, Madanlal Vyas, had gone to meet Baba at Maihar, he could hear the non-stop sound of Ali Akbar practising in a room above where they sat. As a musicologist, Madanlalji was overwhelmed by the beauty of Khansaheb's sarod-playing.

'He plays well, doesn't he?' Baba asked.

'His playing is incredible,' Madanlalji replied.

'शारदामाँ से माँगा था [He is the boon I prayed to Shārdā Ma for.]'

Such was Baba's love for Khansaheb. However, when Khansaheb came downstairs, Baba sternly rebuked him for no apparent reason.

Describing Baba's way of teaching, Ma used to say, 'Learning from Baba was not easy. He demanded complete and unconditional surrender and unquestioned obedience from his pupils. Panditji and I were the studious, disciplined and obedient kind, and we could adapt to these harsh conditions. Thus, we were saved from Baba's wrath. In contrast, Bhaiyā was a born lateral thinker with a gift for dramatic

34

spontaneity. It was neither natural nor easy for him to give copybook renditions or adhere to the strict regimen imposed by Baba.

'Baba with his orthodox mindset believed that sparing the rod spoiled the child. But he overdid it, and was exceptionally harsh towards Bhaiyā and later towards his eldest grandson, Aashish. A single note rendered out of the notations he had taught, and Baba would get angry and beat Bhaiyā. This became such a routine that, regardless of the season, Bhaiyā started wearing a padded jacket while taking lessons from Baba, to protect him from the beatings he would get. It was hilarious during the summer, when the temperature in Maihar would rise beyond 40°Celsius in May and June. Bhaiyā would be dripping in sweat but wouldn't remove his padded jacket. When Baba would ask him why he was wearing such a thick jacket in such scorching temperatures, Bhaiyā's standard excuse was that he was suffering from cough and cold. He would fake some coughing to justify his alibi. It was so funny that it was difficult for Panditji and I to control our laughter.

'Baba's attitude towards Bhaiyā and Panditji was not the same. If Panditji made a mistake—which was rare—Baba wouldn't be harsh, but when Bhaiyā made a similar mistake, Baba would beat him.

Pt Ravi Shankar, Baba Allauddin Khan and Ut. Ali Akbar Khansaheb.

The Great Escape

'In 1937, when Bhaiyā was about fifteen years old, Baba decided to get him married. The chosen bride was Zubeida Begum, daughter of a police officer from Shivpur (now in Bangladesh). It was an arranged marriage, like it used to be in those days. Zubeida Bhabhi (brother's wife is called 'bhabhi' in some Indian languages) was a teenager at the time. She was a pragmatic person, often disgusted by her husband's careless, reckless attitude towards life. Like any other wife, Bhabhi expected her husband to be focused on making name, fame and money. It was one hell of a culture shock for her to see him routinely being thrashed by Baba. Bhaiyā, in his rebellious teens, was finding Baba's pressure a bit too much to handle; the added pressure from his spouse was making his life miserable. One night, Bhaiyā, in all probability instigated by Bhabhi, ran away from home. Of course, he took along his sarod and some personal belongings.

'The next morning, Baba wondered why there was no sound of riyaaz from Bhaiyā's room. Baba went upstairs to inquire. Baba was shocked to see three knotted bedsheets hanging down from the window railing, serving as evidence of the great escape. Baba questioned Zubeidaji, but her defence was that she was fast asleep and totally clueless about her husband's escape. Baba could never buy the story that a wife sleeping in the same room could be completely unaware of her husband's escape, that too if he was carrying a big, heavy instrument like a sarod and a suitcase full of belongings. Perhaps the knotted bedsheet was a mere ruse and Bhaiyā actually escaped after climbing down the stairs in the dead of night. Thereafter, the equation between Baba and Zubeidaji remained discordant. Both Bhaiyā and Aashishda became major victims of this discordance.

'Distressed by Bhaiyā's escape, Baba went and shared the news with Brijnathsinghji, who used a wide array of methods to find him. Baba also started communicating with his friends in music circles, mainly in Calcutta (now Kolkata), to keep an eye out for him, as Baba suspected that Bhaiyā would go there. Instead, he went west to reach Bombay (now Mumbai).'

The following passage was narrated to us by none other than Ali Akbar Khansaheb himself.

'After reaching Bombay, I went straight to All India Radio for an audition. Dinkar Rao Amembal was the programme executive in charge of Indian music, and also the conductor of Bombay Radio Vadhya Vrinda. Dinkar Rao was in charge of auditions, along with the station director Z.A. Bukhari.

'I had applied under the alias of Shibu Dutt [Khansaheb was born in Shivpur, thus the name]. Dinkar Raoji was not at all impressed by my rustic looks, but granted me an audition out of pure kindness. I started with a short ālaap. Pleasantly surprised, Dinkar Raoji asked me, "Will you be able to play with tablā?"

'I said, "I will try."

'Dinkar Raoji called for a set of tablā and said, "Don't worry; don't be nervous. Play slowly at the tempo you are comfortable with." So, I started with a *vilambit gat*. Though Dinkar Raoji was not a tablā player, he was kind enough to accompany me on it during the audition. Impressed by the rendition of the gat, Dinkar Raoji told me, "Now try to increase the tempo." I kept increasing the tempo until we reached a tempo in which Dinkar Raoji couldn't keep the pace. He stopped and said, "Okay, okay, you have passed

the test! Come tomorrow with your sarod and we will broadcast
you live." Meanwhile, Ashraf Khan, the famous actor-singer of the
Gujarati stage and a Sufi saint, after concluding his live broadcast,
came to greet Dinkar Rao and Z.A. Bukhari. On hearing a single
phrase of my playing, Ashraf Khan told them, "अरे, इसका क्या
audition ले रहे हो! यह तो शेर का बच्चा है, सीधा प्रोग्राम दे दो [What is the point
of taking his audition? This kid is a born genius.]'"

The famous industrialist Rajabahadur Laxminarayan Pittie, a
good friend of His Highness Brijnathsinghji, happened to listen to
this AIR Bombay broadcast by Khansaheb. It was indeed a sarod
recital of high calibre. The true identity of an artiste is known
from his music. Despite the name of the artiste being announced
as Shibu Dutt, Rajabahadur Pittie was pretty sure that it could be
none other than Ali Akbar.

Rajabahadur Pittie went to the AIR station in his Chrysler
limousine. As Ali Akbar was leaving the building, Rajabahadur
opened the door of his car and commanded young Ali Akbar to
get inside. The car zoomed back to his residence. Rajabahadur
sent a telegram to Brijnathsinghji to convey that Ali Akbar was
in his custody, and was being sent by the Allahabad-bound train
to Satna junction (about 40 km from Maihar). Back then, Maihar
didn't have a railway station. When the train arrived at Satna, the
maharaja's men pulled Ali Akbar from the train and whisked him
home. Corporal punishment was the reason why young Ali Akbar
had escaped from home, and he got that in even heavier doses now
on his return. Ali Akbar's rigorous training resumed and it went
on for another five years.

In 1939, almost a year after Ali Akbar and Zubeida's
marriage, Aashish was born. The year 1943 was a milestone for
Ali Akbar. Baba, as per routine, had gone to Lucknow to play for
a radio broadcast. The British station director came to Baba and
expressed his wish to appoint Ali Akbar Khansaheb as the chief
of the orchestra. In those days, working for a radio station was

a respectable job, so Baba agreed. Ali Akbar Khansaheb became the youngest music director ever to work for AIR, Lucknow. He gave solo performances and composed music for the radio ensemble. There, the famous music director Madan Mohan became associated with Ali Akbar Khansaheb. Years later, in an interview, Madan Mohan mentioned that his musical career had been greatly influenced by listening to and hobnobbing with Ali Akbar Khansaheb. In 1945, after hearing Ali Akbar Khansaheb's recital on the radio, the maharaja of Jodhpur, Umed Singh, appointed him as the court musician and bestowed the title of 'Sarod Nawaaz' upon him.

Thus, Ali Akbar was able to make an exit from Maihar. At last liberated from the iron shackles of Baba. He returned only for the rare social visit, that too without his sarod. In October 1944, Ravi Shankar too left Maihar for good and moved to Mumbai, where he joined the Indian People's Theatre Association (IPTA). Ali Akbar's solo renditions were regularly broadcast on radio, giving him widespread fame and recognition. Soon, he became the star of music conferences.

Going back to the story narrated by Ali Akbar Khansaheb: 'A couple of years after my first broadcast from AIR Bombay, I again encountered Dinkar Rao Amembal during one of my early solo concerts. Just before going on stage to begin my recital, I went to the washroom, where I bumped into Dinkar Raoji. He spotted me and called me by the alias "Shibu Dutt" that I had adopted while I was at AIR Bombay.

"'Have you come to listen to Ali Akbar's sarod recital?" he asked me. I nodded in affirmation. "Listen to him carefully, and learn from his rendition. He has been trained by his father Ut. Allauddin Khan, the greatest of them all." I again nodded and went for my performance. Later, as I was getting down from the stage, Dinkar Raoji came and hugged me, and laughingly said, "You sure fooled me, didn't you!"'

Marriage

As a musician, Pt Jotin Bhattacharya may not have reached the heights of Baba's star disciples like Annapurna Devi, Ali Akbar, Ravi Shankar, Nikhil Banerjee, Panna Babu, Aashish, Bahadur, etc., but his closeness to Baba was unmatched. He was not only Baba's personal secretary but also his confidante.

Quoting Pt Jotin Bhattacharya from his book *Ustad Allauddin Khan and Us*:

'. . . अन्नपूर्णा की संगीत की नींव तैयार कर रखी थी। लेकिन, जहाँनारा की मृत्यु ने उन्हें कितना बाधित कर रखा था यह तब मालूम हुआ जब बाबा ने उससे कहा, "माँ मैंने तुम्हारी शादी तुम्हारे यंत्र के साथ कर दी। तुम्हारे सारे जीवन की व्यवस्था मैं कर जाऊँगा। तुम मन प्राण से बजाओ। जनता के सामने बजा कर तुम्हें अर्थ-उपार्जन करना नहीं होगा। तुम अपने चिदानंद के लिए बजाओगी और अपना वादन सुनाओगी उस ऊपर वाले भगवान को। संगीत ही तुम्हारा पति होगा। साज़ बजाकर रुपया मत कमाना, वरना असल संगीत नहीं रहेगा।

'दीदी से दुःख की कहानी सुनकर, अन्नपूर्णा देवी में भी विवाह के प्रति वितराग जगा था। दीदी की बात कान में सुनाई देती, 'बहन, शादी मत करना।' इसी मानसिक अवस्था में बाबा ने दिन-रात सिखाना शुरु किया। अन्नपूर्णा देवी ने खुद को संगीत के प्रति समर्पित कर दिया। तब उन्हें क्या पता था कि उन्हें भी शादी करनी होगी और उसका परिणाम जहाँनारा से भी बदतर होगा। जहाँनारा तो एक ही बार में दग्ध हुई मगर उन्हें सारा जीवन दग्ध होना पड़ेगा।'

'... माँ शारदा देवी के मंदिर में, उदय शंकर की करबध्द प्रार्थना बाबा अस्वीकार नहीं कर पाए, इसलिए अन्नपूर्णा का विवाह रवि शंकर से करने की मंजूरी दी।

[Baba had laid the foundation of Annapurna's music training. However, the trauma of his elder daughter Jahanara's death manifested when Baba told Annapurna, "Ma, I have married you to your surbahār. I will leave sufficient provisions for you to meet the basic expenses of your entire life. Put your heart and soul into your music. You won't need to play in front of the audience for money. Just play for the Supreme Self. Music will be your life partner. If you use music to earn money, the purity will be lost.

Hearing the story of what happened to her elder sister, Annapurna was disinterested in matrimony. As if Jahanara's warning against marriage haunted her. Considering this mindset she was in, Baba commenced her intensive training, and Annapurna devoted her heart and soul to music. Baba never imagined that Annapurna too would get married and her marriage would result in a bigger tragedy than Jahanara's marriage. Jahanara's acute suffering ended quickly with her early death, while Annapurna suffered for more than seven decades.

While at Shārdā Ma's temple, with folded hands, Uday Shankar prayerfully proposed Baba for Ravi Shankar's marriage with Annapurna Devi. Baba just couldn't refuse and gave his consent.]'

Many, including His Highness Brijnathsinghji, advised Baba against the marriage, saying, 'भात कैसा है समझकर घी डालना, और लड़का कैसा है समझकर ही बेटी देना [You need to be very careful about where you are marrying your daughter.]' However, Baba was adamant, saying he had given his word to Uday Shankar and it was therefore final.

On 15 May 1941, the Hindu marriage ceremony was arranged at the Uday Shankar Cultural Centre, Almora. Annapurna Devi was converted back to Hinduism just before the marriage ceremony.

On their wedding day.

Ravi Shankar, Annapurna Devi and their newborn Shubho.

Switched

'Bhaiyā's biggest enemy was his careless nature,' Ma used to tell us.
'His impulsiveness and lack of caution have got him into trouble
too often. For instance, once, he had gone to a remote part of India
to perform. The Muslim hosts introduced an extremely beautiful
woman to him. The woman was so beautiful that Bhaiyā was
spellbound by her looks. Then and there they proposed Bhaiyā
to marry her. Bhaiyā committed a blunder by giving his instant
consent, despite the fact that he was already married at that time
and had two sons, Aashish and Dhyanesh.

'The very next day they performed the *nikaah*, the Islamic
marriage ceremony. On the first night, as Bhaiyā went to his bride
and lifted the *ghoonghat*, he had the shock of his life. It was not the
same woman he had given consent to. She didn't have the slightest
resemblance to her.

'Bhaiyā rushed out of the room. He wanted to break up the
marriage then and there, but those people started blackmailing
him with threats of passing on the story to the media and taking
the case to Baba. Bhaiyā, in his distress, contacted his one and
only friend, Panditji, and sought his help. Panditji rushed there
and solved the problem by annulling the marriage, but he wasn't
a shrewd negotiator either. Bhaiyā had to dish out a ridiculously
large amount of money to bury the incident.'

Ut. Ali Akbar Khan.

Pt Ravi Shankar and Ut. Ali Akbar Khansaheb.

Elaboration of a Rendition

न विद्या संगीतात् परा

[*There is no art greater than music*]

I grew up in a domain of overexposure to the golden era of Bollywood music (1949–79, an era ruled by Lata Mangeshkar, Asha Bhosle, Mohammad Rafi, Kishore Kumar, Manna Dey, etc). In those days, the standard duration of a song was about three and a half minutes (that was the capacity of the standard 10 inch 78 rpm shellac disc record). Imagine, therefore, my revelation in hearing the profound depths and richness of the music I heard and learnt (in my limited capacity) at Ma's house. My experience was akin to a child sighting the ocean for the first time.

For instance, once during the early eighties, I happened upon a lesson Ma was giving Basant Kabra. Thanks to my schooling, I had an elementary knowledge of about thirty raags. I tried my level best to figure out which raag was being taught to Basant, but I could not. The notes were of Kaafi Thaat but the effect, the feeling, the mood it created was excessively serious, full of pathos, as if it were a variation of Raag Darbari Kanada with Shuddh Dhaivat. The ālaap and *jod* went on for almost a couple of hours.

As soon as they took a break, I asked Basant Kabra, 'Which raag is this?' Disappointed at my lack of knowledge, Basant sternly replied, 'Bhimpalaasi.' As per my understanding then, Bhimpalaasi was a light raag used for devotional bhajan kind of songs or some light music that could be readily identified with the bandish 'बिरज में धूम मचाए श्याम'. It was beyond my imagination that such a serious and detailed approach was possible in rendering *Bhimpalaasi*.

'I've never heard Bhimpalaasi with such ornate elaboration,' I exclaimed. Ma, with a gentle smile, said, 'The way Baba has taught us, if we cover all the *ang*s [elements], we can perform any raag for up to three to four hours without repetition. The ālaap Baba taught us is a blend of Dhrupad and Khayaal, but in the format inclusive of Sthāyi, Antarā, Sanchāri, Abhog, gradually stepping up the tempo. The various elements include *meend, sparsh, krintan, chhoot-taan, gamak,* etc., followed by *bol* which has *ladi, ladgunthaav, laag-lapet.* So much in ālaap, followed by *jhala,* including *thok jhala,* a variety of *ultaa jhala, taarparan, dhooya, maathaa* and *armaathaa.*

'Next, accompanied by tablā is *ati*-vilambit [very slow] gat, followed by vilambit [slow] gat. Baba taught us all the three styles of gats: *Maseetkhani, Razakhani* and *Wazirkhani.*

'Wazirkhani gats are created by Baba's Guru Ut. Wazir Khan, the very first to alter the twelve-*maatra* Dhrupad gats into sixteen-*maatra Teen Taal. Maseetkhani* gats always start on the twelfth beat of *Teen Taal,* while *Wazirkhani* gats have no fixed starting point. This is followed by *madhyalay* [medium-paced] *gat, razakhani drut* [faster] *gat,* and *ati drut* [very fast] *gat.*'

Basant Kabra.

'Nothing is good enough. So let us do what is right, devote the best of our efforts to reach the unattainable, to develop to the maximum the gifts that God has given us, and never stop learning.'

—Ludwig van Beethoven

Music is Music is Music

Pt Ravi Shankar.

In 1944, a youthful Ravi Shankar had just begun performing publicly. One time, he gave a recital at Lucknow's Marris College of Music, established in 1926 by the legendary musicologist Vishnu Narayan Bhatkhande. There were many prominent musicians and musicologists in the audience. At the end of the recital, Sakhaavat Khan, the sarod teacher of Marris College, commented, 'यह तो सरोद का बाज सितार पे बजा रहा है [He is playing the sitār like a sarod].'

Baba gave such a hostile rebuke that I dare not quote the exact words he spoke as it may create misunderstandings. Baba explained to the effect that music is music. The message of the letter is far more important, than the pen it is written with. A poem could be written using various colours of paper and various colours of ink, but the poem is far more important than the shade of the paper or the colour of the ink. 'संगीत माँ शारदा की आराधना का साधन है, जो कोई भी साज़ पे किया जा सकता हैं। मैंने बीन के कठिन अंग का हर साज़ में प्रयोग किया है [Music is but a means of worshipping Shārdā Ma, which can be done on any instrument. I have tried to imbibe the most difficult beenkaar style in all the instruments.]'

> 'Let there be no noise made, my gentle friends;
> Unless some dull and favourable hand
> Will whisper music to my weary spirit.'
>
> —William Shakespeare (Henry IV, Part 2)

Why Music?

नाहं वसामि वैकुंठे योगिनां हृदये न च।
मद्भक्ता यत्र गायन्ति तत्र तिष्ठामि नारद॥

[*I neither live in heaven, nor in the hearts of yogis.*
I reside wherever My devotees sing my name. O Narad!]
—*Padmapuran, Uttarakhand* (14/23)

Guru Ma never learnt Sanskrit, nor did she ever read Vedant philosophy, yet she would impart the wisdom of the Upanishads. She imbibed such wisdom from Baba, who had spent his formative years in the compounds of the Dakshineswar Kali Temple, at the eastern bank of the Hooghly (Ganges) river. There, Baba had a chance to meet Ramakrishna Paramhansa and Swami Vivekanand. For a long time, Baba learnt from and participated in the orchestra of Habu (Bhupendranath) Datta, who was Swami Vivekanand's younger brother. Habu Datta had studied both Indian and Western music. He composed his music within the raag and taal framework and conducted an orchestra using the Western as well as a few Indian instruments. Perhaps this was the foundation on which Baba later formed the Maihar Band.

Often, Ma would tell us, 'There are several spiritual paths to self-realization—the highest attainment of human life. The Bhagavad

Geeta classifies three yogas, *Jnāna Yoga* (self-knowledge), *Karma Yoga* (selfless, virtuous deeds) and *Bhakti Yoga* (unconditional surrender to God). In the *Kaliyug* (the age of moral downfall and degeneration we are currently in), *Bhakti Yoga* is prescribed as the easiest of them all. There are many ways of practising *Bhakti*, or devotion, but music is the easiest of all. Yet, music is so difficult that it may take the persistent endeavour of a few births to attain self-realization.'

> In Hindu culture, dance, music and drama were performed mostly in the theatre room constructed in the precincts of temples. This was because the act of both performing and witnessing were considered to be spiritual exercises with the purpose of transporting the audience to a parallel reality where they could introspect and ponder over the subtle emotions of their subconscious.
>
> It was much later that the kings and emperors made the artistes perform in the royal courts.

Was Anyone Playing Malkauns?

वीणा वादन तत्वज्ञ: श्रुति जाति विशारद: ।
तालज्ञश्चाप्रयासेन मोक्षमार्गम् च गच्छति।।

[*He who is the maestro of veena-playing,
has mastered the shrutis (microtones),
is adept in taal, attains moksha effortlessly*]
—*Yajnavalkya-smriti*

Annapurna Devi in the 1940s.

Learning from Baba meant being under an extremely strict regime.
Ali Akbar Khansaheb was compelled to practise for eighteen hours
a day, and Ma around fourteen to sixteen hours because Ma also

helped her mother in the kitchen. Panditji and Nikhil Banerjee's riyaaz hours too were comparable to these. When we asked Ma the story about Raag Malkauns, she said, 'I used to practise only two raags at a time, for months on end. Before noon, I would practise the morning raags, and post late afternoon, I practised evening raags. During the afternoon, I practiced *taiyari*—exercises of *murchhanaa, paltaa, taans, jhala*, etc.

'We all tried to adjust our riyaaz hours to match the recommended time of day for playing each raag, but our sessions lasted so many hours that it was not possible to remain within the recommended time segment.

'Once, when Baba returned after a long tour, Zubeida Bhabhi and a few others went to Baba and complained about the scary ghostly apparitions they had experienced on the peepal tree opposite their house.'

There are many superstitions among Indians about the peepal tree (*Ficus religiosa* or sacred fig tree). Some consider the tree to be sacred, believing that devas reside on them, and some believe that ghosts or unhappy souls dwell on them.

'When Baba asked them to be more explicit, they said, "Ghosts are dwelling on the peepal tree. We must cut it down."

"This tree has been here for many years," Baba reasoned. "What made you suddenly suspect ghosts on it?"

"Often, during the night, when all is quiet and tranquil," Zubeidaji explained, "the leaves of this tree start trembling violently even though the air around is still and no perceptible wind is blowing. We have experienced this many times, especially between 11 p.m. and midnight, and it is scary."

"Are you the only one, or are there others who have also experienced such a phenomenon?" Baba asked.

'As a witness, Zubeidaji produced my mother [Madina Ma], and a few others, who all confirmed that they too had experienced such a phenomenon. Baba thought for a couple of minutes and then asked, "Was anyone playing Malkauns when you experienced this?"

"I don't know which raag, but whenever we had such experiences, Annu was playing her surbahār at that time."

"Call her," Baba said.

'I had no idea why Baba had called me. When I went to him he asked me, "What have you been practising in my absence?"

"For the last three months, my focus has been on practising Raag Bhairav in the morning and Raag Malkauns after sundown," I replied.

"For how many hours a day were you practising Malkauns?"

"About eight hours a day."

"Oh!" Baba exclaimed. After a few moments of contemplation, he recovered and told me, "From now on don't play Malkauns."

'I was sad, because Malkauns was my favourite raag. Baba could discern my disappointment. He looked at me and explained, "A pure rendition of Malkauns is known to trigger parapsychic experiences. You may play Malkauns for a very short duration, or you may teach it to others, but not the detailed renditions you are playing now. I will create a new raag for you."

'Then, Baba created a new raag especially for me. It was an unthinkable combination of Bhairav and Malkauns. Baba named the raag Kaushi Bhairav.

'I stopped playing Malkauns. Thereafter, nobody ever experienced ghosts on the peepal tree.'

~

During the late eighties or early nineties. Rooshiji's elder brother, Krish Pandya, who had migrated to Canada, was visiting India. Krishbhai was an expert in Shiatsu (a form of Japanese therapy similar to acupressure) and held seminars teaching it. I too had attended his seminar.

We went to the airport to receive Krishbhai. But at that point in time I had a hatchback car, not useful to store luggage. Notorious as we were for our mischievous traits, Rooshiji and I hired a 1976 Oldsmobile 98 Regency four-door hardtop. That was the longest car I ever drove. I reached Akashganga to pick up Rooshiji. We informed Ma that we would not be back before 4 a.m.

We received Krishbhai at the airport and dropped him at his nephew's residence at Sonawala building, Tardeo. Krishbhai took along one of the two large suitcases, and requested us to take the other one with us to Akashganga. We reached Akashganga at about a few minutes past 4 a.m.

The reason behind my going up at such a ghastly hour was to help Rooshiji carry the heavy bag, and also because I badly needed to use the washroom. On reaching the sixth floor, Rooshiji opened the main door with the latchkey. Just as we were toiling to carry the heavy suitcase, Ma opened the door of her room.

An overwhelming sandalwood-like fragrance flooded out. I say 'sandalwood-like' because although it strongly resembled sandalwood, it was a fragrance I had never experienced before. I had visited sandalwood shops and factories at Mysore and Bangalore earlier, but never encountered a fragrance like this. Well, my olfactory receptors are not as sensitive as my audio receptors, but what follows is my attempt to describe it.

The fragrance of sandalwood is always accompanied by overtones of secondary aromas, additional smells like pine, freshly cut lumber with a little varnish, or perhaps a creamy or spicy overtone, but I had never encountered such a clean and flowery fragrance as I experienced at Ma's house that day. I was so astonished I asked Ma, 'Is that the smell of a sandalwood incense stick?'

'No.'

'Some oil, or garland, of sandalwood?'

'No, nothing like that.'

'Are you wearing perfume?'

'You know I never wear perfumes.'

'Then what is this divine fragrance?'

Ma just lowered her eyes and smiled shyly, evading my question.

I turned to Rooshiji and asked him.

'She has just finished her riyaaz,' Rooshiji explained. 'Sometimes such things happen to her.'

As I rushed home, even though I was drowsy and exhausted, I couldn't get a wink of sleep as that divine smell kept haunting me.

The next time I met Ma, I requested her to explain.

'I don't know what it is,' she humbly said. 'I don't even know how and why it happens. But Baba used to say, "During your sādhanā, you'll encounter many such milestones. You need to be extremely careful to not let these experiences inflate your ego or distract you from the path of your sādhanā. No matter how attractive such milestones may seem, they are not your destination. Your destination is beyond the sensory world."'

Once, we asked her to share with us her paranormal experiences.

'While playing, if you concentrate very deeply, play truthfully, and bring forth the purest *swars*, without violating the purity of the raag, Shārdā Ma at times acknowledges your efforts.'

'Apart from the sandalwood fragrance, have you experienced anything else?'

'Well, sometimes it is some sweet fragrance, sometimes you hear footsteps as if someone wearing *payal* is walking towards you, or as if someone is dancing to the music you are playing. Sometimes from the corner of your eye you can see a young goddess in a red or white sari with gold jewellery sitting beside you while you are immersed in your playing. If you turn your head to see her, she disappears.

'However, if you practise sādhanā with expectations of any reward, it is no more a sādhanā.' Ma didn't know much Urdu, nor did she indulge much in Urdu poetry, but in her own quaint manner, she used to quote a *sher*, a couplet, which I later realized was penned by the great Iqbal:

सौदा-गरी नहीं ये इबादत ख़ुदा की है
ऐ बे-ख़बर जज़ा की तमन्ना भी छोड़ दे

[It is not a business deal, it is worship of the Almighty
O ignorant one, shun the very desire for a reward]

Annapurna Devi.

Tejomay

In 2011, Nityanand Haldipur visited Bangladesh to perform in
a concert. He was invited by Taufik Nawaz, a senior advocate
of the Bangladesh Supreme Court, and the husband of Dr Dipu
Moni, the then foreign minister of Bangladesh. The venue of the
concert was their palatial house in Dhaka. Taufik Nawaz's father
Ameen Ul Rehman used to learn the bansuri from Baba's disciple
Pt Pannalal Ghosh. As the foreign minister of Bangladesh, when
Dr Dipu Moni visited Mumbai, she paid a visit to Guru Ma. She
was so overwhelmed meeting Ma, she started sobbing like a child.

At Nityanand's Dhaka concert, sitting in the front row among
other dignitaries was Pratiti Devi, the writer, singer and twin
sister of legendary filmmaker Ritwik Ghatak, who had made a
documentary film on Baba. After the concert, Pratiti Devi shared
a memorable incident from her childhood:

'I was about eight or nine years old when Baba was in Dhaka
for a concert. My father was a district magistrate and we had a
huge house. We were fortunate that Baba had agreed to stay at
our house. In the late hours of night, Baba used to do his riyaaz
in seclusion. All of us were instructed not to disturb him. We
could hear the sound of his sarod flowing out of his room. My
mother, Indubala Devi, and I were watching and listening to

Baba, who was unaware of our presence. He was playing with his eyes closed, totally immersed in his music as if he were in a state of samadhi. As his riyaaz progressed, we experienced something which cannot be described in mere words. My mother and I saw Baba's body glowing with a golden halo around it. I asked

Baba Allauddin Khan.

my mother what it was. Her only reply was, "He is a divine soul." Only someone who has witnessed what we had witnessed that night can understand it. Such a phenomenon cannot be explained.'

Swami Shardanandji in *Ramakrishna Lilamrut* has described a similar phenomenon experienced by people around Ramakrishna Paramhans. Whenever Paramhans went into deep meditation, his whole body would radiate a golden glow. When people started gathering to watch this divine phenomenon, Paramhans pleaded with Ma Kali to take it away from him.

Mandukya Upanishad and Ma

नास्ति नादात्परो मन्त्रो न देवः स्वात्मनः परः

[Music is the best among all the forms of worshipping]
—*Yogashikhopanishad*

Apart from my foolish attempts to understand women, the most difficult task I have ever attempted is to learn the sarod, that too at 6A Akashganga. Apart from several instructions bombarded on me by Ma, the most baffling was while learning to play ālaap and vistaar. Ma's instructions were repeated by my senior gurubhais Suresh Vyas and Nityanand Haldipur. When teaching me they would constantly say, 'Wait, slow down, you are too hasty, your strokes are too quick in succession . . . allow the note to decay . . . take a split-second pause between them . . .'

Predominantly influenced by the Bollywood music (of the fifties, sixties, and seventies) I was uncomfortable in pausing between notes. In Bollywood music, some or other instruments compulsively fill the gaps within the vocal rendition or obbligato. From that point of view, I wondered, 'How can there be a gap, a blank space between musical notes?' For decades, I remained unconvinced about this point until, while reading Mandukya Upanishad, I came across '. . . नामात्रे विध्यते गति.' When one ॐ (AUM) chanting ends, before the meditator can bring forth the next ॐ in the series, there must certainly be a moment of blissful silence, which leads to the *turiya* state in which the individual soul rests in his own *sat-chit-ananda svarupa*, the highest Brahmic consciousness, the embodiment of knowledge and bliss, which has neither beginning nor end.

Ma never imparted her wisdom using the first person point of view. Whatever she wanted to teach us, about music or about life, she attributed to Baba. For example, she would say, 'Baba said, always do your sādhanā in seclusion. In the presence of someone, the instinct of seeking validation and showing off your prowess to impress them awakens in your mind. During riyaaz, you have to refine every phrase you are unable to execute with grace and precision. You must repeatedly play the parts you find difficult to perform until you gain mastery over them. However, when someone is sitting in front of you, you won't be able to do so. Therefore, you ought to exercise caution in your sādhanā. Riyaaz without introspection is not sādhanā. No matter how learned and technically proficient you may be, without renunciation and divine grace your true destination will elude you.

'Whenever anybody showered praises on Baba, he would cover his ears and exclaim "*tauba*". Baba would compare laudations to growth of weeds in your farm. If you don't get rid of them soon, it will damage your crop. Sādhanā is like farming. A good farmer must constantly work to remove weeds. Baba used to say, "A crowd invariably disturbs me". Being surrounded by encomiastic extollers and laudatory fans is addictive. Once you get addicted to them, you can't live without them in isolation, and sādhanā is possible only in solitude.

'Baba never denied that you need money to survive in this world. But there are two ways of making a living. One is the way of a bootlegger and the other is the way of a gardener. The gardener makes much less money compared to the bootlegger, but is in congruence with nature and is not swayed from the righteous path. The bootlegger spreads toxicity, while the gardener spreads colours and fragrance from nature's bounty. You have to choose the path you want to tread.'

Excellence Has No Limits

There is a world of a difference between listening to the sarod through a loudspeaker and listening to it in person just a few feet away from the instrument. Most sound engineers are clueless about the complexities and intricacies of the sarod. Dynamic microphones are not meant for the sarod. Although they capture the sound of the main strings quite well, they exaggerate the level of *chikaaris* (the filler-drone strings), and fail to capture the sympathetic resonance of the *tarab* strings as well as the subtle beauty of the harmonic overtones produced by the *jawaari* of the *chhed* (drone) strings. To use Oscar Wilde's analogy, they are able to reproduce every aspect of the peacock except its colours. Sitārists too face this problem, but to a lesser degree. The vocalists and the tablā players are the fortunate lot. Even film music recordings do not do justice to the sarod.

In a concert, the artiste begins with ālaap, followed by *jod*. Then he begins *vilambit* gat. This is when the tablā joins. This is when the stage is transformed into a battlefield for a 'war of volume'. Far too many tablā players keep signalling the sound engineer at the console to continually increase the amplitude levels of the tablā. This triggers a phenomenon called 'masking'. Everybody knows that a low amplitude (volume) sound is masked by the high amplitude sound. But very few know that as per the laws of physics, a low frequency sound masks a high frequency sound. In a tablā pair, the *dāyaa* is tuned to the tonic, say middle C, for example; the *bāyaa* is ideally tuned to the lower C (an octave below, though not all bother to tune the *bāyaa* accordingly). Thus, the tablā being both of louder amplitude and of lower frequency, it invariably masks the delicate sympathetic resonance of the sarod.

In Maihar Gharana, it was unanimously accepted that when it came to the sarod, Aashishda was next only to his father, Ali Akbar Khansaheb. As this is being written, Aashishda is the only person alive who has been trained by Baba Allauddin Khan. Also, Aashishda was the first one to play sitār-style *sapaat taans* on the sarod. I had attended a few concerts of Aashishda, but had never heard him in close proximity, except while he was tuning his sarod in the green room. When I came to know that he was taking lessons from Ma, I made it a point to be there.

I reached Akashganga at around 8 p.m. Sitting in Rooshiji's room, Aashishda was engrossed in playing a raag which I could not identify. His rendition was terrific. Each note was crystal clear, in the sweetest sonorous tone, and in perfect pitch. What he played was extremely beautiful, but I was baffled because it sounded much like Bihaag sans *Teevra Madhyam* with greater importance to *Dhaivat*. It had a distinct flavour of Raag Hemant. When Aashishda looked at me, I humbly asked him the name of the raag. 'The name of the raag is *Hem Bihaag* and it was created by *Daadu* (Allauddin Khansaheb),' Aashishda replied with his million-dollar smile.

While waiting for Ma to come out of her room and teach him, Aashishda kept practicing *Hem Bihaag*. Listening to his sarod in such close proximity was a profound, incomparable experience. I would rate it as the best music listening experience I had until then.

Suddenly, Ma's door opened. Standing in the passage outside Rooshiji's room, she called out for Aashish (none of us ever saw Ma entering Rooshiji's room). Aashishda had been waiting for Ma,

Ut. Aashish Khan.

and yet when Ma called his name, his instinctive reaction was like someone hearing a fire alarm. He jumped up and rushed to the living room. Rooshiji and I followed him.

'What were you playing?' Ma asked.

'*Hem Bihaag*,' Aashishda said.

'Okay, let's see how you play *Hem Bihaag*.'

Aashishda played, perhaps even better than what he was playing in Rooshiji's room. Ma kept listening with a poker face. Although the fan was on, Aashishda had broken into a sweat. After a few minutes, Ma sternly commented, 'राग का तो सत्यानाश कर दिया है [You have ruined the raag.]'

Aashishda wasn't dejected upon hearing this, but I was in shock. What could possibly be wrong with Aashishda's rendition which sounded so exquisite to me? Ma asked him to begin the ālaap, and kept correcting the phrases or giving better options. I am not educated enough in music to fully understand and explain in detail what exactly was going on, but what I perceived was that Ma's phrases were much longer and more complete than Aashishda's phrases, which were beautiful but fragmented. Aashishda could instantly grasp the phrases Ma was singing to him. What followed was divinely beautiful.

Mataṅga Muni in *Brihaddeshi* stated:

योऽसौ ध्वनिविशेषस्तु स्वरवर्णविभूषितः।
रञ्जको जनचित्तनां स रागः कथितो बुधैः।।

[*The organized sound of chosen notes, structured, ornamented,
Which pleases the mind, is called Raag by the learned*]

Ma explained, 'Music is non-verbal communication. Music is a language, which has letters (notes) which make words, which put together make phrases, which form sentences, to create paragraphs, and most importantly, convey a non-verbal message.

'*Raagdari* is like storytelling. No matter how beautiful the independent sentences may be, they ought to collectively make a thematic sense, they should create a mood, an abstract image visible only to the subconscious.'

There is an interesting story behind *sapaat taan* on the sarod. Once, a visitor asked Baba, 'Is it possible to play *sapaat taan* on the sarod the way it is played on the sitār?' Baba's reply was, 'Nobody has played it so far, but it is possible, if one trains himself to develop that skill.' Ma heard this and encouraged Aashishda to take up this challenge. When Baba was on a tour, Aashishda, under Ma's guidance, worked relentlessly to develop the skill of playing *sapaat taan* on the sarod. On his return, Baba was thrilled by young Aashish's newly acquired skill. 'Who taught you this?' Baba asked in amazement. Aashishda's reply brought a proud smile on Baba's face. Ma wasn't his favourite disciple without reason!

'Music expresses that which cannot be put into words and that which cannot remain silent.'

—Victor Hugo

Navarasa

'Our sweetest songs are those
that tell of saddest thought.'
—Percy Bysshe Shelley

The most audible lament from people who don't like Indian classical music much is, 'This music is too sad!'

My usual reply to them is, 'Music is subjective, in the sense that it triggers catharsis. It leads to purification by the release of suppressed emotions.'

Recently, I came across a thought-provoking quote by the great Bhavabhuti:

एको रस: करुण एव निमित्तभेदाद् भिन्न: पृथक पृथगिव श्रयते विवर्तान्।
आवर्तबुद्बुद्तरङ्गमयान्वि कारान् अम्भो यथा सलिलमेव तु तत्समस्तम्॥

[*The fundamental emotion is karuna—compassion.*
Water keeps changing forms like whirlpools, bubbles, waves, etc.,
but fundamentally it is but water]

—*Uttarramcharitam 3:47*

The *Nātya Shāstra* is an ancient Sanskrit text on the performing arts, attributed to the sage Bharata Muni, with its first complete compilation estimated to have been made as early as 500 BCE.

According to the *rasa*, the human emotions theory of
the Nātya Shāstra, entertainment is the desired effect of any
performing art, but never the primary goal, which fundamentally
is meant to transport the audience into another parallel reality,
full of wonder and bliss, where they experience the essence of their
own consciousness, and reflect on spiritual and moral questions.
The aim is to enlighten, not entertain.

The eight primary rasas are:

1. *Shringār* (श्रृङ्गारः): Romance, love, attractiveness
2. *Hāsya* (हास्यं): Laughter, mirth, comedy
3. *Raudra* (रौद्रं): Fury
4. *Kaarunya* (कारुण्यं): Pathos, compassion
5. *Bibhatsa* (बीभत्सं): Disgust, aversion
6. *Bhayānak* (भयानकं): Horror, terror
7. *Veer* (वीरं): Heroism
8. *Adbhut* (अद्भुतं): Wonder, amazement

The ninth rasa is:

9. *Shānta* (शांतं): Peace or tranquillity

Ma used to say, 'The ultimate rasa is the shānta rasa, where all
rasas merge into a transformed and transmuted form. Whichever
rasas your rendition may cover, it should ultimately lead to shānta
rasa.'

'The poet ranks far below the painter
in the representation of visible things, and
far below the musician in that of invisible things.'
—*Leonardo da Vinci*

The Magic of Manj Khamaj

Here is an interesting anecdote narrated by Nityanand.

Monday evenings used to be when I would learn from Ma. I was working in All India Radio, and my duty hours were from 8.30 a.m. to 4.30 p.m. Although I was employed as a bansuri player, I acted as a recordist.

On that particular Monday, there were so many recordings going on at the radio station that my day was exceptionally hectic. I had to go up and down the stairs many times and had to keep standing for long hours while working. By the time the day's work was done, I took the local train home. I was so exhausted I had no energy to take my bansuri, and travel 15.5 km by bus to reach Ma's house for my lesson. I was hoping that for some reason, Ma might send me a message to not come that day. However, this did not happen and I went to Ma's house.

Ma opened the door and let me in. Before I could request her to allow me to opt out of that day's lesson, she went to the kitchen. I waited for about fifteen minutes for her, fretting all the while because of my exhaustion.

When she came out, she looked at me and remarked, 'आज आप बहुत ही थके हुए लगते हो [Today you look extremely exhausted.]' I was glad that she was able to empathize with what I was going through and hoped she would ask me to go home. But, contrary to my wishful thinking, she said nothing of the sort.

Ma asked me to alter the tuning of the tanpurā from *pancham* (dominant) to *madhyam* (subdominant), obviously keeping the *sa* (tonic intact). Then she gave me the *āroha–avaroha* of Raag Manj Khamaj, informing me that she was teaching me a raag created by Baba.

God! I was in no mood to learn anything new, much less a raag created by Baba, because those are the raags that are invariably complex, with a multitude of intricacies.

She began teaching me ālaap, going on for two full hours. Then she suddenly stopped to inquire about my fatigue. Only then I realized that I had completely forgotten about my exhaustion and I was feeling highly rejuvenated and energetic. 'Oh! My fatigue has disappeared like magic,' I said.

Ma smiled and said, 'This is the effect Baba's Raag Manj Khamaj can have on us. If rendered with purity, it has such magical effects.'

When Baba visited Shantiniketan, Rabindranath Tagore asked the sculptor Ram Kinkar to create a statue of Baba. It was Tagore who bestowed the title 'Acharya' on Baba.

How to Render a Raag?

*'There is nothing in the world
so much like prayer as music is.'*
—William Merrill

Rooshiji was a Gujarati, born and brought up in Ahmedabad, with limited exposure to music. He emigrated first to the USA, and then Canada, occasionally visiting India to hold seminars. Becoming Ma's disciple was a reverse culture shock of sorts for him.

What Rooshi had learnt studying psychology (behavioural science) in the USA and Canada routinely contradicted the Vedic wisdom and traditions Ma adhered to.

In the words of Nityanand:

'Rooshiji was rather unhappy with my body language during stage performances. Following the footsteps of Ali Akbar Khansaheb, Pt Ravi Shankar, Pannalal Ghosh and Ma herself, in order to fully focus on my performance, my attempt has always been to immerse myself in the raag I render. Like all the greats of Maihar Gharana, I too am used to shutting my eyes and ignoring the audience while performing.

'One day, over a cup of tea and the snacks and sweets that Ma habitually served us, Rooshiji advised me, "Performing live on stage is very different from performing for radio broadcasts. While you are performing live, eye contact with the audience is critical. It establishes not only a rapport with the audience, but projects authority and confidence. It helps one gauge the level of the audience's musical quotient and play according to their taste."

'Ma was quietly listening to this without bothering to react to what Rooshiji was advising me. Rooshiji's advice was quite contrary to what was being practised by the great masters of Maihar Gharana, so I turned to Ma to seek her opinion.

'I asked her, "The audience has various compositions in terms of age, gender, education and social status. Which segment should I play for? How do I gauge their level of understanding, their likes and dislikes? Also, I play what you have taught me, I don't know how to tailor my renditions to the tastes of the audience."

'Ma laughed and said, "Baba used to say, when you are on the stage, be like an owl. No matter how luminous the lights may be, no matter how colourful the crowd may be, turn a blind eye to them. When you shut your eyes to the external world, only then will your inner eyes open to see within. Play for the one within you. Because the one within you is the one within all. Whenever you play a raag, begin by worshipping it. Imagine it to be a deity. Pray for her mercy on you, that she may manifest herself through you. Let the music emerge out of the purest feelings of your heart. Let your music be an oblation—a holy offering to the God."'

After World War II, the two Cold War rivals, the USSR and the USA, were engaged in the Space Race. On 4 October 1957, the Soviet Union launched Sputnik I. It reached outer space at a record altitude of 577 miles above the Earth's surface.

When a Bengali scientist asked Baba, 'What makes music so difficult?' Baba explained by saying, 'Everyone is racing to scale the heights of outer space. Is anyone bothered to explore the depth of inner space?'

Bheem and Shakuni

'If you have any young one, who
aspires to be a pitch-perfect sarodist,
shoot him now, while he is happy.'
—*Jataayu*

Each Saturday rendezvous at Ma's was all about dining, laughing and listening to whatever we could get Ma to share with us. Its members varied, but Prof. Pandya, Nityanand, Suresh Vyas and Pradeep Barot were the most frequent attendees. I too was a regular except for the few years when I was in China and the USA. Hemant Desai was the eldest member who attended regularly until he moved to Pune.

On Saturday nights, 6A Akashganga would suddenly be abuzz with the presence of Ma's disciples—all of us—and our laughter, feasting and storytelling. By Sunday morning, the house would sink back into a mood of desolation. But this is my observation; Ma herself remained inert, unaffected, indifferent to both, the frolicking Saturday nights and the sullen weekdays.

While we waited for Ma to come out of her room and talk to us, I would receive my music lessons. The music was not only difficult to learn, but very difficult to teach. A single phrase could be so long that someone with my kind of filmy tendency could conjure a three-and-a-half-minute film song out of just two phrases from

73

it—one for *staayi* (chorus), and the other for repetitive *anatarās* (verses).

A Saturday music lesson followed by a joke session.

At Ma's house, I first started learning from Rooshiji, but there would be so many arguments between us that Ma intervened and asked Suresh Vyas to assume the responsibility of teaching me. With the sole exception of their language skills, there was nothing in common between Suresh Vyas and Rooshikumar Pandya. Though both of them imparted the lessons they had learnt from Ma, their understanding, interpretations and approach were quite different. If two students of the same guru could be so different, imagine the differences among different gharanas.

I wasn't the only one who had problems learning from Rooshiji; Dr Sunil Shastri too experienced the same, and with Ma's permission, he switched to the bansuri and started learning from Nityanand. Till date, there hasn't been a single problem between them. Sunil and I were fortunate compared to Jaykishore and Qamar Ali, who were far more talented and promising than us, but instead of complaining to Ma, they stopped coming to Akashganga.

All of us found it very difficult to learn under Rooshiji. Perhaps because Indian classical music was not Rooshiji's forte. The other students who stopped learning from Rooshiji were Smarth and Naresh. I offer these details only to demonstrate how Ma kept close track of each and every one of us. Quite often, she scolded Rooshiji for teaching us in a wrong way. Music was of paramount importance to Ma and it didn't matter to her whether the person she was reprimanding in front of others was someone with whom she had signed a marriage bond.

As a rule, whatever was taught or learnt in Ma's house was all under her supervision. If I made a mistake, she would scold Suresh. It was rather humorous because whenever I went for my lessons, Suresh would be more nervous than me. He used to literally beg me, 'अबे साले, ठीक से बजा वरना मुझे माँ की डाँट खानी पड़ेगी [Play properly or Ma will scold me.]'

Suresh was very fond of cracking jokes on Gujaratis, and whenever I played a note at a frequency a cent or two lower than the optimum frequency, he would taunt me, saying, 'You Gujjus are born misers. You people have a tendency to "play less" and "pay less" than what is due.'

I used to respond by threatening him, saying, 'ज़्यादा होंशियारी मत दीखा वरना ऐसा बेसुरा बजाऊँगा की माँ आके तेरी पिटाई कर देगी [Don't act smart or I'll play so poorly that Ma will come and fire the hell out of you.]' Nityanand and Rooshiji used to find these exceedingly funny and would laugh out loudly, often drawing Ma's attention.

Once, when I was sure Ma was in her room and the door was locked, in order to tease Suresh, in the middle of the Ahir Bhairav lesson he was teaching me, I abruptly began playing a filmy song. Although that film song too was in Ahir Bhairav, Suresh and Nityanand panicked. Although I had played the song for just a few seconds, to my utter surprise, Ma heard it all from behind the closed door. An hour later, when she came out of her room, she laughed at me and said, 'बड़े नसीबवाले हो [You are so lucky!]'

With the series of misfortunes that I've faced in my life, I certainly can't be called lucky. So, I asked her, 'Me lucky? How?'

'आप की और बाबा की दोनों की ख़ुशक़िस्मती है, कि आप उनके पास नहीं सिखे [It is your good fortune, and Baba's too, that you never had to learn from him.]'

We stared at her in bewilderment as we couldn't understand what she was hinting at. With her signature laughter, she explained, 'अगर आप बाबा के पास सिखते होते तो बाबा मार मारकर आपका ख़ून कर देते, और बाबा को फाँसी हो जाती [If you were learning from Baba, he would have flogged you to death, and he would have ended up behind bars on charges of murder.]' Everyone was rolling around in laughter, while I hid my face.

During one of our Saturday rendezvous, Suresh said, 'गुजराती लोगों को राग भूपालि पसंद नहीं [Gujaratis don't like Raag Bhupali.]'

Ma asked, 'क्यूँ? [Why?]'

Suresh said, 'भूपालि में म-नी जो वर्जित है [Bhupali does not have Ma–Ni, that's why.]'

Everyone present burst out into loud laughter, but Ma didn't laugh as she didn't get the joke, and I didn't because being a Gujarati, the joke was on me.

Ma asked innocently, 'म-नी वर्जित है तो क्या हुआ? [So, what if Ma–Ni is omitted?]'

Suresh explained, 'मनी माने पैसा, बिना पैसे की चीज़ गुज़रतीयों को कहाँ पसंद आएगी? [Ma–Ni meaning money. Gujaratis won't be interested in anything without money.]'

Ma burst out into her typical childlike laughter.

> 'Art ought to be a sādhanā; an endeavour for perfection. What is the point of running after popularity when most of what is popular is mediocre?'
>
> —Annapurna Devi

Nityanand's Story

योगीन्द्रः श्रुतिपारगः समरसाम्भोधौ निमग्नः सदा
शान्ति क्षान्ति नितान्त दान्ति निपुणो धर्मैक निष्ठारतः।
शिष्याणां शुभचित्त शुद्धिजनकः संसर्ग मात्रेण यः
सोऽन्यांस्तारयति स्वयं च तरति स्वार्थं विना सद्गुरुः॥

[The elevated yogi, master of the scriptures, unagitated by the worldly currents, serene, forgiving, pacified, practising forbearance, committed to virtuosity; the one who purifies the minds of the disciples with his own concourse, such a true guru, selflessly emancipates others as well as himself]

Nityanand Haldipur.

Though my father, Niranjan Haldipur, was a chemical engineer who owned two factories, he was very fond of music. Thanks to

77

his cousin, Devendra Murdeshwar, my father ended up becoming
Pt Pannalal Ghosh's disciple.

Devendra Murdeshwar was an accomplished tablā player.
One day, he chanced upon listening to Panna Babu's bansuri
recital. Panna Babu's music had such an impact on him that
Murdeshwarji decided to become a disciple of the great master.
Murdeshwarji practised day and night with exemplary diligence,
and soon became Panna Babu's prime disciple, and a well-
known flautist. He later married Pannalal Ghosh's daughter,
Shantisudha.

As a child, I got my initial lessons from my father. My
grandfather was the first to recognize my talent and suggest to my
father that I should be formally trained in music. Therefore, my
father took me to Panna Babu who, upon hearing me play, was so
impressed that he not only started teaching me, but also gifted me
one of his bansuris, which I treasure to this day.

Young Nityanand learning from Panna Babu.

After Panna Babu's death in the year 1960, I started learning from Pt Chidanand Nagarkar for the next three to four years, and thereafter from Pt Devendra Murdeshwar.

Allow me to narrate the interesting story of how I ended up being accepted as Annapurna Devi's disciple.

In the year 1950, Murdeshwarji had joined AIR (All India Radio) as a flautist in the National Orchestra under the directorship of Pt Ravi Shankar. As one of his trusted assistants, Murdeshwarji became very close to Pt Ravi Shankar and had a faint acquaintance with Annapurna Devi as well. Pt Ravi Shankar left AIR in 1956 for a series of international performances. By then, Annapurna Devi had stopped giving public performances and was living the solitary life of a recluse.

Sometime in the early seventies, the AIR authorities wanted Annapurna Devi to perform in a national programme, but they knew that it wasn't an easy task to convince her to do so. Knowing that Murdeshwarji belonged to her gharana, and had a close association with Pt Ravi Shankar, the AIR authorities decided to put the onus on Devendra Murdeshwar to convince Annapurna Devi to perform for the programme.

Murdeshwarji sought an appointment with Annapurna Devi, and on behalf of AIR proposed that she play in the prestigious national programme. As expected, Annapurna Devi flatly refused. During the meeting, Murdeshwarji made several attempts to coax her, but she remained adamant, sternly telling him to never bother her again. As the defeated Murdeshwarji was leaving, he requested her, 'As you may remember, my wife, Shantisudha, is Panna Babu's daughter. She is desirous of meeting you to seek your blessings.'

This was a request Annapurna Devi could not refuse, not only because Panna Babu was Baba Allauddin Khan's disciple, but also because she had tremendous respect for him as a pioneer of bringing the bansuri into the classical domain.

Moreover, he was a freedom fighter too, and, most importantly, a saintly soul.

It is worth mentioning that as a freedom fighter, to escape from the clutches of the British police, Panna Babu migrated to Calcutta and joined New Theatres as an artiste, and also worked as the independent music director for some films. Panna Babu wanted to learn from Baba Allauddin Khansaheb, and so sought Pt Ravi Shankar's help. However, Pt Ravi Shankar suggested that Panna Babu become his student instead. Panna Babu refused, insisting he wanted to learn from Baba.

Once, when Baba happened to visit Bombay. Panna Babu invited Baba to his house for dinner. Here, in a childlike manner, he clasped Baba's feet and pleaded with Baba to accept him as his disciple. Baba was moved by this, and accepted his request. The rest, of course, is history. However, Panna Babu's relationship with Pt Ravi Shankar thereafter became less than cordial.

Returning to my story, Murdeshwarji requested me to drive them in my car to Annapurna Devi's house. This is when I met her for the first time. During the visit, Shantisudhaji and Annapurna Devi interacted in Bengali and I sat in a corner without any interaction with Annapurna Devi. Murdeshwarji left for AIR Churchgate, and Shantisudhaji and I returned in my car. On our way back, Shantisudhaji said, 'In everyone's life, there comes a time when he feels stranded, all the doors seem shutting on him. I can see that happening to you, and when you feel so, please go to Annapurna Devi and make her your guru; she is the rishi of our gharana.'

Shantisudhaji's words were a shocking revelation of the state of mind I was in at that point in time. That was the time when my musical progress had come to a halt. Despite my sincere efforts and practice, I was stuck on a plateau of mediocrity. There was no improvement in my music.

Pt Rajeev Taranath.

After this conversation, the idea of making Annapurna Devi my guru kept haunting me, but I didn't know how to approach her. Also, I was deeply committed to my guru back then, Pt Devendra Murdeshwar, with whom I shared a very candid and friendly relationship. Finally, after more than a decade, an opportunity arrived through Pt Rajeev Taranath, who was a disciple of Ali Akbar Khansaheb, but one who occasionally visited Annapurna Devi for guidance.

Rajeev Taranathji had a doctorate in English literature and worked as a professor in Mysore. One of Ali Akbar Khansaheb's oldest disciples, he had left everything behind and moved to Calcutta to learn the sarod at the Ali Akbar College of Music. When Khansaheb emigrated to the USA, Rajeev Taranathji's *tālim* (training) was forsaken, prompting him to learn from Annapurna Devi.

While in Calcutta, Taranathji fell seriously ill. He was in dire
financial straits and couldn't afford proper medical treatment.
He decided to quit music, sell his sarod, and return to Mysore.
During those days, Annapurna Devi, who by then was virtually
separated from Panditji, was at Calcutta. As Ali Akbar Khansaheb
was perpetually on concert tours, Annapurna Devi taught at the
Ali Akbar College of Music.

When Nikhil Banerjee learnt of Taranathji's decision, he
shared it with Annapurna Devi. The next day, Rajeev Taranath
was surprised to see Annapurna Devi standing next to his bed. She
inquired about his health, consoled him, encouraged him not to
quit music, and gave him some money for his medical treatment.
She also assured him that he need not worry about the medical
expenses as long as she was there. 'I am alive because of her kind
gesture,' Taranathji stated. 'Being only four years younger than
Annapurna Devi, I used to address her as "Didi" (elder sister).
However, after that incident, I started addressing her as "Ma"
(mother).'

Whenever Taranathji visited Bombay, he used to stay with
me at my place. In the year 1986, Taranathji came to my house
and shared with me his desire of learning from Annapurna Devi.
He requested I drive him to her house, but with a warning that I
would not be allowed inside. I would need to wait downstairs.

After three days of this ordeal, I refused to drive Taranathji to
Annapurna Devi's place unless and until he promised to take me
upstairs to her house along with him. Taranathji knew that he was
being blackmailed, but had no choice but to agree with me.

When we reached Akashganga, Taranathji went in and told
Annapurna Devi about my waiting below her house for the last
three days. She scolded Taranathji, saying, 'How unfair! The poor
boy is driving you here every day, and you make him wait in the
scorching sun for hours on end. Please bring him up.'

So, Taranathji brought me inside Annapurna Devi's house. Upon seeing her, I paid my obeisance. With much kindness and affection, she asked me to take a seat and offered me tea and sweets. While we were leaving, I requested Taranathji to ask Annapurna Devi about my tālim with her. Taranathji conveyed my request to her, but at that time she ignored it.

Luckily for me, before leaving for Bangalore, Taranathji gave me a message to convey to Annapurna Devi. I went to her house to deliver it. I rang the doorbell, and fortunately she opened the door. I paid my obeisance and gave her Taranathji's message. She made me take a seat and served me tea and sweets. I once again pleaded with her to accept me as her disciple. This time, she said, 'Give me some time to think about it.'

At that time, Atul Merchant was present at Ma's place, taking music lessons from Rooshiji. I'll let him narrate the conversation which took place after I left Annapurna Devi's house that day.

A poker-faced, well-built man with a comical, heavy moustache came to meet Ma. His appearance and body language made him look like an off-duty policeman. His conversation with Ma lasted only for a few seconds, and yet as always, Ma asked him to take a seat, and served him tea and sweets. Ma seemed to be in some contemplation after he left. When Rooshiji asked her what was bothering her, she said, 'क्या मुसीबत [What an awkward situation!]'

We asked her, 'Why, what happened?'

With a sigh, she replied, 'The person who just left is Nityanand Haldipur, a flautist. He has been after me to teach him.'

'What's the big deal? Refuse him,' Rooshiji said.

'That would be committing a sin,' Ma explained. 'According to Baba, not teaching a seeker of knowledge is a sin.'

'Then start teaching him,' Rooshiji said with a laugh.

'But he is Devendra Murdeshwarji's disciple,' Ma said in a tone of caution. 'If I accept him as my disciple, Murdeshwarji may feel offended.'

'Murdeshwar!' I exclaimed. 'What a name! Literally it means the god of the corpses. Who is he?'

'Well, he is Panna Babu's disciple and his son-in-law as well,' Ma explained.

'Ask Nityanand to seek Murdeshwarji's permission allowing him to learn from you,' Rooshiji suggested. 'If Murdeshwarji has no problem you have nothing to worry about.'

Ma turned to me and asked me for my opinion. Perhaps she was testing me. 'Ma,' I said, 'After Panna Babu's demise, and after Hariji followed Panditji and Khansaheb in altering Baba's music so as to please the audience, we now have no flautist in our gharana to keep alive Baba's legacy in its pure form. These days, with you teaching so few disciples, can't Nityanand be accommodated once a week?'

Nityanand resumes the story.

After two days, I again went to Annapurna Devi. This time too, she opened the door, but instead of allowing me in, asked me, 'You again? I told you I need some time to think.'

With a mischievous smile, I said, 'You had two full days to think.'

She started laughing and let me in. She said, 'Okay, I can teach you, but only if you have Murdeshwarji's permission to learn from me.'

I made a beeline to Murdeshwarji's house. When I reached, Murdeshwarji was pouring whisky into his glass. Upon seeing me, he asked me to join him and poured one for me too. Before he took the first sip, I stopped him and asked if he would grant me permission to learn from Annapurna Devi.

Murdeshwarji was shocked. He asked me, 'How did you end up meeting Annapurna Devi?'

'I went to meet her with Rajeev Taranathji.'

Murdeshwarji was speechless. He immediately granted me permission, saying, 'She is the greatest of all, by all means please go and learn from her.'

This is how in the year 1986 Annapurna Devi became my Guru Ma, more than a decade after Shantisudhaji had asked me to become her disciple.

On my first day of learning, she asked me to play something so she could gauge my level of proficiency. To be on the safe side, I started with an ālaap in Yaman, the raag I had learnt from three earlier gurus. I must have played for about fifteen minutes when she asked me, 'Are you a performing artiste, or are you playing for yourself in seclusion?'

'I perform at concerts and radio–TV broadcasts,' I replied, wondering why she could be asking me such a question despite knowing my profession.

'If you are a performing artiste,' Ma explained, 'you can't afford the luxury of taking so much time to establish a raag. Audiences these days have a very short attention span. If you fail to establish the mood of the raag within the first couple of minutes, the audience won't be able to relate with the rest of your rendition.'

I paused and thought for a while. I was very much aware of the problem she was explaining, but clueless about the solution. Realizing my mental state, she explained, 'The beginning of your rendition should manifest the raag vaachak—the thematic phrase which denotes the essence of the raag and establishes its mood.'

The revelation astonished me. I had been learning from so many gurus, but no one had ever taught me something so important and crucial. She then went on to teach me Raag Yaman itself. I had been playing Yaman for years, but the phrases she taught me were so outstanding that I had never thought they could exist in the Yaman framework.

I was so overwhelmed by the quality of Yaman she taught me that I thought of quitting my job at AIR and stopping the tuitions I was giving to devote myself to learning from her full-time. When I met Ma the next time, I was amazed by her prescience. Before I could even open my mouth, she asked, 'Are you thinking of quitting your job?'

'Yes, Ma, I want to devote my full-time learning from you.'

'That is not right. You must earn to support your family.'

'But my wife has a job and she earns a decent salary.'

'Never depend on your wife's earnings. You too must earn something. It is up to you whether or not to teach others, but please don't quit your job.'

It is said that our subconscious mind picks up our guru's traits. After becoming Guru Ma's disciple, I went through a major transformation, not only as a musician, but as a person as well. My previous Guru Devendra Murdeshwarji loved whisky and by forcing me to drink with him he had also made me a habitual drinker. After coming to Ma, Atul, Sunil Shastri and Rooshiji all tried to convince me to stop drinking, but I was finding it very difficult to do so. I was a chain-smoker too.

During a Saturday rendezvous, with his typical aggression, Atul went to the kitchen where Ma was cooking. From outside the kitchen, not visible to them, I was overhearing their conversation. Atul was trying to convince Ma, 'Ma, as his guru, please give Nityanand a diktat that he shouldn't touch alcohol ever again.'

Ma was not convinced.

Atul asked her, 'Why not?'

'As an addict, such a diktat would be too harsh on him.'

'But wouldn't it be good for him?'

'On the contrary,' Ma explained calmly. 'If he goes against my diktat, his guilt may have an adverse effect on his psyche. He may stop coming for his lessons.'

Atul was disappointed because Ma didn't agree with him and give me a diktat; however, Ma's simple one-liner worked better than any diktat. Upon hearing Ma's reply to Atul, at that very moment I gave up alcohol.

Under Guru Ma's guidance, I progressively acquired *raagdari*, depth, refinement, maturity in my renditions, and a whole new dimension in music and in life I had never known existed.

It is said that familiarity breeds contempt. That is true even for celebrities. The closer you become to them, the more you discover various faults you never knew were there.

Once, Ali Akbar Khansaheb graced Atul's house for dinner. After dinner, as we all gathered around Khansaheb, Atul asked the Swar Samrāt a tricky question, 'Khansaheb, how come such great celebrities of art have such dark sides to them?'

Khansaheb, the king of lateral thinking in music, who was also famous for witty one-liners, asked Atul a counter question, 'Do you like art?'

'Of course, I do,' Atul promptly replied.

'Do you want to continue loving art?' Khansaheb asked with his signature mischievous lopsided grin.

'Of course I want to,' replied Atul.

'Then keep away from artists, or you'll stop loving art.'

This was somehow true in the context of all the celebrities I encountered as a performer and a recordist at AIR. However, my experience with Guru Ma has been quite contrary to this rule. Instead of discovering her darker side and negative traits, I kept discovering more and more goodness in her character and the greatness of her *siddhi* (attainments). Despite my initial scepticism, I was subsequently convinced beyond doubt that she was truly a saintly person.

यस्त्वात्मरतिरेवान्तः कुर्वन्कर्मेन्द्रियैः क्रियाः ।
न वशो हर्षशोकाभ्यां स समाहित उच्यते ॥ ३७॥

[*But the lover of the inner Self, though operating through
the organs of action, is unaffected by joy and sorrow;
he is held to be in equanimity*]
—*Annapurna Upanishad* (1.37)

Therapeutic Hostility

यः समः सर्वभूतेषु विरागी गतमत्सरः ।
जितेन्द्रियः शुचिर्दक्षः सदाचार समन्वितः ॥

[Guru is the one who treats all equally,
without favouritism or discrimination.
Who has risen above sensory pleasures,
pious, versed, and virtuous]

Contrary to the popular myth that Annapurna Devi had inherited her father Baba Allauddin Khan's fiery temper, Guru Ma was exceptionally kind, empathetic and patient with her disciples even while teaching them. Guru Ma never charged any fees whatsoever, nor did she accept any gifts. On the contrary, she not only cooked meals for her disciples, but also lavishly showered gifts and gave monetary aid to the needy ones. I have narrated this in detail in the chapter titled 'Mysterious Benefactor'.

When I left my job to start my business, I went to seek Ma's blessings. She asked me to wait, went inside her room and returned with two brand-new Rolex watches. One was 14k gold and the other stainless steel.

'Keep the one you like and give the other to Rooshiji,' she instructed.

The gifted Rolex watches.

I refused but she insisted. I definitely didn't have the cheek to take the gold Rolex, so I kept the stainless steel and gave Rooshiji the gold one.

I asked Ma, 'Ma, these are very expensive watches! Where did you get this from?' Ma didn't reply, but later I learnt that she had acquired these for Panditji and Shubho. The watch was in mint condition even though the year of manufacture was more than a decade ago.

Of course, when it came to music, Ma was strict and demanding of her disciples, but she varied the degree of strictness in proportion to the disciple's capability.

For example, on one occasion, Basant Kabra was learning Raag Desh from Ma. As mentioned earlier, Ma always taught in the living room. The session had started at around 4 p.m., and by the time it was 7 p.m., Stuti Dey had arrived for her lesson. No one had the temerity to disturb Ma while she was teaching. Rooshiji had to wait quite a few minutes to find a window of momentary pause during the lesson to intimate Ma about Stuti Dey's arrival.

'Oh god!' exclaimed Ma. 'I forgot to inform her not to come today.'

Ma was unaware that Stuti Dey had already entered the room and was standing right behind her.

After deliberating for a few seconds, Ma instructed Basant to pack up for the day.

People may wonder what is so unusual about such a story. Well, let me explain that in Ma's case it was. Ma adhered to the principles of the guru–shishya paramparā, therefore, as a rule, she taught one disciple at a time. Yet, there were exceptions like the brother–sister duo of Sandhya and Sudhir Phadke; the trio of Leena Vaze, Meena Sukthankar and Nanda Sardesai; and a few others who learnt in pairs right from the beginning. Each disciple was given a fixed day and time several days in advance.

Whenever there was a disciple from a far-off land, such as Basant Kabra (Jodhpur), Amit Bhattacharya (Benaras), Daniel (Austria), etc., the lessons would last for six to eight hours (albeit with breaks and depending upon the disciple's stamina). No other disciple was taught on that day.

As Stuti Dey heard Basant learning Raag Desh, she reminded Ma about her own incomplete lesson of the same raag. I note that it is impossible for anyone to 'completely' or 'perfectly' learn any raag. The deeper you dive, the more you discover.

When Stutiji's training session started, I was surprised to realize she was allowed certain liberties which were not allowed to Basant. Phrases given to her were relatively simpler and shorter, and unlike Basant, she was allowed an extra stroke to complete a phrase.

After Stutiji left, I asked Ma, 'Weren't you too strict with Basant and rather lenient with Stutiji?'

Ma habitually gave Baba's example. 'You know, Baba had all kinds of students learning from him. What was taught and expected from Bhaiyā and Panditji couldn't have been taught and expected from the orphans of Maihar Band.'

Ma continued, 'A student who went on to become a respected ustad came to learn the sarod from Baba. However, in those days, Baba was not keeping too well, so the onus was on Panditji to teach him. The grasping power of the student was so low that Panditji kept repeating the instructions but the student just couldn't follow him. Now, Panditji always had a reputation of being the "one who never gets angry", but on that day, I could see his face becoming red with rage and his forehead sweating profusely. I understood the situation and came to the boy's rescue. Panditji whispered in my ears, "Please take him away from me before I beat him up." I took over teaching the boy after that, but, believe me, it was truly a Herculean task. The boy was otherwise extremely talented in music. On his own, he learnt to play the harmonium, sing along to film songs, and even entertained us all.'

Not only the music lessons, but Ma's interpersonal equation too varied with each disciple. For instance, for some inexplicable reason, I was given the licence to tell her the way I saw it. With Dr Shastri, the conversation invariably revolved around Vedanta philosophy.

During our Saturday evening gatherings, we had a friendly competition to see 'who made Ma (and everyone else) laugh the most'. I had a reputation of being very witty and funny, and Suresh was a master of one-liners. Rooshiji was good at memorizing jokes, and his timing was superb. Nityanand was extremely creative.

Ma's relationship with Basant Kabra was all music and no conversation. On the other hand, Nityanand and Ma would have excessively long discussions which none of us could understand. Nityanand worked as an artiste and recordist in AIR, mainly handling the classical music parts, and he would always give Ma the latest news from the goings-on there.

We feel that the wiring of Nityanand's brain should be a subject of research in neuroscience. He has an astonishing ability to meticulously remember music and conveniently forget everything else. He could be the sure winner of a 'World's Most Forgetful Person' contest.

Nityanand's conversations with Ma sounded like a perfect comedy skit. For example, every Saturday he would stand at the kitchen door and give her a detailed report about what had happened that week in the classical music world at AIR. Ma, while cooking for us, would listen attentively. Expecting high-grade comedy, we used to stand behind Nityanand and listen to their conversation. Our aim was to count how many times the word 'that' got repeated. We used to call it 'that' conversation.

'Ma, today *that* female singer came for recording.'

'Which one?'

'I keep forgetting her name. Remember *that* singer who had messed up her rendition a few months ago?'

'Oh, *that* singer! Why was she called again?'

'What to do? She has a clout with *that* politician.'

'What raag did she sing this time?'

'She sang *that* raag.'

'Which raag?'

'I forgot the name. It was *that* rare raag very similar to Jhinjhoti.'

'Raag Khambavati?'

'Ya, ya, *that* one.'

'Who accompanied her on the tablā?'

'*That* funny guy.'

'Which one?'

'Remember *that* one, whose *bāyaa* sounds like knocking on a cardboard?'

'Oh God! *That* one again!'

Such conversations would go on for about an hour. Nobody except Ma could understand what Nityanand ever said, but it was funny enough to keep us laughing for the next few hours.

By the time our lot came to Akashganga, Nikhil Banerjee had totally abandoned Ma and shifted to the camp of her elder brother Ali Akbar Khansaheb, with whom he went for many concert tours playing numerous *jugalbandis* (duets). Nikhil Banerjee's sudden death in 1986, at the age of fifty-four, was yet another source of enormous grief for Ma.

Hariprasad Chaurasia had become such a busy star both in film music and the classical domain that he had no time to visit Ma for lessons or socially. Nevertheless, as an annual ritual, he used to make it a point to visit her on the day of Guru Purnima.

We were shocked to witness Ma's harsh attitude towards Hariji. In his absence, Ma would generously and repeatedly praise him. She used to say, 'You all make terrible disciples. With the exception of Basant, you all are lazy bums and not *riyaazi* enough.'

'Ma, you've taught so many during your lifetime,' I asked. 'According to you, who was your best pupil?'

'Nikhil and Hariprasad were the best I got,' was her obvious answer. 'They both were extremely hard-working. Nikhil was like a karma yogi, totally focused and devoted to riyaaz. Unlike others, he was never after name, fame or money. Right from the days of *Basant Bahar* (1956) when Nikhil played with Bhaiyā and Panna Babu, the music director Jaikishan was extremely fond of Nikhil's sitār-playing, and used to invite him to the Famous Recording Studio at Tardeo, not far from here. However, Nikhil was least interested.

'One day, Nikhil ran out of money. I could help him a bit, but I too was in a severe financial crisis. I reminded him, "Why don't you go to Jaikishan? He became so fond of you during the recording of *Basant Bahar*. Just for a few hours of recording session he pays you so well."

Pt Nikhil Banerjee.

'Following my advice, Nikhil went to Famous Studio. Shankar-Jaikishan used to record songs during the pre-lunch sessions, and post-lunch Jaikishan would record the background music. Nikhil reached the studio post-lunch. Jaikishan was thrilled to see him. However, at that point in time, he had no specific sitār piece suitable for Nikhil in the score he was recording. Nonetheless, Jaikishan gave the "pack up" order to the rest of the orchestra and requested Nikhil to play whatever he was in the mood for. Jaikishan explained that he would use the recording as background music, fitting it in as the situation allowed.

'At the end of the session, delighted with Nikhil's playing, Jaikishan handsomely rewarded Nikhil with an envelope of currency notes and asked, 'Nikhilda, can you come tomorrow morning at 10 a.m. to play for a song recording?'

Nikhil expressed his inability saying, 'Sorry, I can't come.'

'When can you come?' Jaikishan asked.

'When I run out of money I'll come,' smirked Nikhil.

Bemused by such an answer, Jaikishan asked, 'Are you unhappy with the fees I am paying you? Or is there any other problem? Has anyone been disrespectful to you here?'

'Nothing of the sort,' Nikhil replied with an assuring smile. 'You know I want to spend as much time as possible learning from my guru, Annapurna Devi. I take concerts and recordings only to meet my living expenses.'

Shocked to hear this, Jaikishan gave him an open invitation, saying, 'Nikhilda, my doors are always open for you. Just walk in anytime you need money or feel like playing.'

Speaking of Hariji, Ma used to say, 'For a long time, Hariprasad was after me to accept him as my disciple. After testing his tenacity for quite a few months, I accepted him. He was already recording for films, but at that point in time, his playing was not suitable for classical renditions. My precondition with him was, "You'll have to start all over again, from ABC."

Pt Hariprasad Chaurasia.

'I thought he wouldn't agree, but he started learning from scratch. Every day he worked hard for long hours at recording studios, and in the evenings, he would come to me to learn classical music. He would eat without fuss whatever I cooked, and after the meal, he would immediately resume learning. What has made him such a big star is his hard work and perseverance.'

Remarkably, all her praises for Hariji were in his absence. Once, during the lessons, Hariji realized that Ma was suffering from a severe cough. As Ma used to sing and teach, with such a bad throat, she had to strain herself. Next evening, he brought some medicines for Ma and gave them to her just before the lesson, explaining how and when to take them. Ma chucked the medicines in the trash, saying, 'आप यहाँ संगीत सीखने आए हो या डॉक्टरी करने? [Have you come here to learn music or to practice medicine?]'

Whenever Hariji visited Ma (annually on the day of Guru Purnima), all those present would be shocked by Ma's harsh attitude towards Hariji. On one Guru Purnima day, Hariji visited Ma. In his usual jovial manner, he mentioned his recently concluded Europe tour. He boasted a bit about his international fanfare and the awards and rewards he got. He then pulled out a quartz wall clock, and offered it to Ma, saying, 'आपके लिए

Switzerland से यह घड़ी लाया हूँ। भारीवाली है [For you I bought this wall clock from Switzerland. It is an expensive one.]' (For the benefit of those who don't know Hindi, the term '*bhaari*' in Hindi could be a synonym for both 'heavy' and 'expensive'.)

To everyone's shock and surprise, Ma took the slim, round wall clock in her left hand, and with a flick of her wrist, like a Frisbee champion, tossed it out of the balcony. The balcony was at a distance of about 8 feet on the left of where she was sitting. The shutters were but partially open. Through that opening, the wall clock landed six storeys below, on the terrace of the adjoining bungalow.

Everyone was shocked and stunned. Ma looked at Hariji and said, 'भारी चीज़ ज़ोर से गिरती है [The heavier they are, the harder they fall.]' Saying that, Ma got up and went away to her room and didn't come out for the rest of the evening. That was the end of the Guru Purnima event that year.

On another occasion, Hariji came with a bagful of currency notes. Showing off the rich booty, he said, 'I dedicated yesterday's concert at Jalandhar to you. I played exactly the way you have taught me. Look at these currency notes that people showered on me. Since the concert was dedicated to you, I would like to offer this money to you.'

Keeping a straight face, Ma took the bag and started walking towards the window. Remembering the clock incident, Hariji quickly snatched away the bag from Ma and asked in an alarmed voice, 'Ma, what are you doing! Throwing away the money?'

'Why? What difference does it make to you?' Ma argued. 'Since you have given the money to me, I can do whatever I feel like with it.'

Hariji, with the bagful of currency notes, made a beeline out of the house. Ma kept laughing after that in her typical carefree manner.

The most famous incident is of Ma throwing the tanpurā at Hariji. Those were the days before electronic tanpurās were invented. Ma was kind enough to play the tanpurā for Hariji during the lengthy teaching sessions which lasted for hours. Like Baba, Ma was very strict about *mudrā dosh* (shaky or faulty stance). If music is a form of meditation, the *saadhak* must remain still. However, that day, despite a couple of warnings, Hariji couldn't refrain from excessively shaking his head. Ma angrily warned him, 'Will you stop behaving like a restless monkey!' Hariji promptly steadied his stance for a while, but after a few minutes again began shaking his head. Ma lost her temper and threw the tanpurā at him. It shattered into pieces as it landed with a loud bang on the floor, just a few inches in front of Hariji. Hats off to him for passing the acid guru-*bhakti* test, signifying unconditional surrender to the guru. Calm and composed, Hariji gathered the pieces of the tanpurā, placed them at Ma's feet and kept staring at her. The pregnant pause lasted for a few seconds, and both ended up laughing aloud for several minutes.

The saddest example was on the day of Hariji's seventieth birthday bash when the who's who of the music world were to attend the function. Hariji was to be felicitated and the book *Bansuri Samrat Hariprasad Chaurasia*, authored by Surjit Singh, was to be unveiled by none other than Bollywood superstar Amitabh Bachchan.

A few days in advance, Hariji had sent a message to Ma that at the given day and time he would be coming to seek her blessings, as it was possibly to be the happiest day of his life. With a bouquet of flowers, Hariji arrived at Ma's house sharp at the appointed time. Naturally, he was in a hurry as he had to reach what was perhaps the biggest ever felicitation function in his honour.

However, to his utter dismay, Ma refused to open the door. Hariji kept pleading from the other side of the door, but Ma stayed firmly inside. Ma timed Hariji, who, for about forty minutes kept ringing and pleading with her to allow him to come in and seek her blessings. Hariji was getting delayed for the function so he went away, leaving behind a floral bouquet at the door.

I knew that Hariji was going to come meet Ma. I therefore made it a point to be at her house. However, I got delayed and could reach only half an hour after Hariji had left. I saw a floral bouquet lying outside the door. Ma opened the door within a few seconds of my ringing the bell. I paid her my obeisance, placed the bouquet in a vase and inquired about Hariji's visit. She said, 'Yes, he came, but I didn't open the door. He kept ringing for about forty minutes, then went away. He must have left this bouquet of flowers at the door.'

'Ma! He is your best disciple. You've loved him like your own son,' I said in surprise. 'How can you be so harsh with him?'

After a brief pause, Ma said, 'An artiste ceases to be a seeker the moment he achieves stardom. Stardom is the ultimate test imposed by Shārdā Ma on Her seekers. Very few are able to pass this test. Stardom is the greatest challenge encountered by an individual to remain grounded as a good human being, a good friend, a good spouse, a good parent, a good disciple, a good teacher, a good role model. You know, awards and felicitations can trigger spiritual अधः पतन [abjection],' Ma said in a very serious tone. 'The easiest way to spiritually destroy a person is by felicitating him. The claps, applause, praises, rewards, awards are sure to inflate an artiste's ego to monstrous levels and trigger his spiritual downfall.

'Guess what must be going on in that function right now?' Ma asked me. 'Dozens of celebrities and hundreds and thousands of fans must be singing and showering praises on Hariprasad, who is not too spiritually evolved. As his guru, it is my sacred duty to be watchful and keep my disciple's ego under the tightest rein. It is not easy to be a guru.

'A guru has to teach different disciples with varied intelligence quotients, varied emotional quotients, varied musical quotients and varied spiritual quotients, without discrimination. एक ही कुंभार

के बनाए हुए है हम सब [We are all created by the same god. There must be some reason why god shaped us differently.]'

Sharing an instance of Ma's humour.

Compared to the rigorous riyaaz of Ma, Khansaheb, Panditji, Nikhilda, Hariji, Aashishda and Shubhoda, the subsequent lot of Ma's disciples were relatively too lazy.

Ma would often call Nityanand and Hemant 'Peepu' and 'Phishou'. Whenever she called them by these comical epithets, 'O Peepu! O Phishu!', her way of speaking was so musical and so comical that we all would burst out laughing.

Peepu–Phishu are from the Bengali version of an ancient fable of the two laziest possible siblings. The two were such sloths that one night when their neighbours alerted them that their roof was on fire, they lazily went back to sleep. The house was soon enveloped in flames. When the flames started scorching the back of one of them, he uttered, 'Peepu', the abbreviation of *'peeth purchhe* [my back is burning]'. The other brother replied, 'Phishu', the abbreviation of *'phire shou* [turn over and sleep].

Jeetendra Prasad, a minor prince from Nepal, was learning sitār from Baba. Once, while conversing with Panna Babu, Prasad learnt that Baba was teaching Panna Babu Raag Deepak. He pleaded with Panna Babu to teach him the āroha-avaroha and pakad of Raag Deepak. Panna Babu obliged.

In a sudden fit of anger, Prasad ran to Baba and shouted, 'You are partial. You taught Raag Deepak to Pannalal but not to me. I don't want to be your disciple any more.' Saying this, he banged his sitār and broke it.

Baba calmed him down saying, 'I didn't teach you Raag Deepak because I didn't find you capable of handling it. If learning just the āroha-avaroha has made you so angry, imagine what learning the raag in detail would have done to you.'

Tailormade Sargam

Speaking of Baba, Ma said, 'Baba never ever took any money from any of his pupils. He ended up wasting too much time teaching pupils who had no aptitude for music. Some of them were tone-deaf, and no matter what Baba did, they would have never become musicians. Baba's performing career and the income from it suffered because of the time he spent on teaching. However, Baba believed that god had sent him to Earth to teach music, and that it was his duty to fulfil this divine mission.

'For example, in those days, Baba regularly played for AIR Allahabad. An old man named Munnulal, a goldsmith by profession, would come to Baba to learn the sitār. Baba was fully aware of the fact that old Munnulal neither had the aptitude for music nor the dexterity to play the instrument, but he never disappointed him. Baba said, "After working for the whole day at his shop, if he comes home and plays music for joy and peace, I am not going to disappoint him."

'There were several such examples, like a case of a *panhaaraa* [water-bearer], who would draw water from our well. Baba called him and asked him if he had learnt music. The poor labourer was so dumbfounded by this unexpected encounter with a dominating personality like Baba that all he could do was shake his head in negation.

"What? You've never learnt music!?" Baba asked.

"I never got the opportunity," answered the poor man.

"Do you prefer to lead the life of a beast, or would you rather evolve as a human?" Baba taunted him. The poor man was speechless.

"Come in right away," Baba said. "I'll teach you music." Thus began the poor man's music lessons. Despite a few days of sustained effort, Baba couldn't make him sing a single note. Baba was in no mood to give up, but soon the poor man escaped from this ordeal, never to be seen again.

'Then there was the *pujāri* [temple priest] who came all the way from Satna, about 42 km away from Maihar, to learn music from Baba. The commute of 42 km each way to and fro was a considerably long distance in that era, and that too for an elementary music lesson. The pujari was a real simpleton. His lessons with Baba were so hilarious that we had to lock ourselves in our room as we couldn't control our laughter. For starters, he arrived with a strange-looking instrument which he believed was the sitār. At first, Baba tried to persuade him to shift to another instrument, but the priest was adamant. Baba had to spend hours restoring it.

'The funnier part was that the priest wanted to sing along while playing the sitār—something nobody has ever done, not even in Bollywood films, but Baba for whatever reason allowed him. (Stalwarts like Baba and Ut. Vilayat Khansaheb have sung while giving instrumental recitals, but never have they sung and played simultaneously. They would stop playing their instruments while singing, and resume playing once they finished singing.)

'As always, the training started with the basic Bilāwal—Major scale: Sa Re Ga ma Pa Dha Ni Sa.

'But the pujari failed to understand why he was being made to sing the notes Sa, Re Ga, ma. After just a few repetitions, he pleaded, "Baba, this is not what I want to learn."

'Knowing Baba's fiery temper, we expected some serious fireworks, but fortunately the priest got nothing of the kind.

"Then what is it that you want to learn?" Baba was deeply puzzled.

"I want to sing devotional chants while playing the sitār."

Bemused, Baba thought for a moment, and the genius that he was, he came up with an incredible idea. Baba took the instrument from the priest's hand and started playing the notes of Bilāwal—Major scale:

Sa Re Ga ma Pa Dha Ni Sa'
Sa' Ni Dha Pa ma Ga Re Sa.
[C D E F G A B C']
[C' B A G F E D C]

'However, while playing, Baba sang the following lyrics:

See-ta Ram jai See-ta Ram jai
[C D E F G A B C']
See-ta Ram jai See-ta Ram jai
[C' B A G F E D C]

'The priest was thrilled. He joyfully began playing and singing the āroha and avaroha, chanting the lyrics Baba had just invented for him. The priest finally got what he was seeking. Baba created some more such pieces for him, but I can't recall them all now.

'The pujari's musical quotient was so low that we asked Baba what was the point in wasting time on him. But Baba explained that as a teacher, it was his duty to teach whoever came to learn regardless of his aptitude.'

This story Ma told us was so amusing that all of us exploded with laughter. Nityanand and I tried to sing the scale with the 'Sitaram' lyrics, but it wasn't easy to sing while laughing so loudly.

Baba's room.

Baba Goes to the Cinema

Pt Jotin Bhattacharya has narrated numerous anecdotes in his book on Baba. Below is a translated version of a funny anecdote which gives an insight into Baba's idiosyncrasies.

One day, Baba took his grandchildren, Aashish, Dhyanesh, Shubho and Shree to see a mythological film, *Jai Hanuman*. Kailash Talkies was the only theatre in Maihar. Although Baba was the one who had inaugurated that cinema hall, he had never seen a single movie there.

That film was a C-grade low-budget mythological film. Within half an hour of the start of the show, Baba walked out, with the children in tow, and returned home.

Surprised to see them returning so early, we asked Baba, 'What happened?' Baba said, 'फ़िल्म में एक गाना बहुत बेसुरा था [A song in the film was too out of pitch.]'

Later, when Jotin Babu visited the cinema hall, he was told that though there was no need for Baba to purchase tickets, Baba had insisted on buying them, that too the cheapest available for the lower stalls. In those days, the lower stalls used to have bare wooden benches without backrests. The upper stalls used to have cushion-less seats with backrests, and the most expensive balcony seats used to be cushioned seats with backrests.

When the manager, Mr Ilaviya, came to know that Baba was in the theatre, he came running down and pleaded, 'Baba, why are you sitting here? Please come with your grandchildren and sit in the balcony. The stalls are meant for people of lower classes and not someone of your stature. Baba, however, refused to budge, saying, 'मुझे निम्न श्रेणी में बैठकर ही आनंद आता है। क्योंकि मैं भी निम्न श्रेणी का व्यक्ति हूँ। इसके अलावा, नाती-पोते अगर अभी से ऊपर गद्दी पर बैठने की आदत डालेंगे तो बाद में बेंच पर बैठने में असुविधा होगी। शुरू में कष्ट करना बहेतर है। उपयुक्त होने पर गद्दी पर बैठने में आनंद मिलेगा। [I prefer sitting with people from the lower classes as I consider myself to be one of them. Besides, if my grandchildren get used to the luxury of sitting on cushioned seats in the balcony at this age, they will be uncomfortable sitting on the benches later on in life. Migrating from hardship to luxury is much better than the other way round.'

In 1952, the film *Aandhiyan* was released. Its music director was none other than Ali Akbar Khan. Baba was furious to learn that his son was now making lowbrow film music. He went to the theatre, but refused to take a seat, as a mark of his disapproval. Baba bluntly said, 'I didn't waste all those years teaching him music so that he would stoop down to the pedestrian level entertainment.'

However, the film began with the title music of an Indian orchestra which was quite in congruence with Baba's Maihar Band, albeit played by the more efficient cine musicians. The title music was immediately followed by Lata Mangeshkar's song '*Hai Kahin Par Shaadmani*'. With a contented smile, Baba walked away saying, 'If such is the quality of film music, I have no objection.'

Baba was extremely fond of Lata Mangeshkar's singing. He called her 'आसमान से आयी हुई परी [An angel who has descended from the heavens.]'

There is another interesting incident shared by Suresh.

In 1960, Tapan Sinha made the film *Kshudhita Pashan*, based on the story 'Hungry Stones', written by Rabindranath Tagore. Arundhati Devi, the actress, singer, writer, director and wife of

Lata Mangeshkar rehearsing with Ali Akbar Khansaheb.

Tapan Sinha, played the female protagonist in the film. Arundhati Devi was a student of Visva Bharati University, where she was trained in Rabindra Sangeet. Arundhati was like a daughter to Baba. When Baba was on a visit to Calcutta, Arundhati went to Baba and requested him to attend the premiere of *Kshudhita Pashan*. However, Baba was reluctant, mainly because he was sceptical of the music given by his son Ali Akbar Khan.

After a lot of persuasion, Baba agreed to attend the film show with the condition that he would walk out in just a few minutes. However, Baba was rather touched by the music and he sat through the entire film.

'Drama and Music are inseparable yet contradictory art forms. Drama is all about putting on the mask, while Music is about bringing out the innermost emotions.'

—Jataayu

Punitive but Not Greedy

पूर्ण संतुष्ट हूँ अब किसीकी चाह नहीं है मुझे
एक कतरा भी अब तो समंदर सा लगे है मुझे

[Fully contented, I am free of desires now
A tiny drop seems like an ocean to me now]

Baba Allauddin Khan.

Here is yet another anecdote from Pt Jotin Bhattacharya's book.

'The day was 11 June 1950. While taking lessons from Baba, young Aashish played the ālaap, jod and jhala very well, but when

Baba asked him to play the gat, Aashish could not remember it. He was indeed a prodigy, but poor memory was his weakness. Baba got very angry at him for forgetting the gat and beat him mercilessly. It was inhumane in every sense. Madina Ma and I tried to stop Baba, but he paid no heed to our pleas. Every time, after beating Aashish, Baba would go to his room and cry for a long time.'[6]

Those who have learnt music may agree it is next to impossible to remember all that is taught to you without taking notes and writing down key passages. For music as complex as what Baba taught, it was even more difficult. It is beyond my imagination how Ali Akbar, Ravi Shankar, Annapurna Devi and others managed to learn so much from Baba in conformance with the oral tradition of Vedic knowledge. Baba neither gave them written notations nor dictated them.

The day after the beating, Aashish had a fever. When I went to the hospital to get him some medication, a huge crowd had gathered there. Someone told me that a renowned saintly person of Maihar had just committed suicide by self-immolation. People had brought him to the hospital but he was declared dead on arrival.

The deceased was indeed a saintly person. At the Shārdā Ma temple of Maihar, a wandering Hindu sage had given this man a sacred mantra, saying, 'With this mantra, you can convert any metal to gold. But remember, it can only be used for philanthropy. The mantra will lose all its power should it ever be used for selfish reasons.'

So, this saintly person then used the power of this mantra to help various people. Some days passed and the man's own family faced a severe financial crisis. His wife earned a living by making beedis (rolled tobacco leaves used for smoking), while he immersed himself in philanthropy and meditation. His children lived in extreme poverty. This situation made his wife demand some of his magical gold to reduce their family suffering. At first he refused, but eventually his wife's insistence made him yield. He made a lot of gold for his family. They moved to a bigger and better house, and his wife expanded her business by employing many workers to roll tobacco for her.

However, soon the man realized that his mantra had lost its magic. In a dream, the wandering sage came and told him that because he had used the mantra for self-interest, it had lost its power. The man went insane and committed suicide.

On my return from the hospital, I told Baba about this suicide. To my surprise, he knew this man. Baba said, 'The man had helped a lot of people by creating gold for them. A Bengali doctor at Maihar hospital used to be my family doctor too. This doctor had saved the life of the wife of this saintly person. In deep gratitude, the saintly person converted the doctor's two brass pots to pure gold. The doctor quit, moved to Katni, built a large house there, and entered into private practice. This saintly man had once approached me, saying, "Let me help you. With my help, you'll never have to worry about money for the rest of your life. This will allow you to pursue your music without any worldly anxieties." With folded hands, I told him, "I don't need more money, just give me your blessings."' Baba was not interested in any rewards without karma (effort).

When Panditji and Khansaheb became the highest paid artistes, they requested Baba to hike his fees, saying, 'Baba, times have changed. Inflation has made everything dearer, yet you keep charging the same old fees for your concerts. As your disciples, it is disrespectful to you that we get paid more than you do.'

'Oh really!' Baba responded. 'Then why don't you charge less than I do?'

Ma's Driving License

The separation became obvious when Ma and Shubho moved to Akashganga. Panditji continued living with his paramour, Kamala Chakravarty. They had a chauffeur-driven black Ambassador car, but since Panditji used to be out of town or out of the country most of the time, the car and the chauffeur were at Shubho's disposal. Panditji sold the Pavlova apartment and chose to stay at hotels during his visits to Bombay.

The Ambassador car.

Panditji terminated the employment of the chauffeur, and the car was soon to be disposed of, but for some reason that did not occur and the car remained unused in the Akashganga garage for quite some time.

The anecdote I am narrating here is a classic example giving insight into how naughty and manipulative Hariji was and how gullible Ma was.

Concerned about Ma's reclusion, Hariji tried to pull Ma outdoors. He managed to convince her that if the car remained unused for a long time, the parts would get rusted and it would prove to be an expensive affair to repair.

'क्या मुसीबत [What a problem]!' Ma exclaimed. 'What can be done about it?'

'Every few days, you must drive the car.'

'But I don't even know how to drive the car.'

'It is very easy, I'll teach you.'

Thus began Ma's adventure with an automobile. Here, the roles were reversed. Hariji was the guru and Ma the obedient disciple. With an able guru like Hariji, and with her high IQ and exceptional dexterity, Ma quickly learnt to drive. Every week or so, on the pretext of driving lessons, Hariji would get Ma out of the house for a drive to Worli Seaface, etc., mostly at nights to avoid the traffic.

Suddenly, a realization dawned on Ma. She asked, 'I've heard that you need a licence to drive a car. If you drive without a license, the police may arrest you.'

'That's right,' Hariji replied.

'Then go and get me a licence,' Ma demanded. 'I don't want to be a law-breaker.'

Now Hariji was in a Catch-22 situation. It was almost impossible to take Ma and make her stand in a long queue for hours at the formidable Road Transport Office. But clever as Hariji was, he made another woman who was an efficient driver give the test on behalf of Ma. Sure enough, the woman easily passed the driving test. Next, they needed a photograph (black and white in those days) to be affixed on the licence. For the photograph, Hariji's better half, Anuradhaji, sans her spectacles, was made to dress and groom to resemble Ma as closely as possible. Hariji submitted a blurry photograph to further the trick. The licence was issued with the name and address of Annapurna Devi, but the photograph was of Anuradhaji.

However, this driving adventure soon ended in a tragicomic manner. The comedy was that Ma had been conditioned to learn from Baba with total surrender and unquestionable obedience. Ma was in the same mindset during her driving lessons with Hariji. Once, at a parking lot opposite her house, Hariji was teaching Ma car-parking skills. The car was going at a very slow speed, but another car driven on the wrong side came from the opposite direction, and they had a head-on collision. It was the other driver's fault, but neither car suffered much damage.

The funny part was when Ma started scolding Hariji, 'Why didn't you tell me to apply the brakes? I was waiting for your instructions but you said nothing.'

Shocked, Hariji asked Ma, 'You mean to say when Baba was teaching you music he dictated each and every note you played?' Hearing this, Ma burst out into laughter. The other car's driver came out to apologize, but was taken aback to see Ma and Hariji convulsed with laughter.

Soon after this, a sycophant of Panditji's reported to him that the car was being misused. Within a few days, Panditji arranged to dispose of the car. Ma lost another reason for the momentary getaway from the incarceration of her house.

A word about this sycophant. He was a sitārist who kept visiting Ma. In front of Ma, he would speak ill of Panditji, especially his sexual affairs, and keep lamenting that although he was Panditji's disciple, he wasn't much taught by Panditji. He wanted to learn from Ma, who said, 'Without Panditji's written permission I can't teach you.' Needless to say, that never happened, but he kept visiting Ma, and, every now and then, shamelessly sought monetary help from her. He kept reporting Ma's activities to Panditji. This included the names of those who came to learn from her, who visited her, etc.

The Gharana War

आनोभद्राःऋतवोयन्तुविश्वतः

[*Let noble thoughts come to us from all directions*]
—*Rigveda* (1.89.1)

During a Saturday rendezvous, while waiting for Ma to appear from her room, we asked our senior member Hemant Desai how he ended up learning from Ma. To our utter surprise, Hemant replied, 'Niloufer suggested that I learn from Ma.'

'Niloufer who?' we asked.

'Ut. Rais Khan's sister; Ut. Vilayat Khan's niece,' Hemant explained.

'You mean to say she knew Ma and used to visit her?' we asked.

'Not only that,' Hemant grinned. 'She was learning from Ma.'

'Wait! How did you end up knowing Niloufer?' we asked.

'Well, it's a long story,' Hemant said as he reclined in his chair. 'I had returned from the US, and had a desire to seriously pursue the sitār. Before going to the US, I was learning the sitār under Niloufer and Rais Khan's father, Mohammed Khan, who played both the rudraveena and the sitār. However, my learning was sporadic and not serious. One day, after my return from the US, while taking an evening walk at Breach Candy, I bumped into

Niloufer. I shared with her my wish to learn the sitār in a serious and systematic manner. Niloufer pointed to a tall building in the vicinity which was the Akashganga building and said, 'If you really want to learn seriously and systematically, your only choice is to go to Annapurna Devi, who lives on the sixth floor of that building. No one can teach you better than her. I too am learning from her. But please don't ask me to take you to her.' Back then, I had no idea who Annapurna Devi was, but I was intrigued simply because Niloufer was my guru Mohammed Khan's daughter and the famous sitārist Rais Khan's sister. In spite of having such masters at home, she was learning from Annapurna Devi and was recommending her name to me so strongly. I thought she must be a teacher of the highest order.

'So, I made a beeline to the sixth floor of Akashganga and rang the doorbell. The door didn't open. I left a note with my address and telephone number, but there was no response. I made several visits to her house, and rang the doorbell; she never opened the door and never responded to the many notes I left in her letterbox.

'By chance, I happened to meet Mr Soli Batliwala, a lawyer by profession and the chairman of the Bhulabhai Memorial Institute operating from Akashganga, which also used to host the National Centre of Performing Arts [NCPA] until it shifted to Nariman Point. This is where Pt Ravi Shankar established his Kinnara School of Music. However, when Pt Ravi Shankar started globetrotting, the onus fell on Annapurna Devi to teach Panditji's pupils. As Mr Batliwala frequently visited Annapurna Devi, I too joined him during his next visit. However, we kept ringing the doorbell, but she didn't open the door.

'With Anantramji, the sitārist and tablā player, I finally met Ma, and on his request, she accepted me as her disciple.'

Although Hemant's story was interesting, more intriguing was the fact of Niloufer learning from Ma. When Ma came out of her room and served us dinner, I asked her, 'There is so much animosity between different gharanas, each claiming to be the best. Vilayat Khansaheb never misses an opportunity to belittle Pt Ravi Shankar. Instead of appreciating the Herculean efforts of Baba in adopting the orphans and teaching them music and enabling them to earn a livelihood with something as ingenious as the Maihar Band, Vilayat Khansaheb ridiculed Baba by calling him a mere bandmaster and not an ustad.[7] They have also criticized the creation of new raags by Baba, Panditji and Ali Akbar Khansaheb. On the other hand, Panditji has never spoken a word against Vilayat Khansaheb ever. In such a situation, why did you accept Niloufer as your pupil?'

Ma smiled and said, 'This gharana war is a recent phenomenon. Things were rather amicable a few years ago. Jealousy is a natural instinct and part of human nature, but back then it was never publicly expressed. Baba opposed gharana snobbery as he himself learnt from so many gurus from different walks of life. Baba used to say, "If any seeker of knowledge approaches you, you should impart your knowledge without hesitation. In my life, I have experienced that ustads were reluctant to teach those who were not their family members. You can't even imagine the adversities, pain and suffering I have gone through in learning from different gurus. With all the hardship, whatever I was able to collect in my begging bowl, I generously distribute it all. It is a sin not to teach someone who is hungry for knowledge. But remember not to teach or preach unasked. Otherwise it will be an act of ego gratification."

'In the year 1945, while he was a court musician of Jodhpur, on behalf of the maharaja of Jodhpur, Bhaiyā organized a mega Indian classical music event. Numerous music celebrities were invited. During his Dhrupad rendition, Ut. Dabeer Khan was unhappy with the *pakhawaj* player who was accompanying him. On his own initiative, Baba volunteered to accompany Dabeer Khan and played the pakhawaj for the rest of the performance. Such was the mutual respect among the artistes back then.

'Vilayat Khansaheb was also invited to this event. After it was over, he extended his stay in Jodhpur by eight months and lived in Bhaiyā's house, learning and playing with Bhaiyā. One day, as a response to the maharaja's request, both played a *jugalbandi*. After one rendition, the maharaja requested them to play Raag Megh. Vilayat Khansaheb whispered in Bhaiyā's ears, "Dada, I don't know Raag Megh." Bhaiyā explained to him the *chalan* (series of note patterns or the grammar of the raag) and *pakad* (the melodic theme of the raag) and they played it together.

'Vilayat Khansaheb was not bitter against Bhaiyā. As narrated by more than one person to me, once, in Calcutta, before playing a jugalbandi with Bhaiyā, Vilayat Khansaheb announced to the audience, "Please don't consider this a duet. I am not capable of playing with Dada [Ali Akbar Khan]. He, out of affection for me, has made me sit with him. Therefore, please pardon my flaws and errors."'

When Vinay Bharatramji asked Ma the difference between Pt Ravi Shankar and Vilayat Khansaheb, Ma said, 'Vilayat Khansaheb is master of *murkis* [a taan-like ornamentation cluster of three notes played in rapid succession]. Like Thumri singers, he plays murkis very quickly, yet clearly and in perfect pitch.'

However, as time passed, Vilayat Khansaheb's bitterness towards Panditji kept growing. He would play for AIR only if he was paid one rupee more than Panditji. Vilayat Khansaheb also publicly announced his displeasure in the year 1999 when Panditji was awarded the Bharat Ratna—India's highest civilian honour.

It should be noted here that Vilayat Khan was awarded the Padma Shri and Padma Bhushan in 1964 and 1968 respectively, which are India's fourth and third highest civilian honours. However, he refused to accept them, declaring the committee was musically unqualified to judge him. In January 2000, when he was awarded the Padma Vibhushan, the second highest civilian award, he again refused, calling it 'an insult'. This time, he publicly announced he would not accept any award that other sitār players, his juniors and, in his opinion, less deserving people, had been awarded before him. Pt Ravi Shankar was the only sitārist who had received this award, so the implication was clear. 'If there is any award for the sitār in India, I must get it first,' he said, adding, 'This has always been a story of the wrong time, the wrong person, and the wrong award in this country.'[8]

Ma continued: 'Vilayat Khansaheb's relations with his sister's husband Ut. Mohammed Khan [his guru at the time] too were far from cordial. Ditto was his attitude towards his nephew Rais Khan. Niloufer herself had spoken to me at length about their discordance. Niloufer, though not as talented and focused as her brother Rais Khan, was a dedicated student. However, there was something more to it. During her lessons, she would never ask a single question, but on her next visit would invariably come up with many. Once I asked her why she never asked these questions while I was teaching her, and she candidly stated that all the lessons she got from me she passed on to her brother Rais Khan, and these were actually his questions.'

'Why did Niloufer stop learning from you?' we asked Ma.

'I started getting anonymous phone calls threatening me with dire consequences if I didn't stop teaching Niloufer. Some unknown man used to bang my front door and shower all sorts of abuse on me, screaming at the top of his voice that I need to stop teaching her. Niloufer too was receiving such threats. It was difficult to guess who could be threatening both of us. But for the sake of her safety, I had no choice but to advise Niloufer to stop coming to me. For a long time, there was no news of her until the day I got the news that she was murdered.'

In this context, we found it extremely surprising that on one Guru Purnima day, Pandit Hariprasad Chaurasia came to Akashganga with Vilayat Khansaheb's daughter, Zilla. Hariji is known for doing unexpected things, but this surprised all of us. Of course, Zilla was pretty, elegant and a dignified lady. Though she didn't pay obeisance either to Ma or Baba's photo or bust, she was extremely warm, polite and charming. She addressed Ma by calling her '*foofi*'—father's sister (aunt).

I tried to serve her a plateful of our standard Guru Purnima menu of chhole, samosa, pizza, assorted mithais, pakoras, etc., but she flatly refused them all. When Ma insisted, saying, 'अरे, कुछ तो लेलो! [Have something at least],' Zilla said, 'Okay, give me something that is without salt.' I quickly offered her a plateful of assorted mithais, which had more than half a dozen varieties. To our surprise, she said, 'No, mithais too contain some salt.' After some back and forth, she said, 'Okay, I'll have a cup of tea with one spoon of sugar but without masala, as masalas too have some salt.'

The burden of preparing a cup of tea fell on Nityanand. As he was preparing the tea and I was arranging the cup and saucer on a tray, our gurubhai Qamar Ali came to the kitchen to help.

'She looks quite healthy!' I exclaimed. 'What kind of disease could she be suffering from that she can't tolerate a grain of salt?'

'She is suffering from the gharana disease,' Qamar Ali said, looking into my eyes.

Puzzled by his reply, I asked, 'Meaning?'

'The meaning is very simple,' Qamar Ali explained. 'उसे इस घरका नमक नहीं खाना है [She doesn't want to eat the salt of this house.]'

It was clear that Zilla and Hariji had come with an agenda they intended to discuss with Ma. After the ritualistic pleasantries, Zilla and Hariji initiated a discussion with the topic of the domination of tablā players in the Indian classical music genre. It was assumed that both Vilayat Khansaheb and Guru Ma were rather unhappy about the increasing dominance of percussion instruments over the melodic ones. In congruence with Zilla's viewpoint, Ma told Hariji, 'Whom can we complain to, and how can we complain?

We are the ones [indicating Panditji and Khansaheb] who created such a situation.' Both Hariji and Zilla smiled in agreement.

Then Zilla and Hariji switched the topic of discussion to Raag Jaijaiwanti, lamenting how the current popular version had deviated from the authentic original one. Saying this, Hariji took out his bansuri and played just the *mukhada* (chorus) of the currently popular version of the Jaijaiwanti bandish '*More Mandire*', expecting Ma would teach the authentic version of Jaijaiwanti in front of Zilla and all present. However, Ma's strong intuition could comprehend the design and said, 'मैंने कभी आपको जयजयवंती सिखाया ही नहीं, और अब इस माहौल में नहीं सिखा सकती [I've never taught you Jaijaiwanti, and this is not the time and environment to teach music.]'

Failing to get what they wanted, they began lamenting about the habit of many people in the audience who sing along with the artiste's rendition and that too off-key. Zilla gave a short comical demonstration, making everyone roll in laughter. Soon, both Hariji and Zilla departed.

During one of the annual concerts of the Acharya Allauddin Music Circle, Ma allowed Hemant Desai to give his maiden public performance. Hemant Desai started with an expansive ālaap. Throughout the ālaap and jod, the tablā player kept looking at the audience and waving at the people he made eye contact with. Hemant Desai was so focused on his playing that he didn't notice, but I was furious. After the concert, I went to Ma's house and complained about this to her. Ma agreed with me that what the tablā player did was ridiculous, but looking at his age, Ma chose not to tell him anything.

Ma quoted Baba's lament, 'How to play in such concerts! Here I was playing the ālaap, but the tablā player was so disinterested he wasn't even listening to my playing. He was restlessly and impatiently waiting for the beginning of the gat, where he could show off his prowess. His very presence and body language spoilt my mood.'

As narrated by Pt Jotin Bhattacharya, 'Sometime during the sixties, while discussing the state of Indian classical music with Panditji and Khansaheb, Panditji lamented, "Jotin, please understand that we are now professional or, should I say, commercial musicians. We are in the business of making a living by pleasing the audience with our music. Unfortunately, the audience is paying us to be entertained, and not to be enlightened. We have to give them what they want. All they want is thrills and gimmicks. Nobody cares for the purity and authenticity of our rich tradition." Khansaheb smirked in agreement at Panditji's reply.'

'बहुत ही मुश्किल होता है एक सच्चे संगीत साधक का सफ़र जीवन निर्वाह के लिए श्रोतागण के सामने बजाना पड़ता है और ताली और गाली से अलिप्त रहकर अपने मार्ग पर चलते रहना है'

—अन्नपूर्णादेवी

'The journey of a true seeker is invariably difficult. He needs to give public performances to support his basic expenses. Without allowing the applause and criticism to affect him, he has to tread on the chosen path'

—Annapurna Devi

Remove that Muffler

One of Ma's biggest headaches was how to deal with the daily flood of letters, notes, messages and offers which arrived. She used to ignore most of them but, as a matter of respect, would reply to a few. Mainly Suresh Vyas and I were the ones to write replies. Most of them were requests for meetings. Many wanted her *darshan* (a term used in Eastern cultures for sighting a deity or for a devotee meeting a holy person or guru). It may be what modern-day godmen, politicians or even film stars seek, but for a recluse like Ma, it was as if people were prying into her personal life and violating her space.

Many musicians, some fairly established, some beginners and some absolute novices wanted to learn from Guru Ma. Offers kept pouring in for recitals and recordings with rather tempting fees. I have personally returned some high-value cheques sent to Ma as advances for proposed recitals. Ma refused them all regardless of whom the offers were from or what fees they were offering.

Sometimes it was very difficult to avoid certain visitors. For instance, Prof. Rooshikumar Pandya got to meet her because of a handwritten note from Ali Akbar Khansaheb to Ma, requesting her to accept Rooshiji as her disciple. Ma was in no mood to teach Rooshiji, who back then looked like an Indian version of the

Beatles's George Harrison, but she had no choice but to accept him as her disciple.

Talking about George Harrison, the famed musician visited Ma with the help of a note from Indira Gandhi, the then ruling prime minister. That story has been narrated in a different chapter.

Nityanand was brought to Ma's house first by Panna Babu's daughter and eventually by Pt Rajiv Taranath. There are more or less similar stories when it comes to most of the people who ended up becoming Ma's disciples.

On one occasion, a very famous Indian classical vocalist sent repeated messages to her, asking for a meeting. I should not reveal his identity, but he was known for his strangely acquired mannerism of repeatedly blessing the audience.

At the appointed hour, the maestro reached 6A Akashganga. Ma was mildly surprised to see he had brought his tanpurā with him. After the ritualistic pranam, he sat down and began tuning his tanpurā. Ma politely asked him the reason for his visit.

'I am going through a rough patch,' he explained. 'My singing has lost the impact it used to have on the audience. I have come to seek your advice.'

'You mean to say you sing for the audience?' Ma asked. This was a loaded question.

There was a deafening silence for a moment. Ma broke it, saying, 'You are such a great singer, and I am a forgotten instrumentalist. Who am I to advise an accomplished singer like you?'

Of course, he was an extremely famous and prominent singer, but of late his popularity had been diminishing because of the dramatic rise of Pt Bhimsen Joshi's popularity.

'I request you to kindly listen to my singing for a few minutes and guide me as to how I can improve.' Saying this, he closed his eyes and started singing. With pursed lips and an expressionless face, Ma listened to him. After about twenty minutes of his rendition, he paused, opened his eyes and looked at Ma.

'Any suggestions?' he asked.

Ma got up from her seat and started walking away. She turned back and said, 'सबसे पहले, आपने गलेमें जो मफ़लर बाँध रखा है उसे हटा दीजिए [First and foremost, remove the muffler you have wrapped around your throat/voice.]'

(In Indian languages, the term *gala* means both 'throat' and 'voice'.)

The maestro instinctively touched his neck, but there was no muffler.

Ma left the living room, and locked herself in her room.

The maestro sat there for about twenty minutes more, deep in thought. On his way out, he paid obeisance to the closed door.

We all were aware of Ma's Zen-master-like riddles. For years, this incident remained food for thought to us. We kept debating what she had really meant when she spoke those words. There are a number of possible interpretations.

The maestro used to wear a दुपट्टा (stole) around his neck, and maybe Ma in her ignorance couldn't differentiate between scarf, stole and muffler. But wait, before he started singing, he had already removed the stole.

Perhaps Ma wasn't even talking about something as superficial as a piece of fabric. For all the years we knew her, we never heard her comment or even notice anyone's attire or looks.

Was she hinting at getting rid of his inhibitions? The inhibitions which invariably result from comparison and competition with others.

Annapurna Devi.

'Ma, please teach me how to generate feelings in my renditions,' Nityanand once asked.

'The deeper you can immerse yourself in the rendition, the greater the feeling you can generate,' Ma replied.

Debt-Free

'Ma, why are you teaching your disciples free of charge?' I once asked her.

'ऋणमुक्ति [To be debt free],' she replied. 'I want to be free of all karmic debts so that I don't have to be born again.'

According to the *Rigveda*, *Taittiriya Samhita* (*Krishna Yajurveda*) and the *Satapatha Brahmana* (*Shukla Yajurveda*), human beings are entrapped in the burden of debts. Moksha, the salvific liberation from the karmic cycle of deaths and rebirths, is not possible unless one is debt-free.

The three fundamental debts are:

मातृपितृ ऋण: We are indebted to our **parents** for giving us birth and for our upbringing. It is impossible to repay them; all we can do is pass it on by giving birth and bringing up our progeny.

ऋषिऋण: We are indebted to our **gurus and sages** for imparting to us their invaluable knowledge and wisdom and guiding us to the path of enlightenment. The only way to repay the debt is to selflessly pass on the knowledge, wisdom and guidance to the future generation.

देवऋण: We are indebted to **mother nature**. We ought to be benevolent towards all the creations of nature, and be of selfless service to the ecology and the environment.

Following in Guru Ma's footsteps, Nityanand and Basant Kabra do not accept any fees either in cash or kind from their disciples. Perpetuating the legacy, they too feed exotic meals to their disciples the way Ma used to do.

While teaching Raag Deepak, Baba had warned Panna Babu never to play it indoors, and instructed him to follow it with Raag Megh as the *utaara* (antidote) to recover from its hostile effects. Every Sunday, Panna Babu did the riyaaz of Raag Deepak at his preferred spot in a forest near his Malad residence.

One Sunday, some influential people from the film industry visited his residence. Panna Babu's wife Parul Ghosh, the playback singer, was the sister of Anil Biswas, the doyen of film music. Parulji sent someone to call Panna Babu home and he immediately stopped his riyaaz and returned.

The visitors proposed that Panna Babu do music direction for films, but he refused. When Parulji insisted on him accepting the proposal, Panna Babu, the gentlest of souls, got highly agitated and started leaving his house in a fit of anger. That very moment, all the tanpurās, a pair of tablā and some flutes near him simultaneously cracked loudly.

Panna Babu instantly remembered Baba's warning to play Raag Megh as the utaara to Raag Deepak. After playing Megh, his anger subsided.

Epitome of Integrity

'Music is the highest art, and
to those who understand,
is the highest worship.'
—Swami Vivekanand

During the pre-Internet era of the late mid-eighties, the telefacsimile (fax) was the fastest and cheapest medium of exchanging letters and documents—a boon for overseas communication.

After the very disturbing threats and suffering surrounding her teaching Niloufer, Ma stopped using the phone. She neither dialled out nor answered incoming calls. After much pleading from Rooshiji, he was allowed to use the phone for an hour each day. Convincing Ma to install a fax machine was too difficult a proposition.

Because of my overseas business, I had installed a fax machine at my home, and I told Rooshiji he could use it. Rooshiji used to communicate with his brother and nephews in Canada, as well as with a large number of other people, being a hypersocial personality. This was in stark contrast to Ma's reclusive nature. Also, Smarth Bali had shifted out of Bombay, and would fax letters addressed to Ma and Rooshiji.

The incoming fax messages had a degree of comedy. It was a standard practice to begin the fax message with the headings:

'Message From: __' and 'Message To: __' so the recipient would know to whom the fax should be routed. However, Smarth in his fax messages used to write, 'अगर माँ के सिवा किसीने भी यह message पढ़ा उसका मुँह काला' (literally meaning that if anyone other than Ma read his message they would have a 'blackface', implying intense disgrace or shame or loss of honour, resulting in metaphorical defacing). The funnier part was that Ma herself never read letters or messages. She would invariably ask one of us to read them out to her. We would all have a good laugh reading Smarth's messages.

Akashganga was 7 km from my house, but only 2 km from my office at the time. Although it was troublesome to go all the way to deliver the messages received and collect the messages to be faxed, I didn't mind as long as I had the opportunity to meet Ma. However, there was an understanding that if the message didn't have 'URGENT' written on it, I should not make a special trip, but instead bring it when I would go for my weekly lessons.

One early morning in 1986–87, a message popped up on my fax machine which read, 'Message for Prof. Rooshikumar Pandya— URGENT'. On my way to the office I took a detour and went to Akashganga to deliver the message to Rooshiji. As I went in, Rooshiji was having his morning tea. In a minute, Ma joined us. It was a funny contrast—Rooshiji always had three large cups at a time, and Ma would have no more than half a cup, that too just once in the morning.

Ma appeared drowsy and tense, but not grumpy. As I got up and paid my obeisance, she remarked, 'आज सुबह सुबह कैसे? [How come so early?]' There was something funny about her voice. Because of the sore throat, her Lata Mangeshkar–kind of voice was sounding like Bhimsen Joshi singing *kharaj* notes.

'पता नहीं आज मैं क्या करूँगी [I don't know what I am going to do],' she lamented. 'आज मेरी आवाज़ ही ख़राब हो गई है [Today my voice has become so hoarse!]'

Rooshiji ridiculed her, saying, 'क्या सुबह सुबह फ़िज़ूलका टेन्शन लिए हो? [Why are you so tense about matters of no importance?] आपको कौनसा प्रोग्राममें या रिकॉर्डिंगमें गाना है [You don't have to give a singing performance or go to a studio for recording a song.]'

'This evening Shashwati is coming for her lesson,' Ma explained. 'How am I going to teach her with such a hoarse voice? I can barely talk, how am I going to sing to teach her?'

'Tell her not to come,' Rooshiji said, giving his favourite solution. For some unknown reason, Rooshiji loved to cancel Ma's disciples' lessons. 'Shall I phone and tell her not to come?'

'No way!' Ma sternly disallowed Rooshiji. 'Last time also I had asked her not to come. It is unfair to keep cancelling lessons.' The conversation spoke volumes about Ma's integrity in teaching.

'Who is this Shashwati?' I inquired. 'I don't think I've met her.'

'She works as a sitārist in the Films Division. Her mother, Shrimati Shobha Kundu Ghosh, was the first female sitārist to be broadcast from AIR Calcutta.'

Purely out of curiosity, I went to Ma's house that evening. I was amazed to hear her voice had fully recovered. She was singing each phrase perfectly well while teaching Shashwati.

'What medication did Ma take for her throat?' I asked Rooshiji.

'You know she is averse to taking any medication,' Rooshiji replied.

'Then how did her voice return to normality in just a few hours?' I asked.

'Atul! By now you must have realized that she has a habit of doing inexplicable things.'

Linguistic Bias

The dilemma about speaking a native language versus using a common national or international language, known in some circles as the association vs assimilation debate, has been going on for centuries. Those who knew Ma are convinced about the importance of native language.

I was born in a Gujarati family. As a child, I was compelled to learn Gujarati, Hindi, English and Sanskrit as the special language. As a dyslexic child, I kept cursing our education system for burdening me with so many languages. Despite being a Gujarati, my wife speaks very little Gujarati and can't read or write it at all. My son, now seventeen, neither speaks nor understands Gujarati. None of this bothered me until I observed the difference in the quality of Ma's communication with those who spoke and those who couldn't speak Bengali, her mother tongue.

Fundamentally, Ma was a person of few words, and in her last years she spoke even less. When she was bedridden, all of us tried our best to have a conversation with her, but we usually failed to get anything more than a brief exchange of pleasantries. However, with Shashwati, Ma would invariably become talkative. We non-Bengalis were extremely jealous of Shashwati because, except for Suresh, none of us in Mumbai could understand what Ma and Shashwati were talking about. Moreover, Ma would also converse with Shashwati's husband (also a Bengali), who had nothing to do with music.

We realized the importance of the language factor when we saw Ma interact with a young journalist from Kolkata named Tathagata Ray Chowdhury. Throughout her life, Ma had avoided journalists like the plague. Therefore, we were shocked when Ma spoke so candidly and for so long with this journalist whom she had never met or heard of before. As they conversed in Bengali, none of us could understand them. There was no way we could have verified what Ma actually spoke and what was published.

At the fag end of Ma's life, Shekhar Sen came to interview Ma for the Sangeet Natak Akademi documentary. Ma had strictly forbidden us from photographing her, and here Shekhar Sen was shooting her interview with a professional film unit with lights and a movie camera. Why? Because he had requested Ma in the Bengali language. The interview, however, was in Hindi. Sen started the shoot asking questions in Hindi, but Ma just wouldn't respond. He got frustrated, and made one last desperate attempt by asking the question in Bengali, and, lo and behold, Ma responded well and spoke in an animated manner.

Shashwati reminisces the meetings between her mother and Guru Ma. In her words:

'When I got a job as a sitārist in the Films Division, I moved to Bombay. I knew it was a difficult task to approach Annapurna Devi and persuade her to accept me as her disciple. The sarodist Pradeep Barot, who too was working in the Films Division, suggested I write her a letter as the daughter of Shobha Kundu née Ghosh, the first female sitārist to be broadcast by AIR. My mother knew Guru Ma from her Calcutta days.

'Pradeepji gave me Guru Ma's address, and I wrote a long letter to her in Bengali, where I begged her to accept me as her disciple.

But it was the mention of my mother that did the trick. Guru Ma replied by asking me to visit her with my sitār. She said she would listen to my playing first and then decide whether to or not to accept me as her disciple. This was in 1986.

'I went to Ma's house with my mother. I played a bit of whatever I could manage. Ma said, "A lot needs to be repaired in your playing. You'll need to unlearn everything and relearn from scratch." I expressed my commitment to undergo the training.

'Guru Ma candidly told me, "I had no intention of teaching you, but because of your mother I have agreed."

Smt. Shobha Kundu Ghosh (mother) and Shashwati (daughter).

'This was when my mother intervened and told Guru Ma, "I too wanted to learn from you, but never got the chance." Guru Ma responded by embracing my mother and said, "I remember listening to your performances on the radio. You were quite proficient and were a source of inspiration to all female instrumentalists. How difficult it was in those days for a female instrumentalist to perform in music conferences. It is no small achievement to have established yourself as an artiste in that environment."

'My training started. The fourth Monday of the month was the day fixed for my lessons. However, after Shubhoda's demise [15 September 1992], Ma became very depressed. Rooshiji informed me not to come as Ma had stopped teaching. Ma was now avoiding meeting her disciples, except on Saturday evenings when Nityanandji, Sureshji, Atul, etc. used to gather. Pradeepji had told me that Ma would remain locked in her room, so cooking was out of the question. Rooshiji had to order food from outside for the Saturday evening disciples and himself. This went on for a year.

'Then, once again, I messaged Guru Ma that my mother was seeking permission to visit her. Guru Ma didn't refuse. I took my mother to her house. Surprisingly, the meeting proved helpful. My mother initiated the conversation in Bengali and Guru Ma responded quite well and opened up. The conversation slowly became more intimate. My mother's family life too had been filled with deep sadness. Guru Ma started reminiscing about her past, and the struggles Baba, Panditji, herself and Khansaheb had undergone. Guru Ma spoke about Panditji's major illness and how she had to sell off all of her jewellery, and how she and Panditji were left penniless; how Shubho was tricked into migrating to the US, which ruined him both as a sitārist and as a person. Guru Ma and my mother were both sobbing. According to Prof. Pandya the meeting proved cathartic.

'The positive outcome of this meeting was that my training restarted. Gradually, Guru Ma resumed teaching her other disciples as well.'

'Enigma of a Recluse'

On 5 April 1999, an interview of Panditji was broadcast on Indian television, which I recorded on my VCR. I brought the tape to Ma's house and showed her the interview. Needless to say, Ma confirmed the obvious, that what Panditji claimed was not true.

I said, 'There is a famous African proverb, "Until the lions learn to write, every story will glorify the hunter." For years, Panditji has been giving a false version of the facts to both the media and the world at large.' Nityanand and I suggested, 'Once, just for the record, your version should be published; otherwise, the falsehoods Panditji is spreading would come to be regarded as historical truths.'

'Show me the draft statement and I'll think about it,' she said, and went away into her room.

With help of inputs from my gurubhais, followed by factual corrections from Ma, the draft statement was finalized. Though I had taken the initiative, the question was in whose name the article should be published. Nityanand and I were the only ones willing to assume this responsibility. Rooshiji, Dr Shastri, Suresh Vyas, Smarth Bali, Hemant Desai and Pradeep Barot all backed out, and also advised Nityanand and me against publishing the article. Ma was quietly and patiently listening to all this from afar, without any comment or reaction, totally detached, as if the discussion was about some unknown person.

I convinced Ma that Nityanand, being a professional musician, should not be involved in any controversy. Back then, I did business with a few overseas clients who knew nothing about the sitār or Indian classical music, so I had nothing to lose by authoring this article. Nityanand also said he was not worried about the consequences, but Ma decided in my favour, and the following article was published under my name in several newspapers and magazines:

Enigma of a Recluse
By Atul S. Merchant[9]

April 5, 1999. Pt Ravi Shankar being interviewed by Mr Prananjay Guha Thakurta. Both consummate professionals. Well researched questions, savvy answers. And then suddenly a googly by the interviewer:

> I have always been intrigued by one question. Your first wife Annapurna Devi, the daughter of your Guru, is supposed to be a very wonderful musician. But I have always wondered why she never performed publicly? Maybe you can throw some light.'
> The one-time dancer cannot control the choreography of his face muscles. Few seconds of that and the man is in control.
> 'I think it is better if she could answer this herself . . .'

So far so good. But maybe it is the unconscious insecurities . . . 'Why doesn't she leave me alone', he must have wondered. And then the prevarication:

> 'But as far as my analysis goes, as long as we were married I used to force her to play along with me and give programs . . .'
> '. . . But after, she didn't want to perform alone. She always wanted to sit with me. And after we separated she didn't want to perform.'

'. . . She maybe doesn't like to face the public or she is nervous or whatever but it is her own will that she has stopped. This is very sad because she is a fantastic musician.'

'*Maybe not*', some of the viewers speculate. The program over, they search for the real answers.

The lady in question Smt. Annapurna Devi is a recluse. An enigma. But then there are leads. Her students, her well-wishers, the people who knew her and heard her before she divorced Ravi Shankar.

Annapurna Devi was born to Madina Begum the wife of Ut. Allauddin Khansaheb on the auspicious day of *Chaitra Purnima*. The ustad was away on a tour so his disciple Raja Brijnathsingh the Maharaja of Maihar named her Annapurna as there is an ancient ritual of worshipping Goddess Annapurna on the day of *Chaitra Purnima*. Her father lovingly known as Baba had transcended man made religious boundaries. He was a devout Muslim and an ardent devotee of Shārdā Ma. He often said, 'संगीत मेरी जाती है और सूर मेरा गोत्र . . . [Music is my race and sound is my ethnicity . . .]'

She grew up in Maihar in her home filled with *Sur* and *Taal*. Music woke her up and music lulled her to sleep. In a home where music was religion, one would think that learning music would be the most natural thing for her to do. But Baba's older daughter Jahanara had suffered at the hands of her in-laws because she pursued music. Baba did not want to teach music to Annapurna for this reason. But Annapurna's genes were programmed . . .

Once, while Baba was away for a stroll, her brother Ut. Ali Akbar Khan was practicing his lessons. Annapurna noticed a mistake in her brother's playing and was correcting it in her childlike playful ways when Baba happened to enter. He stopped, listened, and summoned her to see him.

Baba had a legendary temper and young Annapurna was petrified. When she went to him, she was hardly prepared for what she saw and heard. Baba was in tears as he held her.

'Here is the tanpurā, I'll teach you all I know.'

And teach he did, prompting Ut. Amir Khansaheb to observe wryly, 'Annapurna Devi is 80 percent of Ut. Allauddin Khan, Ali Akbar is 70 percent and Ravi Shankar is about 40 percent.'

'Baba often used to say,' quotes Batuk Diwanji, 'मेरी लड़की को सुनो, रवि शंकर और अली अकबर उसके सामने मिट्टी के बराबर है [Listen to my daughter, Ravi Shankar and Ali Akbar are nothing compared to her.]'

Ut. Ali Akbar Khan and Smt. Annapurna Devi were imbibing Baba's music, *paltaas, alankaars, jhamhamaas, meend, ghamak, krintan, and boles*. Ali Akbar cradling his sarod and Annapurna mastering the sitār and later surbahār.

Udayshankar, the legendary dancer and the eldest brother of Ravi Shankar invited Baba abroad. Ravi Shankar was a dancer in the troupe. Young, debonair and a man about town. And here was Baba, traditional, orthodox, disciplined and demanding. But Ravi Shankar loved music and there was instant chemistry between the two.

Ravi Shankar left Paris, shaved his head, came to Maihar, and became Baba's disciple. He lived next door and when Baba was away, young Ali Akbar would climb over the wall and help him with Baba's music. Next day he would play well before Baba and Baba would tell Ali Akbar, 'देखो इसका दिमाग़ कितना अच्छा है [Look, how brainy he is.]' This young pair of Ali Akbar and Ravi Shankar later gave some of the most memorable *jugalbandi* performances till date.

It was Udayshankarji who later approached Baba for the hand of his daughter for Ravi Shankar. One would think that the marriage of two of the most gifted and accomplished musicians would be an ideal marriage. But that was not to be.

While Ravi Shankar played sitār for a *jugalbandi* with Ali Akbar Khan, both Ravi Shankar and Annapurna Devi played *jugalbandi* on the surbahār. The audience and the press raved about their concerts but aye there was the rub. The audience *waah-waahed* more to Annapurna Devi's playing and the reviews had an obvious tilt in her favor. She also played solo recitals in Delhi, Calcutta, and Chennai. And maybe it was Ravi Shankar who became nervous. Maybe his ego was too fragile to accept his wife's superiority as a musician.

Literary critics would call this a dramatic irony that just like in her older sister's case it was music again that became the apple of discord in Annapurna Devi's relationship with Ravi Shankar.

In order to redeem her marriage, Annapurna Devi vowed not to play in public and dedicated her life to teaching Baba's music to deserving disciples like Bahadur Khan, Nikhil Banerjee, Shubho Shankar, Hariprasad Chaurasia, Nityanand Haldipur, Basant Kabra, Sudhir Phadke, Sandhya Apte, Pradeep Barot, Amit Bhattacharya, Amit Roy and several others.

Her lasting contribution to Indian Classical music was recognized and accolades followed: Padma Bhushan in 1977, and later Sharangdev Fellowship, Sangeet Natak Akademi Award and Desikottam (Doctor of Literature), the highest award given by Visva-Bharati University founded by Nobel Laureate Tagore.

However, even after her separation from Ravi Shankar all was not well in Annapurna Devi's life.

Shubho, their son, was initiated into Sarod by his illustrious grandfather Baba but later Ravi Shankar made Shubho switch to sitār. Since Ravi Shankar was mostly away on concert tours, Shubho stayed with his mother Annapurna Devi who started giving him rigorous tālim.

Soon rumors started making rounds that Shubho was going to be a better player than Ravi Shankar, that it was Annapurna Devi's revenge. 'How can people think like that?' Annapurna Devi rhetorically asked one of her disciples. 'If Shubho becomes a good musician the credit goes to Baba . . . our music is his gift . . .'

But Ravi Shankar wanted to verify for himself. He summoned Shubho to play for him and a few others. Shubho played what he had learnt. 'Awesome' some of the listeners reported. Maybe Ravi Shankar felt threatened. And before Annapurna Devi could comprehend what was going on, Ravi Shankar lured Shubho away to the land of milk and honey.

New country, new tune. Shubho was discouraged from pursuing music in the States. And it was suggested that since he had studied at J.J. School of Arts at Bombay, he should take up commercial arts as his career.

When you take somebody away from his milieu and tell him to change his métier and that too in an alien environment, even street-smart people would find it hard to succeed, not to speak of someone who had spent his days and nights practicing *surs* and *taans* in a very Spartan environment. Shubho barely managed to survive by doing odd jobs such as a waiter's.

A change of heart. After a long hiatus, Ravi Shankar started teaching sitār to Shubho. Shubho's solid tālim by his mother helped him accompany his father in the concerts. Rumor has it that when Shubho played his passages; microphones were deliberately turned down. Soon Shubho felt alienated from his father and stopped accompanying him.[10] A hat-trick for Ravi Shankar. Neither Ut. Ali Akbar Khan nor Annapurna Devi nor Shubho was playing duets with him.

The tragedy of it all was that Shubho went into depression and was later admitted into a hospital for pneumonia. The financial help was not forthcoming from his father. Ravi Shankar's rationale: he had his own family to support.

Soon after, Shubho died.[11]

When a patient dies because of negligence on the part of a doctor, the death is called Iatrogenic. Does English language have a word 'Patergenic'?

Lately Pt Ravi Shankar is being criticized for promoting his daughter Anoushka. Pt Ravi Shankar's rationale is that it is his paternal obligation to promote and support his offspring. One wonders whether this belated sense of obligation overcompensates for the guilt he might have felt on Shubho's death. But that is food for a Freudian.

After the article came out, I did get some threatening phone calls. The anonymous callers said that they would ruin me, but I paid no heed to them. During one of our Saturday rendezvous, Ma came out of her room and announced, 'Let me tell you this once and for all. I never had nor have any interest in publishing anything about my music, or my story, or my version of the marital discord. This was just a little test for you all. Atul and Nityanand have passed the test. The rest, including Rooshiji, have all failed.'

Then, turning to Nityanand and me, Ma said, 'As your Guru Ma, my blessings are with you both. You may or may not become millionaires, but Shārdā Ma will always provide you for your needs.' Saying this, she went away to her room and shut the door.

Ma's Interview

The year was 1997. Pt Ravi Shankar released a limited edition of *Raga Mala*, his second autobiography. However, the mass-market edition was released only in September 1999, and it took a few more months after that to reach us. Some of the points mentioned in that book were a contradiction to what we had heard from Ma and others like Ali Akbar Khansaheb, Aashish Khan, etc. We decided to put Ma's version on the record. Again, as this was soon after the article 'Enigma of a Recluse' was published, I got the privilege.

Here is the interview:

Annapurna Devi: Interviewed by Atul Merchant

1. **Your memory of your legendary father, Ut. Allauddin Khansaheb, and the relationship you shared with him**.

I always remember Baba with respect, awe and love. I had *shraddha* (faith) in him from my very childhood. He was different from the other mortals I met during my life. He was simple, egoless, truthful, full of love and respect for people, but above all he was an embodiment of compassion when it came to poor people. I always felt very close to him and he was very loving towards me.

2. **Your father had started teaching you with vocal lessons but when were you shifted to the surbahār?**

Baba first taught vocals (Dhrupad) to both Bhaiyā (Ali Akbar Khansaheb) and me. Later, when I was learning the sitār under him he told me, 'I want to teach my Guru's *vidyā* (erudition) to you because you have no greed. To learn, you need to have infinite patience and a calm mind. I feel that you can preserve my guru's gift because you love music. However, you will have to leave the sitār, an instrument liked by the connoisseurs as well as the commoners. The surbahār, on the other hand, will be appreciated only by those listeners who understand the depths of music or who intuitively feel music. The commoner might dislike your playing and may throw tomatoes at you. So, what is your decision?' I was dumbfounded. 'I will do as per your *aadesh* [command]' was my simple response.

3. **We have heard that you can play almost all the string instruments, like your father. Tell us something about you and your music.**

No, I do not play all the instruments that Baba played. I only learnt to sing and to play the sitār and the surbahār. However, I do teach the flute, sarod, sitār and other instruments through singing. For me, music is like worship. Baba used to say that one could reach God through music. He also told me that, if need be, I would be able to earn my living through music and be economically independent. I practise what Baba taught me as a form of meditation. I work towards doing justice to what he taught me. He used to say that every note should touch one's soul. This is extremely difficult and requires eternal sādhanā. It is a process of surrender, submerging of one's ego . . .

4. **In your time, there were only a few female artistes in the field of music. Were there any social or religious taboos that you had to break through?**

I believe that learning music is a very demanding task requiring time, commitment and continuing effort. I have observed that in our society, as long as a woman is not married, she may be able to give what it takes to continue her rigorous riyaaz. I don't think there are any physical limitations that come in the way of a woman mastering any instrument. All she needs is a burning desire, the right guru, discipline and determination.

As far as taboos are concerned let me share what happened to my sister. Baba taught her vocal music with much love. He was very disturbed when she was not allowed to sing by her Muslim in-laws. Due to this experience, he was in a dilemma whether to teach me or not. But I used to listen to and remember what he taught Dada. One day Baba went to the market and Dada was practising his lessons on the sarod. Dada made a mistake and I was correcting him. I was so involved in the music that I did not notice Baba had returned. I suddenly became aware of his presence behind me and got scared. But instead of scolding me Baba called me to his room and gave me a tanpurā. This was the beginning of my tālim.

There was no difference in the way I was taught music just because I was a female child. As a matter of fact, Dada and I were given the same tālim. I think music knows no gender differences. Emotional and aesthetic expression have more to do with the artiste's personality than with the gender. An introspective artiste might go for sur and ālaap while an extrovert might opt for *layakaari*.

5. **A memory of your first public performance. Was it a solo or duet? Where did you perform?**

I recall that my first public performance was a duet in Delhi. I remember Panditji telling me before the performance that I should cater a little to the public taste. My response was that I would play only what I was taught. I think the audience enjoyed my playing also.

6. Which one is memorable in your opinion and why?

I don't particularly like my playing so I don't think of any concert that I played as memorable.

7. Why did you stop playing in public?

Whenever I performed, people appreciated my playing and I sensed that Panditji was not too happy about their response. I was not that fond of performing anyway so I stopped it and continued my sādhanā.

8. Do you think music gives you courage and inner strength to fight back against all the odds in your life?

I look at Baba's gift of music to me as a mantra from a master. It definitely gives me inner strength. Thanks to my music, I have survived.

9. Do you believe in women's emancipation? How do you rate Taslima Nasreen and others who fight for the cause of women?

I strongly believe that women are as capable as men. I am very happy that in India more and more women are realizing their potential, asserting themselves and making their presence felt in various spheres of life. I have great respect for women who stand up for what they believe in, and who fight for the cause of women against all odds.

10. Do you agree that for women, career and marriage do not go together?

No. I do not agree. If there is mutual respect and understanding amongst husband and wife, and if there is absence of jealousy, both can build their careers and still be happily married.

11. Do you think an unsuccessful marriage ruins a woman more than a man in life?

Yes. Unfortunately, this is true. It is more difficult for a woman to start anew than for a man. The problems for her are many: social, emotional, maybe financial.

12. What were the qualities that attracted you to Ravi Shankar?

I was brought up by Ma and Baba in an ashram-like atmosphere at Maihar. There was no question of my getting attracted to Panditji. Ours was an arranged marriage and not a love marriage.

13. What do you think should be the basis of a relationship between husband and wife?

I think the basis of the relationship between husband and wife should be: mutual respect, love, understanding, honesty, sincerity and willingness to sacrifice . . .

14. Why are celebrity marriages less successful?

The absence of the above.

15. How do you rate Ravi Shankar as a person and also as an artiste?

Panditji loves music and he sacrificed a lot to learn it. He worked hard at mastering it. He beautifully presented what he learnt from Baba to the world. And even when doing so he maintained the purity of our raags. As a musician, he deserves every honour and more. He has earned it. However, his giving too much prominence to the tablā has moulded the public taste—the audiences have no patience for sur ka kaam, they want rhythm and speed. In my opinion this is a disservice. Otherwise, Panditji's contribution to our music and its propagation is phenomenal. Dada and Panditji are two creative geniuses who have made the audiences around the world aware and appreciative of the great tradition of Indian classical music. I have no need to say anything that would belittle Panditji as a person.

16. Do you agree that an artiste should be a good human being too?

It would be great if all artistes could be like Baba, who was a great artiste as well as an exceptionally good human being. However, I think it is difficult for all mortals to be that way.

17. Recently, your private life has become more public just after the release of an autobiography of Ravi Shankar, *Raag Mala*. In this book, he has mentioned a few incidents/events from your conjugal life, especially about Shubho. If we say your long absence from the music field and your dignified silence regarding everything only gave birth to these false and fabricated stories about you and your former husband, would you agree?

I am aware of the false and fabricated stories about me regarding what happened in my married life. I have been quiet about it because I thought of Baba while he was alive. I didn't want to hurt Baba in any way, so I put up with the injustice and suffering. However, now I feel that your discerning readers should know my side of at least the Shubho part of the story. I was amazed to read the articles. I think Panditji is losing his sense of propriety or his mental balance or that he has turned into a pathological liar.[12] He has exemplified the English proverb: 'No fool like an old fool'. I think he is also angry with me since Pt Jotin Bhattacharya had written about Shubho's departure from Bombay.

It would be nice if he would devote all his time to teaching his *shishyas* instead of wasting his time and energy in such frivolous pursuits. His shishyas would be grateful for his gift and India would be richer with talents.

Anyway . . . the facts are as follows:

That year when Panditji came to Mumbai, he learnt that Shubho was playing very well. He called him and after listening to him, initially he underplayed Shubho's artistry and then suggested to Shubho that he should now go with his father. The people of Panditji's circle pointed out that Shubho was '*taiyar*' and that he could play anything and that he should tour with his father.

According to Shubho, Panditji had added, 'Your mother and I have studied under the same guru so I could also teach you.' My response was, 'He is right but he will not have the time for it. Please stay here and continue your tālim for one and a half years more. After that you can go anywhere you like. I will not stop you then because by then you will be ready to take on the world.'

This is when Panditji and Shubho hatched the plan about Shubho's taking sleeping pills—a stage-managed drama to malign me and to take him away from me. Shubho was immature at the time and hence unwittingly became a party to his father's plot. I think he realized this later and stopped communicating with his father a few months before his untimely and possible preventable death.[13]

Let me share with you what happened . . . When I was told that Shubho had taken sleeping pills, I immediately called a doctor, who examined him and confirmed that nothing was wrong with him. We also searched for an empty bottle or any other tell-tale signs but nothing was found. As a matter of fact, Shubho himself called his father at that time and told him to take him away as per their plan.

My only plea to Panditji at that time was, 'You have ruined my life and now you are ruining your son's life. Why?' His only answer was, 'It is because of you.'[14] Till today I have not understood his motives for interrupting Shubho's tālim. Maybe it was because of the rumours making the rounds that Shubho was going to be a better player than Panditji, and this was my revenge against Panditji. I don't understand how people can think like that. If Shubho, or anybody for that matter, becomes a good musician, the credit goes to Baba. Our music is his gift.

I know Panditji is very image-conscious. Maybe he feels that the recently published book on me has made some dents in his image and his articles are an attempt to salvage it and assuage his guilt for the gross injustice he did to his son.[15] Shubho realized this during the last months of his life and refused to see his father. Shubho could have been a great artiste; he was close to it. If he had continued his tālim he would have played great music. But a combination of factors prevented it.

18. **How do you look upon the arrival of Rooshikumar Pandya in your life? Do you feel he is a godsend? Tell us something about him.**

I believe that everyone and everything is godsent. God sends you what you deserve according to your karma. But only when something unexpected and improbable happens do we label it as 'godsent'. In this respect, Prof. Pandya was really godsent. The kind of experience I had with my first marriage, it was highly improbable for me to marry again. But in spite of the odds, it happened. When Prof. Pandya came into my life I was at the lowest point of my physical and mental health. I believe that if I am alive and with you today that has been possible because of Prof. Pandya.

19. After the experience you have had, do you still believe that a woman should give up her career for her home?

I have never believed that a woman can't do justice to both career and home. If she really wants to achieve something in her life, she can work on that and still do full justice to her home, provided her husband is supportive and there is no clash of egos. But sometimes women use the home as an excuse for the underachievement in their career or use career as an excuse for neglecting their duties at home.

20. Do you find peace in anything other than music?

Music and meditation.

21. How would you wish to be remembered among the future generations of musicians?

I don't feel I am anyone special and that people should remember me.

The First Note of Discordance

'When fates deal in human destiny,
they heed neither to pity nor justice.'
—*Charlie Chaplin*

'Ma, if you don't mind,' we once asked Ma. 'Could you share with us how and when things started becoming difficult?'

'The first year of my marriage was perhaps the happiest spell of my life,' Ma said. 'Everything was going so well. An unexpected event spoiled it all. Once, Brijnathsinghji told Baba, "I've been hearing great praises about Annapurna's progress in music. I would like to listen to her playing." When I was born, Baba had been on a visit to Rampur. His Highness Brijnathsinghji named me Annapurna, and called me his baby sister as I was his guru's daughter. However, this would be perhaps the first time I was meeting him.

'When Baba was taking me to the palace, Panditji expressed his desire to join us. Not only that, he too took along his surbahār. Baba was not at all happy about this, but in order to not offend his son-in-law, he refrained from expressing his displeasure.'

'What raag did you play that day?' Nityanand asked.

She thought for a moment and said, 'I am unable to clearly recall which raag I played, but I think Brijnathsinghji had asked me to play Raag Shree or maybe Malkauns. I played exactly the

Panditji and Ma a few days before Shubho was born.

way Baba had taught me. I started with a detailed ālaap, with antarā, sanchāri and abhog, followed by jod in vilambit, madhya and drutlay, concluded by jhala.

'It was nearing 8 p.m., and a palace servant came and signalled to Baba by pointing at the wall clock. Baba realized that it was the maharaja's dinner time, so he asked me to conclude my rendition. The maharaja became very emotional. He recalled the day of my birth, and as a token of appreciation for my performance gifted me some gold and a large piece of land in Maihar.

'Maharaja Brijnathsinghji got up from his throne and was heading for his dinner when Panditji stopped Brijnathsinghji and requested, "Please listen to my rendition too." Baba was the maharaja's guru; Brijnathsinghji did not want to insult his son-in-law. He therefore returned to his throne. Panditji began his rendition on the surbahār. However, Brijnathsinghji was not in the mood to listen to the rendition imposed on him. After a few minutes, he got up and walked away.

'Panditji took this as an insult and sulked for quite a few days after that. But Baba and I knew that Panditji had committed three serious mistakes. First, he went to the palace uninvited. Secondly, he tried to impose his rendition on the maharaja when he was proceeding for dinner. Thirdly, he played the surbahār instead of the sitār.[16] Brijnathsinghji had been learning music for several years and was a connoisseur of music. It wasn't easy to please him.

'Knowing Panditji's personality, Baba never recommended Panditji to take up the surbahār. However, as my first surbahār was so large for my size, Baba made another smaller one for me. Soon after our marriage, Panditji took my old surbahār and requested Baba to teach him as well.'

That incident at the palace, which first seemed like a minor fissure in their matrimonial bond, soon developed into a deep crack, which eventually became an ever-widening rift as Panditji continually failed to keep the green-eyed monster at bay.

समेट लेती शिकस्ता गुलाब की ख़ुशबू
हवा के हाथमें ऐसा कोई हुनर ही न था

[The wind just didn't have any capability of
Gathering the fragrance of the withered rose]
—*Parveen Shakir*

Brijnathsinghji was so fascinated by Ma's rendition that he requested Baba to teach him the surbahār. That was easier said than done, but Baba had to respect the wish of his employer.

After 1947, the state of Maihar acceded to the Union of India. Brijnathsinghji moved to Jabalpur. Yet, he kept visiting Maihar to take music lessons from Baba. Brijnathsinghji died in 1968. The following photograph seems to have been taken shortly before his demise.

Madina Ma, HH Brijnathsinghji and Baba.

The Duel of a Duet

*'Art should never try to be popular.
The public should try to make itself artistic.'*
—Oscar Wilde

Pt Ravi Shankar and Ut. Ali Akbar Khan.

In December 1939, Pt Ravi Shankar made his debut by playing a jugalbandi with Ali Akbar Khansaheb. They went on to play numerous other jugalbandis. Following the mega success of their concerts, there was a fad in the classical domain for duets between artistes across gharanas. However, in those days no other pair ever had half the success Khansaheb and Panditji had with their jugalbandis. A jugalbandi is harmonious only between artistes trained by the same guru, such as the Gundecha brothers, Rajan–Sajan Mishra, etc. The Shiv–Hari pair is perhaps the only exception to the rule as they had an incredible understanding between them. However, music is as subjective as food, and there is no logical explanation regarding what works and what doesn't. I personally find the jugalbandis between north Indian classical and Carnatic classical out and out ridiculous.

According to the Upanishads, the ego is a major obstacle in the path of a seeker. The seed of ego is present in all of us to a lesser or greater extent. Ego is like a bunch of weeds in a farmer's field. Until the weeds are uprooted completely, one cannot cultivate a healthy crop. The way one needs to constantly uproot the weeds, we need to uproot our ego. Our ego is so deeply ingrained in us that although the very objective of sādhanā is destruction of the ego, we struggle to eliminate it even with dedicated spiritual practice. We need to make conscious and constant efforts to destroy our ego.

Ego thrives on the instincts of comparison and competition. Those on the path of spirituality don't encourage jugalbandis as they bring out competitive instincts among the performing artistes and lure the audience into comparing the performers. Each member of the audience, with or without an elementary knowledge of music, renders his verdict about who played better. In every jugalbandi concert, 'the green-eyed monster' invariably arrives as the chief guest to prey on the artistes.

'From February 1949 until 1956,' Ma told us, 'Panditji was working as the music director for AIR, New Delhi. Whenever Baba visited Delhi, he stayed at DCM owner Bharat Ramji's house. Baba used to teach the sitār to Bharat Ramji's wife, Sheela Devi. Baba had proposed to him that if Panditji stayed there he could regularly teach her the sitār. Bharat Ramji was kind enough to agree to give us accommodation in one of the many rooms in his palatial estate.

'There were several baithaks [a kind of music session where the audience and artiste are in close proximity] arranged by Bharat Ramji and the who's who of New Delhi, with top politicians, bureaucrats and foreign dignitaries in attendance. Even Dr Karan Singh had arranged a baithak where Panditji and I played a jugalbandi. Indira Gandhi too attended a few of our baithaks and, for some inexplicable reason, developed a liking for me. We became quite friendly and met socially as she lived not far from where we were.

'For years, my focus had been the surbahār and Panditji's the sitār, but he wanted to follow Baba's suit and play both sitār and surbahār.

Panditji and Ma during their jugalbandis.

'After our performance in New Delhi, despite my lack of interest in socializing with them, the celebrity audience gathered around me and showered praises on my playing a bit more than they did for Panditji. When this happened repeatedly, Panditji found it very disturbing. We stopped playing jugalbandis, but the problem didn't end. Panditji thought my solo renditions were getting more applause and praise than his. Panditji's lament was that I was deliberately stealing away the limelight from him.

'Back home, Panditji would invariably be in a bad mood and sulk. His point of view was that in order to please the audience we should modify the music by making it lighter, a bit Westernized, and thus more palatable. However, I refused, as I wanted to be in congruence with our rich classical heritage, and had full faith in the power of our ancient classical tradition. I believed that the audience ought to evolve and learn to appreciate the richness of our heritage in its pure form; the artistes should not stoop down.'

This is an age-old debate:

मार्गोदिशीतितद्द्वेधातत्रमार्गः सउच्यते।
योमार्गितोविरिंच्याधैः प्रयुक्तोभरतादिभिः ।।

Since the Vedic era, two branches of music have developed. मार्गी (Mārgi) and देशी (Deshi). One for the 'class' and the other for the 'mass'. The aim of the Mārgi music was moksha, salvific liberation. It was piously sacred, well researched by the *rishi-muni*s (sages and ascetics) of the Vedic Era, and therefore adhered to strict discipline.

देशे-देशेजनानांयद्रुच्याहृदयरंजकम्

On the other hand, Deshi music has been for pleasing and entertaining the masses. It was a genre that was highly flexible to make it suitable to the varying taste and preferences of different people from different regions.

The problem was that Panditji wanted to venture on the path of the Deshi branch of music, while Guru Ma wanted to walk on the path less travelled, that of the almost extinct Mārgi music. Ali Akbar Khansaheb, as usual, went along with Panditji on this too. When asked about this in an interview, Khansaheb responded with his brilliant one-liner, saying, 'Classical music is my mother, but experimentation is my inamorata with whom I can take a lot of liberties.' Khansaheb went on to explain, 'Classical music should be reformed in such a way that it flows with the current of the time. Our challenge is then to bring depth and feelings into this reformed music.'

Returning to the story, Ma said, 'During one of our jugalbandis, Panditji became highly disturbed and agitated. He kept complaining that the microphone was not loud enough. I passed on my microphone to him. Instead of giving his microphone to me in exchange, Panditji kept both the microphones throughout the rest of the performance. The audience saw Panditji with two microphones, while I had none. Panditji ended up facing a lot of criticism, which added fuel to our marital discord.'

Quoting Sakuntala Narasimha on Annapurna Devi:[17]

On 31 December 1955, I was present at her duet concert with her [then] husband, sitār maestro Pt Ravi Shankar, at the annual conference of the Madras Music Academy. I later realized that it was a historic occasion, for it was the last time Annapurna and Ravi Shankar shared a platform. The two, it is said, never played together again. I was then a teenager, and since I was learning music, my mother took me along to attend all the concerts during that December season. On New Year's Eve, when Ravi Shankar and Annapurna took the dais at 9 p.m., the pandal was full [there was no hall at that time]. The recital went on well beyond the billed duration. As soon as midnight approached, I remember Ravi Shankar stopped playing, lowered his surbahār, leaned towards the microphone and wished the audience a Happy New Year.

None of us knew at that time that the two were playing together for the last time. What I remember very clearly, six decades later, is that during the recital, an unforgettable concert, Ravi Shankar [better known as a professional artist among the two] would play a phrase and pause for Annapurna to do her bit, and each time she outdid him, to the delight of the audience. Especially during the jhala and fast improvisations, he threw her several challenges but each time she went one better and outperformed him in terms of speed and breath-taking flights of fancy. He tried playing faster, and unfazed, she responded in equal measure. It was an unforgettable treat. I remember the moment when he, almost in desperation, played a super-fast phrase, and she coolly took up the challenge and outdid him. He then threw up his hands dramatically, almost as if saying 'I give up', and the audience burst into ecstatic applause. Ravi Shankar clearly meant to lead, although it was a duet concert, but again and again she outshone him, without fanfare, flamboyance or theatrics. I can clearly recall Annapurna seated on the stage, on his left, dignity personified, taking the musical presentation to great heights. She was not dressed in a flashy 'pattu' sari like all the other women who performed at the conference. Whether it was an ālaap, gat or a *tihai* to arrive at the *sam*, it was she who carried the day.

Annapurna's father, Ut. Allauddin Khan, and her brother, Ali Akbar Khan, have both gone on record to say that between Ravi Shankar and Annapurna, she was undoubtedly the better artist, and that probably rankled Ravi Shankar. The Music Academy concert was reportedly the last time they played together. A few months later, in 1956, Ravi Shankar left her. That was the end of her public appearances and concerts. The couple went on to secure a divorce much later. Fame and accolades do not always come automatically and commensurately to those with talent. She became a recluse . . .'

Shubho too lamented, 'Papa drastically lowers my microphone levels.' At New York's Lincoln Center concert, Panditji used two high-tech expensive microphones for himself, but Shubho was given just one very ordinary microphone.[18]

When I was with Ali Akbar Khansaheb, I asked him if this was true. Khansaheb laughed and said, 'पंडितजी, मेरा microphone कम कर देते थे, तो शुभोकी तो बात ही क्या? [If Panditji used to lower my microphone, what to speak of Shubho?] This is one of the reasons I stopped playing jugalbandis with Panditji and started playing with Nikhil Banerjee instead.'

The ticket of the concert of Shubho with Panditji.

In his days, Baba used to tune his sarod to the tonic of B. With modern technology better strings became available, so Ali Akbar Khansaheb and Bahadur Khansaheb were able to standardize the tuning of their sarod to C. However, in those days, their C was a few cents lower than the current international standard of C=261.63 Hz (A=440 Hertz). During his Maihar days, Pt Ravi Shankar too used to be at par with Baba and Ali Akbar Khansaheb by tuning his sitār to C. Subsequently, Panditji opted for a smaller sitār and started tuning with C#=277.18 Hz as the tonic.

This is when the problem of tuning while playing a jugalbandi with Ali Akbar Khansaheb began. They reached an agreement to compromise for a frequency which would be the midpoint between their usual tonic frequencies. As per simple maths,

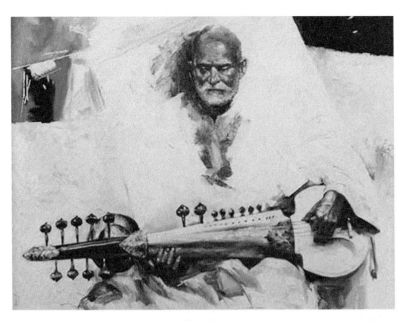

Baba Allauddin Khan.

Madina Bhavan.

Baba Allauddin Khan.

Annapurna Devi.

Ut. Ali Akbar Khan.

Pt Nikhil Banerjee.

Pt Hariprasad Chaurasia.

Shubho and Aashish Khan.

Nityanand Haldipur.

Basant Kabra.

View from Ma's house.

Some of the members of our Saturday rendezvous at Ma's house
(L to R: Rooshiji, Suresh, Atul, Nityanand and Smarth).

Naresh Bhargav, Pradeep Barot, Dr Lalita Rao, Suresh Vyas, Govind Bhargav, Prabudh Banerjee, Rajdeep Barot, Nityanand Haldipur, Milind Sheorey, Atul Merchant, Qamar Ali and his daughter, and Nanda Sardesai at the annual concert sponsored by Annapurna Devi under the banner of Acharya Allauddin Music Circle.

L to R: Suresh Vyas, Qamar Ali, Nityanand Haldipur, Jaykishore, Pradeep Udyavar,
Rooshikumar Pandya, Atul Merchant, Sadanand Naimpalli, Sunil Shastri,
Smarth Bali and Pradeep Barot.

Annapurna Devi.

Ut. Ali Akbar Khansaheb with Pt Nikhil Banerjee.

halfway between C and C# would have been 269.4 Hz, but Panditji dominated over Khansaheb in every aspect of life, so why not in tuning too? Panditji would pull Khansaheb to a higher and higher frequency all the way to 274 Hz. But this proved disastrous for Khansaheb. Often during their jugalbandi concerts, Khansaheb's strings would break due to excess tension. For instance, during the jugalbandi concert in Banaras, Khansaheb's strings kept breaking throughout the performance. Panditji kept playing whenever Khansaheb was busy fixing the string, but the audience got disappointed.

Pt Kishan Maharaj, Pt Ravi Shankar and Ut. Ali Akbar Khan.

Sometime in April 1950, as a response to public demand, there was a recital in Delhi of the trio of Ali Akbar, Ravi Shankar and Vilayat Khan, with Kishan Maharaj on the tablā. When reports of the recital reached Baba, he asked Jotin Bhattacharya, 'तीनों में अलीअकबरने सबसे कम बजाया। ऐसा क्यों? क्या इसी लिए मैंने उसे बचपनसे सिखाया है? अलीअकबरमें जितनी क्षमता है वह सबके हाथ बंद कर सकता है, लेकिन उसने ऐसा नहीं किया।[19] [Among all three, Ali Akbar played the least. Have I trained him since childhood for this? Ali Akbar is capable of restraining any artiste, but he chose not to do so.]'

The American author Robert Greene, famous for his books on power and strategy, never met Guru Ma, nor did Guru Ma ever hear about him. Yet, while reading the very first page of his most famous book, *The 48 Laws of Power*, we couldn't help remembering Guru Ma.

'Make the people above you feel comfortably superior. When you outshine your boss, superior, captain, husband, parent, you will inspire fear and insecurity and they will want to punish you.

'In your desire to please or impress them, do not go too far either, or you might accomplish the opposite.

'Instead, make your masters appear more brilliant than they are, and you will be successful.'

An Error Applauded

Ma told us a funny story from many years ago.

'During one jugalbandi, Panditji and Khansaheb played Raag Shree. Those trained in Indian classical music know that the *shruti* [micro-frequency of the note] of the *komal rishabh* is lower than normal in Raag Shree. However, due to his typical carefree and careless attitude, Bhaiyā kept playing the normal komal rishabh. Bhaiyā, while playing, habitually closes his eyes and refrains from looking here and there except for a quick rare glance at the tablā player, and that too occasionally. Panditji kept trying to catch his attention, but Bhaiyā, typically immersed in his playing, just didn't look at Panditji. Then Panditji kept playing the lower frequency komal rishabh of Raag Shree again and again to point out to Bhaiyā his mistake.

'However, as komal rishabh is the *vaadi swar* [the prominent note most frequently played] of Raag Shree, Bhaiyā kept playing pancham the samvaadi [the sub-prominent note] in response by sliding from komal rishabh to pancham. Bhaiyā's glissando went beautifully with the movement of Raag Shree, and created a terrific *sawaal–jawaab* [call and response improvisation] kind of effect. The audience was thrilled and clapped each time this happened. The mistake became an act of genius.

'After the rendition, Panditji told Bhaiyā, "Alu [that was how he always addressed Ali Akbar Khan], I was trying to draw your attention to point out that you were playing the wrong shruti of komal rishabh, but you just didn't look at me. I kept playing the lower shruti of komal rishabh to point out your mistake, but you kept playing pancham in response." By then a crowd had gathered on the stage. They congratulated Bhaiyā for his genius.

'Later that night, at home, when Panditji narrated this incident, all of us, including Bhaiyā, had a good laugh.'

Pt Ravi Shankar and Ut. Ali Akbar Khan.

During her final days, Ma was bedridden. Once, when Suresh Vyas was attending to her, he saw the above image on the Internet. He ran to Ma and showed it to her. At first Ma couldn't recognize who the two people were. Then she joyfully exclaimed, 'अरे! यह तो भैया है [Oh! This is Bhaiyā!]' The next second she could recognize Panditji too, and started laughing like an amused child.

The Critics Who Knew Too Much

'Critics are like eunuchs in a harem:
they know how it's done,
they've seen it done every day,
but they're unable to do it themselves.'
—Brendan Behan

A music critic once stated in his review of a Khansaheb concert that at certain points in his rendition, he was *besura* (off-pitch). This was after Khansaheb had been awarded the title of '*Swar Samrāt*' (Emperor of Musical Notes), by none other than Baba Allauddin Khan himself.

Those were the days of the spool (reel-to-reel) tape recorders. Khansaheb asked for the reel and listened to the entire recording. The next evening, another concert was scheduled and Khansaheb knew that the same music critic was going to attend. Khansaheb kept the recording ready, and refused to start the rendition until this critic arrived. When he did, Khansaheb told him, 'Here is the recording of my last concert. You have published in the newspaper that I was off-pitch at certain places. I will now replay the recording. Please be kind enough to point out to me where I have erred, and which notes I have played off-pitch.' The humiliated music critic publicly apologized, and the concert started.

A similar incident took place with Panditji. A music critic wrote that Panditji's renditions were mediocre. Unlike Khansaheb, Panditji took a very different approach. He invited that music critic, along with a group of connoisseurs, to his residence for dinner, and played for them for six hours. What Panditji played was music of the highest calibre. After the performance, while having dinner, he politely asked the music critic, 'I know I am not good enough. I know I need to improve. Could you please guide me regarding what improvements I need to make?' The critic was too stunned to utter a single word.

Another instance was pretty funny as well. During the season, it was not unusual for Bombay to have multiple classical music concerts on a given weekend. It was not possible for the critics to attend them all; they would ask the artistes beforehand what they were going to perform and write a review without attending it. Once, it so happened that because of some unforeseen circumstances, an artiste's performance was delayed. In order to adhere to the tradition of raag timings, the artiste had to change the raag. However, the next morning, a newspaper published a detailed review of the rendition of the raag the artiste never rendered.

> Ma was an extreme example of the artiste–audience rapport.
> For stage performances, Ma practised and preached 'negative hallucination', that is, as if the audience were non-existent.

Struggle of the Superstars

जीवन में जितना दोष और दुःख दिखाई दे,
उतना ही अच्छा है; इसी से वैराग्य आएगा।

[The more faults and sorrows you come across in life,
the better it is, for it will lead you to asceticism]
—*Acharya Allauddin Khan*

Nobody else had Pt Jotin Bhattacharya's proximity and closeness to Baba. Often, Baba would tell him, 'तुम मेरी बूढ़ी उमर के बेटे हो' [You are my old-age son]'. Jotinbabu lived in Baba's house from 1949 to 1956 and played multiple roles: Baba's disciple, his personal secretary who handled all of Baba's correspondence, his ticket bookings, shopping, etc. He was also the guardian and academic tutor for Baba's grandchildren. Baba never allowed anyone outside the family to live in his home, not even Pt Ravi Shankar, who during his Maihar days had to live in a rented cottage next to Madina Bhavan. Only after he married Annapurna Devi did he shift to Madina Bhavan.

There was a reason why Baba was so protective of Sharan Rani. After 1947, Maihar acceded to the Union of India. Maharaja Brijnathsinghji moved to Jabalpur. The native princes of India were living on the privy purse money they were getting from the government of India. With nothing better to do, they wiled away

Pt Jotin Bhattacharya.

Vidushi Sharan Rani.

their time in wining, dining and womanizing. The reputation of
the neighbouring Holkars of Indore was so bad that Baba didn't
want to take a chance with any of his female disciples.[20]

Pt Jotin Bhattacharya was from Banaras, and had a double
graduate degree—considered to be a very high academic qualification
in those days. As noted above, Baba had made Jotinbabu the
guardian and tutor of his grandchildren at Maihar. Khansaheb had

left his sons Aashish and Dhyanesh, and his daughter, Shree (Baby), at Maihar, while the two younger sons, Pranesh and Amreesh, were with Zubeida Begum and Khansaheb in Bombay. To Jotinda's surprise, Annapurna Devi with her son, Shubho, was also at Maihar.

After the accession of Maihar, Baba stopped receiving the money he used to get from Maharaja Brijnathsinghji. It was ironic that Panditji and Khansaheb were in Delhi and Bombay, pursuing their careers, while Baba had to look after his grandchildren. Neither of them sent any money to Maihar. Baba had to manage the entire expenses all by himself.

Once, as Baba was leaving for Allahabad. Jotinbabu asked him where he was going. 'I am going to Allahabad to beg for money by playing the sarod. Your brother Ali Akbar has sent his children to me, but never sends me a penny to raise them. Therefore, at my age, I have to perform on the radio to earn a little money.'

As recorded by Pt Jotin Bhattacharya in his book, in October 1949, when he moved to Baba's house in Maihar, Annapurna Devi was at Maihar with Shubho, who was seven years old at that time. Panditji was in Delhi working as the music director for All India Radio. A few days prior to his arrival there, Panditji had told Jotinda that all the money he earned while working at All India Radio went towards repayment of his debts.

At times Ma used to tell us, 'You people can't even imagine how much Baba struggled throughout his life. Panditji and Bhaiyā too struggled relentlessly. At that time, Panditji was in debt and we were facing a severe shortage of money. We had rented a small apartment far from the city in the suburb of Borivali. तब आर्थिक स्थिति भी ख़राब थी। संगीत बजा कर कमाने में तब एड़ियाँ धिस जाती थी। देर रात तक रियाज़ करना और दिनभर काम माँगने जाना [Till the late hours of the night, he used to do his riyaaz, and then during the day he ran from pillar to post to beg with the organizers to give him concerts to perform in and earn some money].

'We were so short of money that we couldn't afford laundry expenses. We didn't even have enough money to buy an iron to

Panditji and Guru Ma in happier days.
When all the world was young,
And all the trees were green.

press Panditji's clothes. From that time on, I have stopped ironing my clothes. However, for Panditji's clothes, I used a heated metal pot as a hot press to remove the wrinkles from his kurtas.

'Panditji suffered all sorts of humiliation from the organizers, who disrespected him without realizing his musical prowess. These influential people shamelessly exploited Panditji in numerous ways. For example, under the pretext of introducing him to film producers, they would keep baithaks of Panditji's recitals at their wine-and-dine parties. I feel sad to mention that it was all free entertainment in the guise of promises they had no intention to fulfil. They didn't pay him a dime. Sometimes he had to pay the tablā accompanists from his own pocket.

'Shubho's health was a constant problem. A catastrophe struck when Panditji fell seriously ill. I don't know what ailment it was, but Panditji was running a high temperature. One day his body temperature went as high as 107°F. In medical terminology it is called hyperpyrexia, a life-threatening condition. To pay the medical bills, I had to sell all my jewellery. With medical treatment, Panditji's condition improved, but it was a long road to a full recovery. He had become so weak that he struggled even to get out of bed. His high fever had affected his nervous system, giving him bouts of amnesia. Panditji started moving around within the house, but when he tried to resume playing the sitār, he experienced a total loss of memory.

'Over the previous several years, I had switched completely to the surbahār, but I resumed playing the sitār for his sake and made him play along with me, simply to refresh his memory of what he had learnt from Baba. After a couple of months of playing together, his memory returned, which restored his confidence and he then resumed his public performances.

'Bhaiyā too went through a bitter struggle. For instance, he was the music director for Nav-Ketan's film *Aandhiya*, directed by Chetan Anand, with Dev Anand as the actor and writer. Bhaiyā had to shuttle between Dev Anand and Chetan Anand for his dues.

'Nikhil Banerjee too faced hardships when he came to Maihar. He sought lodging accommodation in a temple at Maihar.'

About his struggle, Baba said, 'While learning in Raipur, my entire day was spent in the household service of my Gurudev Wazir Khan, so I practised my music throughout the nights. To stay awake, I used to tie one end of a rope to my collar and hook the other end to the ceiling, so that if I fell asleep, the rope would be pulled, thus preventing me from falling asleep. I practised in the dark because I couldn't afford to burn the oil to illuminate the lamp throughout the night. I used to practice the raags of all the *prahars* and conclude my riyaaz with Shuddh Bhairavi. Then I would offer namaaz and eat a breakfast of stale rotis (Indian unleavened bread) with salt.'

Annapurna Devi.

There is an ancient folktale oft told in music circles.

After having completed his training, and before venturing out into the world, a disciple went to his guru seeking his blessings.

The guru said, 'I wish you a life full of suffering.'

The disciple was aghast!

The guru explained, 'Suffering will give you pain, and this pain will manifest as pathos in your music.'

Persecuted by Fanatics

ज़ाहिद-ए-तंग-नज़र ने मुझे काफ़िर जाना
और काफ़िर ये समझता है मुसलमान हूँ मैं

[The narrow-minded devout considers me a kafir
And the kafir thinks I am a Muslim]

Baba used to say, 'मैं न तो मुसलमान, ना ही हिन्दु हो पाया। एक अपदार्थ रह गया हूँ [I could neither be a Muslim nor a Hindu. I am devoid of an identity].'

Throughout his life, Baba faced hostility from Islamic fanatics. With the exception of his family relations, Baba didn't have a single Muslim disciple. With some rare exceptions, most of the tablā players who accompanied Baba were Hindus. Baba created several raags in his life; all the *raags* had Hindu names. To counter this criticism, Baba, as late as 1956, created a raag and named it 'Raag Muhammed'.

Ma had been named 'Annapurna' by Brijnathsingh. Nonetheless, the maulvi compelled Baba to give Ma a Muslim name: 'Roshanara'. When we asked Ma about this, she replied, 'Roshanara was the name imposed upon us. Throughout my life, I've never used it, nor has anybody ever called me by that name.'

Terrible atrocities were committed upon Baba's daughter Jahanara by her fanatical in-laws for the mere act of practising music. She was sent back to Maihar, and when she arrived there, she was in very bad health and promptly died of suspected arsenic poisoning. Jahanara's suffering and death was an acute trauma from which neither Baba nor Guru Ma would recover.

When Baba finally became financially comfortable, he wanted to do something for his birthplace Shivpur (now in Bangladesh). The locals requested him to build a mosque for them as there was none in the vicinity and they had to travel a long distance to visit one. Baba therefore bought a piece of land and sought the permission of the local Muslim religious leaders to build a mosque. However, they denied his request, saying, 'The money you have earned is through music, which is declared as *haram* [forbidden] in Islam. We can't allow any paid labourers to build the mosque. If you want to build a mosque, you must do so with your own hands.'

Baba was very sad, but he went ahead and built the mosque single-handedly with his own hard labour, injuring his back in the process. Even after the recovery, his back pain remained for the rest of his life.

Baba also created a reservoir pond for the local people. Villages in Bengal for ages had man-made rainwater-harvesting ponds to solve water supply woes and enable fish farming.

When Ma was about seven years old, the maulvi approached Baba and told him that it was his duty to teach his daughter Islamic religious practices. His argument was, 'No matter how much you worship Hindu gods, you are legally a Muslim and shall always be one. You'll have no choice but to find a Muslim son-in-law. Therefore, please start teaching your daughter about Islam.'

Baba relented, and the maulvi began visiting their home to teach Ma Islamic prayers. In Ma's words, 'Out of curiosity, Bhaiyā watched Maulvisahib teach me, and afterwards he would tease me saying, "Now that you have become a Muslim, you should start wearing a burqa."

'The maulvi had a body odour like that of a dead animal. Also, I didn't understand a word of the prayers he was teaching me as it was in some Arabic dialect. After a couple of lessons, I told Baba, "I don't want to learn from the Maulvisahib. I can't tolerate his body odour." Fortunately for me, Baba respected my wish and asked him to stop teaching me.'

Aashish Khan was engaged to Alla Rakha Khansaheb's daughter. Despite the most harmonious relationship between Panditji, Alla Rakhaji and Ali Akbar Khansaheb, the engagement broke off because of religious differences. Both Aashishda and Raziaji were happily looking forward to the marriage but the differences in the religious beliefs thwarted their plans. Fortunately, the cancellation of this marriage had little effect upon the warm relations between the Qureshi family and Khansaheb's family. Ali Akbar Khansaheb forever remained extremely fond of Zakirbhai.

When Baba died, the mullahs and maulvis of Maihar created a problem in his burial. To the dismay of the maulvis, the priests of the Shārdā Ma temple joined Baba's funeral procession, and of their own accord performed the traditional last rites puja ceremony for him.

Baba's humility is conveyed by the words he uttered towards the end of his long life: 'संगीत की थोड़ी समझ आने लगी तब जाने का वक़्त आ गया [By the time I started understanding a bit about music, alas it's time to go.]'

Promiscuity and Jealousy

'Men are more moral than they think and
far more immoral than they can imagine.'
—Sigmund Freud

The problem with stardom is that there is no privacy or secrecy. Whatever you do is reported by the media to the public. Therefore, it is almost impossible to hide your indulgences, especially when you cheat on your spouse.

In music, Ali Akbar Khansaheb was a disciple of his father, guru Allauddin Khan, but when it came to promiscuity, Ravi Shankar was his mentor and guru. In fact, the two had always been partners in crime. The pot couldn't call the kettle black. The only difference was that Khansaheb was less brazen than Panditji, who suffered from the Casanova complex. For whatever narcissistic psychological gratification, Panditji was proud of his promiscuous behaviour and would proudly flaunt his affairs rather than trying to be discreet. Panditji had multiple affairs and Khansaheb had multiple marriages, and each had numerous one-night stands.

A Casanova complex is when a man desires a large number of sexual partners, and indulges in a constant active pursuit of women, seducing them into sexual acts without any emotional relationship or commitment. The complex is named after Giovanni Jacopo

Casanova (1725–98), an Italian memoirist and adventurer noted for his sexual conquests.

Annapurna Devi was totally unaware, or rather not bothered about what was going on outside the four walls of her house. However, Zubeidaji was a police officer's daughter. Khansaheb was too naive to withstand Zubeidaji's persistent interrogation. Eventually, he confessed to both his and Panditji's promiscuity. After this, things were never the same between him and Zubeidaji.

Zubeidaji reported it all to Annapurna Devi, which ended the marital harmony between her and Ravi Shankar. Life took an ugly turn. The rest of the Maihar Gharana, including all the children, Baba, Madina Ma and even Baba's disciples suffered the aftermath.

Annapurna Devi's first reaction was to cease all kind of physical contact with Panditji. If she had returned to Maihar, Baba would have guessed the disaster. Therefore, for a year she with Shubho went and stayed with Ali Akbar Khansaheb at Lucknow.

In Ma's words: 'After hearing all this, I lost interest in life. For a long spell of time, I went and stayed with Bhaiyā. Baba was disturbed when he came to know about this. For Baba's sake, Bhaiyā begged me to return to my husband's house. So, after about a year of staying with Bhaiyā, I returned to Bombay. There, Panditji fell seriously ill.'

From February 1949 until 1956, Panditji was working as the music director for AIR in New Delhi. On 7 October 1950, he arrived in Maihar with his spiritual guru, Tat Baba. *Tat* means sackcloth. Tat Baba was called so because he used to wear a threadbare sack which looked like a jute robe. In 1948, despite his musical prowess, Panditji had been hit by numerous adversities and was contemplating suicide. Tat Baba assured him that stardom lay ahead of him. Needless to say, Panditji was spellbound by Tat Baba. He had received a guru mantra from Tat Baba, but Ma refused to do the same, saying, 'For me the only guru is Baba, who has already given me the guru mantra.' Most believe this refusal antagonized both Panditji and Tat Baba.

Another bombshell was dropped on Baba and the rest of the family when they received Ali Akbar's letter declaring he was marrying a woman named Rajdulari. Despite having five children (four sons and a daughter) from Zubeida Begum, a second marriage, that too while he was in dire financial straits, was shocking.

Ut. Ali Akbar Khan with Rajdulariji.

On 14 December 1951, Ali Akbar Khansaheb sent Zubeidaji, along with their two youngest sons, Pranesh and Amaresh, to Maihar.

As per the translated excerpts from Pt Jotin Bhattacharya's book:

10th January 1952. Ali Akbar arrived at Maihar. In the evening, we went to the theatre to watch the film 'Dastaan'. When we returned home, we chatted for hours. I requested Ali Akbar that he ought to keep visiting Maihar every few months and to send money to provide for the children. Ali Akbar complained about his financial struggles. When asked about his second marriage, Ali Akbar said he was going to get married with Tat Baba's blessings.

21st January 1952. Ravi Shankar along with Annapurna Devi and Shubho arrived at Maihar. During Ravi Shankar's stay of four days, we talked a lot. Ravi Shankar confirmed what Zubeidaji had told me about him.

In his words, 'I have already told you what kind of a person I am. I believe we should change and modernize according to the time and age we are living in. However, Annapurna is too stubborn. She just doesn't like to leave the house. She doesn't interact with anyone.

'The first year of our marriage was full of happiness. During those days, Zubeida was not there because Baba had sent Zubeida to her parents. I had confided in Alubhai the secrets of my personal life. Alubhai told it all to his wife Zubeida.

'Shubho was born after a year of our marriage. After a few days, Zubeida returned to Maihar. Annapurna was so naïve then. Apart from her father and brother, she had seen no other man before marriage. Infidelity was beyond her imagination. Zubeida ruined my marriage by informing Annapurna about my promiscuity.[21] Annapurna at once ceased a physical relationship with me. Although I have erred, it wasn't totally unpardonable. In her anger, she went away to Alubhai in Lucknow. Considering Baba's plight, she returned after many months, but things are not the same between us. It is true that I am not a saint, but I ought not be called evil either.'

As we were talking, a *dhobin* [laundress] came to collect the clothes. Seeing Ravi Shankar ogling the laundress, Annapurna said to him, 'What are you thinking? Want to pay her in advance? She has been your laundress for a long time.' Hearing this, Ravi Shankar lowered his eyes in embarrassment and mumbled, 'Give her some money.' Annapurna sternly replied, 'Since you are so desirous of paying her, why don't you yourself give her the money!'[22]

Ravi Shankar was an extremely talented stand-up comedian. One could die laughing at his skill in mimicking people. However, most of the jokes he cracked were either vulgar or sexist. Once during such comedy sessions, Annapurna Devi's voice alarmed us. 'What is all this hilarity about?' she yelled from the adjoining room. 'I know what is going on. You are perverting Jotinda.' However, Ravi Shankar, without paying attention to Annapurna's comments, continued his act.

Baba on sursinghār and Annapurna Devi on surbahār.

Panditji learnt from Baba for about seven to eight years, until 1944. Ali Akbar Khansaheb learnt for about sixteen years, until 1943. After that, both Khansaheb and Panditji pursued their performing careers while Annapurna Devi continued to learn from Baba, uninterrupted. While Panditji was living in Bombay and Delhi, Annapurna Devi and Shubho were sent away to Maihar for several months. When Annapurna Devi was at Maihar, Baba didn't allow her to go to the kitchen to help Madina Ma and Zubeidaji. Shubho spent most of the time with his cousins, Aashish, Dhyanesh and Shree, with Jotinda as their guardian and tutor. While at Maihar, all Annapurna Devi did was learn from Baba and do her riyaaz. In those days, the only other disciples Baba was teaching were Nikhil Banerjee and Jotin Bhattacharya, each once a week. But he taught Annapurna Devi each evening for two to four hours. Should we be surprised that Annapurna Devi ended up learning much more than anybody else?

Ashutosh Bhattacharya was known as 'Kaviraj' (an occupational title given to those practising Ayurveda) as well as a proficient tablā player, being Kanathe Maharaj's disciple. On various occasions, Ashutoshji accompanied Khansaheb, Panditji, Jotinda and others on stage. During Panditji's Delhi years, Ashutoshji regularly came to Panditji to accompany him for his daily riyaaz. Ashutoshji said, 'Whenever Ravi Shankar got stuck in a *taan* or *todā*, he always sought Annapurna's help. Annapurna would come out of the kitchen and immediately set things right. One day, Ravi Shankar and I struggled for more than half an hour to get a todā right, but we kept missing the *sum* [the first beat in the cycle of taal]. Annapurna Devi rushed out from the kitchen and pointed out, "क्या कर रहे हो! तोड़ा इस मात्रा से शुरू करो [What are you doing! Start the todā from this beat]." Panditji played accordingly and voila, the todā ended right on the sum. Panditji was joyous. He said to Annapurna, "I was struggling for half an hour, why didn't you tell me before!" Annapurna went back to the kitchen, saying, "I thought you would be able to figure it out." Such was her calibre.'

'Zubeidaji witnessed Panditji threatening Annapurna Devi, "तुम अच्छा बजाती हो उसको लेकर जो तुममें अहंकार है, उसके लिए तुम्हारी सारी उँगलियाँ तोड़ दूँगा [You have a lot of ego about your playing well, I'll break all your fingers."[23]

Panditji asked Ma and Zubeidaji to leave his house with all the children. While Ma was packing her belongings, Panditji didn't allow her to take her notation books. For Ma, nothing in the world was more precious than the lessons she had learnt from Baba. The green-eyed monster was the greatest villain of the Seniya–Maihar Gharana.

ख़ुद अपनी मर्ज़ी से कहाँ सफ़र करते है हम
तक़दीर जहाँ ले जाएँ वहाँ बसर करते है हम

[The navigation of life is not as per our will
Wherever fate carries us, we keep drifting]
—Jataayu

The Sins of Narcissism

Psychiatrists Sandy Hotchkiss and James F. Masterson[24] identified what they called the seven deadly sins of narcissism: shamelessness, magical thinking, envy, arrogance, entitlement, exploitation and bad boundaries.

Shamelessness: Narcissists are often proudly and openly shameless; they are not bound emotionally by the needs and wishes of others. Narcissists hate criticism, and consider it 'toxic', as criticism implies they are not perfect. Narcissists prefer guilt over shame, as guilt allows them to dissociate their actions from themselves with the excuse 'my actions may be wrong, but my intention was good'.

Magical thinking: They see themselves as perfect, using distortion and illusion, known as magical thinking. They also use projection to 'dump' shame on to others.

Envy: A narcissist may secure a sense of superiority in the face of another person's ability by using contempt to minimize the other person or their achievements.

Arrogance: When feeling deflated, they 'reinflate' their sense of self-importance by diminishing, debasing or degrading somebody else.

Entitlement: Narcissists hold unreasonable expectations of particularly favourable treatment and automatic compliance because they consider themselves special. Failure to comply is considered an attack on their superiority, and the perpetrator is considered an 'awkward' or 'difficult' person. Defiance of their will is a narcissistic injury that can trigger narcissistic rage.

Exploitation: Narcissists often exploit others without regard for their feelings or interests. Often, the other person is in a subservient position where resistance may be difficult or even impossible. This exploitation may result in many brief, short-lived relationships.

Bad boundaries: Narcissists do not recognize that they have boundaries and that others are separate entities and not extensions of themselves. They feel like everyone exists only to meet their needs, or they may well not exist at all. Those who provide such fodder to the narcissist are treated as if they are part of the narcissist and are expected to live up to those expectations. In the mind of a narcissist, there is no boundary between the self and others.

Khansaheb loathed the post-concert gatherings backstage, when the crowd invariably followed him to the green room. Once at the NCPA in Bombay, right after finishing a very successful concert, as Khansaheb was walking towards the green room followed by a huge crowd, he murmured to Rooshiji, 'Let's get out of here as soon as possible.'

'But all these people want to meet you,' Rooshiji said.

'That's the reason,' Khansaheb said. 'I've entertained them for three full hours with music, I don't want to entertain them again with meaningless conversations.'

No sooner had Khansaheb said this, two beautiful women burst into the crowded green room and stood very close to him. Both were bedecked with diamond jewellery, wearing expensive sarees and heavy make-up. Their grooming was exceptionally refined. What followed was an attention-grabbing contest. Both made complete fools of themselves by trying to impress Khansaheb with their knowledge of music. The moment they initiated the conversation, it was clear that they knew nothing about music. Their conversation was so childish that Khansaheb had great difficulty concealing his laughter.

> 'The light that shines from within can never fade
>
> The light and sound of fireworks can never pervade.'

Baba's Will

चाह गई चिंता मिटी, मनुआ बेपरवाह।
जाको कछु नहि चाहिये, वे साहन के साह।।

[Desires are the root cause of all worries.
When desires are abolished, there is no worry
His mind is thus in eternal bliss
The one who wants nothing is the king of kings]
—Rahim

In 1960, Baba summoned Annapurna Devi and Ali Akbar Khansaheb to Maihar. With the help of a civil judge, Baba wanted to make his will. Baba declared, 'I am giving half of all I have to Annapurna and the other half to Ali Akbar.'

Apart from Madina Bhavan with an attached garden of 1 acre, Baba had Rs 1,08,000 as liquid savings. He also owned a piece of agricultural land, three houses in Brahmanbaria (Bangladesh), the reservoir he built, a mosque built and owned along with the land it was on.[25]

Annapurna Devi refused to take anything and gave her entire share to her brother Ali Akbar Khansaheb. However, Baba insisted on her keeping the land which the maharaja had gifted her.

When the will was ready, Baba signed it, and said, 'Today, I have nothing I can call mine. I am just a custodian of this house.

In words of Annapurna Devi, 'Baba told me, "Swear on my head, that all your life you will do your sādhanā. If you get deserving disciples, train them to propagate Seni (Tansen) gharana. Also remember, a woman's place is in her husband's house. However, if for some reason, you are not respected there, act as per your *vivek* [prudence] and discretion."'

It seemed that at that point in time Baba was thinking that his end was near. However, it was written in Baba's fate to live on for twelve more years.

Baba was fond of sankeerna (compound) raags, and created numerous raags of his own, including Arjun, Bhagavati, Bhim, Bhuvaneshvari, Chandika, Dhavalashri, Dhankosh, Dipika, Durgeshvari, Gandhi, Gandhi Bilawal, Haimanti, Hem-Behag, Hemant, Hemant Bhairav, Imni Manjh, Jaunpuri Todi, Kaushi Bhairav, Kedar Manjh, Komal Bhimpalasi, Komal Marwa, Madanmanjari, Madhabsri, Madhavgiri, Malaya, Manjh Khamaj, Meghbahar, Muhammed (Aradhana), Nat-Khamaj, Prabhakali, Raj Bijoy, Rajeshri, Saraswati, Shobhavati, Subhabati, Sugandha, Surasati, etc.

Separation

In October 1944, Panditji left Maihar and came to Bombay with Ma and Shubho. He started working with the IPTA (Indian People's Theatre Association). He rented a room in the northern suburb of Malad, as the next-door neighbour to his elder brother, Rajendra, employed as a screenwriter for Bombay Talkies. Rajendra's wife, Laxmi, and her sister, Kamala, were living there as well.

Shankar wives: Annapurna Devi, Krishna, Lakshmi and Amala.

A physical attraction grew between Panditji and Kamala, causing her family to hastily get her married to the famous film director Amiya Chakravarty in 1945. Following Chakravarty's death on 6 March 1957, Panditji and Kamala renewed their romance.

Panditji used his close friend and confidant Biman Ghosh to cook up a scandal as an excuse to get rid of Ma. Panditji also accused Zubeidaji of adultery.[26] What makes this allegation bizarre is that Zubeidaji and her five children were living in the same Delhi apartment with Ravi Shankar, Annapurna Devi and Shubho. Aashish was sixteen; Dhyanesh and Shubho were fourteen. Yet, Panditji asked them all to pack their bags and leave. Zubeidaji with her five children and Annapurna Devi with Shubho left Panditji's Delhi apartment for Maihar. Baba kept wondering what the problem was, but no one dared to reveal the facts to him. This was the time when Khansaheb founded the Ali Akbar College of Music in Calcutta. He badly needed Ma's help. Therefore, all of them left for Calcutta. Ma and Shubho moved to one of the two apartments Panditji owned at Presidency Court in Ballygunge.

Panditji visited Maihar to influence Baba with his version. However, Baba had absolute faith in his daughter's character. Baba responded by saying, 'अगर मेरी बेटी का चरित्र ठीक नहीं तो उसके टुकड़े टुकड़े कर गंगा में बहा दो [If my daughter's character is dubious, slay her and throw her butchered body in the Ganges.]' After hearing Baba's response, Panditji could speak no more. What really debunked Panditji's abominable bluff was the fact that despite this alleged scandal, Panditji and Biman Ghosh remained lifelong friends. Panditji even accommodated Biman Ghosh in another apartment he owned in the other wing of Presidency Court at Ballygunge.

After ousting everyone, Panditji was now free to pursue what he himself called 'a butterfly lifestyle' of all passion and no commitment. Kamala was back in his life, with the money she inherited from her deceased millionaire husband. Panditji resigned from AIR, and with the help of Kamala, commenced his ambitious tour of Europe and America. Kamala acted as Panditji's secretary and lived as his paramour until 1981.

Ali Akbar Khansaheb became the principal and Ma became the vice-principal of the new college. Bahadur Khan, Nikhil Banerjee, Mahapurush Mishra, etc., were other notable faculty members. On Khansaheb's birthday, under the auspices of the college, an all-night concert was organized at Ranji Stadium (later known as the Eden Gardens), the largest stadium in India. Guru Ma couldn't refuse her brother's request to play at the event. The connoisseurs raved that Ma's performance was the best they had ever witnessed. However, this was to be the last time she ever played in public.

In Indian society, there is a considerable social stigma attached to separations and divorces. This was especially true in the mid-fifties, that too in a sleepy, slow city like Calcutta—this was even more so for a celebrity couple. The juiciest gossip in the music world was the discordance between Ma and Panditji. Ma was least bothered about her public image; however, she was worried about the traumatic impact their separation was having on Shubho, and the reputational damage to Seniya–Maihar Gharana. Ma therefore decided to bury the hatchet and reconcile with Panditji. To convince Panditji, Ma assured him that she would never play in public again. However, Panditji was not convinced. Then, in front of Shārdā Ma's idol, Ma placed her hand on a photo of Baba and took a vow to shun public life and never again play in front of anyone. Ma clarified that because she had promised Baba that she would never stop her sādhanā, she would continue it in seclusion. However, the truce ended shortly after as Panditji kept true to the arrangement only on paper, and continued living with Kamala as his paramour, also continuing his promiscuous flings with several other women. Ma went on living as a recluse within the four walls of her house.

In 1968, Shubho and Ma shifted to Akashganga. Panditji promised Shubho that he would remit Rs 3000 a month as the monthly allowance to meet their household expenses through Soli Batliwala, who acted as Panditji's lawyer.

Thanks to Hariprasad Chaurasia's intervention, the title of the flat was transferred in Annapurna Devi's name. But not the whole property; the flat was divided into two and the title of the smaller portion was transferred in Shubho's name.

In 1970, that is, after Shubho left Ma, Panditji reduced the monthly allowance sent to Ma from Rs 3000 to Rs 2000. Batliwala used to deduct a considerable amount as tax payable. It was beyond Ma's ability to understand the calculation for the tax deductions. Those were the years of Indira Gandhi's economic blunders. There was rampant inflation, and by the year 1972, Ma was struggling to pay her grocery bills.

Gradually, Panditji's allowance started reaching Ma in the middle of the month instead of the beginning and Ma had to keep sending her disciples to Mr Batliwala, who would send them back saying, 'Sorry, so far there is no remittance from Panditji.' All this was extremely humiliating for Ma.[27]

One of Panditji's sycophants instigated Panditji to sell Shubho's part of the flat. Panditji agreed, only to realize later that most of the proceeds from the sale were pocketed by the sycophant.

तेन ज्ञानफलं प्राप्तं योगाभ्यास फलं तथा।
तृप्त: स्वच्छेन्द्रियो नित्यमेकाकी रमते तु य:।।

[He has gained the fruit of knowledge and the fruit of yoga
Who is content, is of purified senses, ever revelling in
his solitude]
—*Ashtavakra Geeta* (xvii–1)

Munna, the Singing Dog

Munna during a music lesson.

At the end of the great Hindu epic Mahabharata, there is a story of King Yudhishthira and a dog. Years after the Kurukshetra war, on the advice of Sage Vyasa, the victorious Pandavas decided to retire and renounce their kingdom. Led by the eldest brother, Yudhishthira, as they began their ascent to the Himalayas, a dog kept following them. First Draupadi fell to her death, followed by the rest of the Pandavas, one after the other. Yudhishthira continued his journey undeterred. The dog was the only one who remained with him.

This is just a metaphorical tale, but it relates to one of Ma's loyal friends. One day, Shubho got home a dachshund puppy and named it 'Munna', a term commonly used in India to address a baby boy. Munna became extremely attached to Ma. First Panditji and then Shubho left Ma. Munna was the only one who remained with her. Ma would often lament, 'Dogs are better than human beings.'

One day Ma, in her torment, told Munna, 'Come, I'll teach you singing.' Thus began Munna's training. Soon, he learnt to howl matching the notes Ma sang. First, he howled in breves, then semibreve, and finally to minim. Over time, he learnt to sing combinations of three to five notes like G R P and D S' D P G. Later, if instructed to sing a particular note from the standard scale Sa Re Ga ma Pa Dha Ni, Munna would sing it on his own, without needing to hear the note as a reference.

The dachshund and husky dog breeds are known for their excessive howling. The Internet is full of videos of dogs howling in tune of the frequency being sung or played on an instrument by their masters. Animal psychologists say that howling is a canine's way of expressing their bond with a human. Living in a house where music was the only activity, Munna soon became renowned for his singing ability.

During one visit, Dhyaneshda witnessed Ma training Munna. Dhyaneshda was so fascinated that he shared Munna's feat with his friends, and soon Munna became the most talked about dog in Calcutta and Bombay. This proved bothersome for Ma, who began receiving a flood of requests to visit her house to hear Munna singing. None of these requests were ever granted.

A prominent maestro of Indian classical music sent a message to Ma to grant him an opportunity to listen to Munna. To avoid him, Ma gave him a witty reply, 'People travel distances to listen to your singing. If you travel all the way to listen to a dog's singing, wouldn't it be outrageous?'

Munna had another remarkable habit. Different disciples with varying skill levels would visit Ma. If the music played was in tune,

Munna would sit near the disciple and quietly listen. If the playing was mediocre, he would simply go to another room. However, if someone played badly, he would start barking angrily at them.

One day a very senior artiste came for his lesson. When it concluded, he tried to impress Ma by saying, "I have composed a beautiful tune I would like you to listen to.' Ma had no choice. The artiste must have played the tune only for a few seconds when Munna started barking at him. Ma started laughing aloud and said, 'Stop it! Even he [Munna] doesn't like it.'

'Music is a higher revelation than
the whole of wisdom and philosophy.
Music is the electrical soil in which
the spirit lives, thinks, invents.'
—Ludwig van Beethoven

An Equation with Indira Gandhi

Renowned violinist Yehudi Menuhin's first visit to India was in 1952, when he was invited by Prime Minister Jawaharlal Nehru. Thus began Menuhin's long love affair with India. Nehru's invitation had stemmed from his desire to invite leading musicians from across the world to expose our people to the best in art and artistes.

During his first visit, Yehudi Menuhin attended a private concert in which Khansaheb and Panditji played a jugalbandi with Chatur Lalji on the tablā. Yehudi Menuhin was so impressed by the two maestros that he first took Khansaheb and then Panditji to the USA.

In his autobiography *Unfinished Journey*, Menuhin acknowledged, 'Indian music took me by surprise. I knew neither its nature nor its richness, but here, if anywhere, I found vindication of my conviction that India was the original source. The two scales of the West, major and minor, with the harmonic minor as variant, the half-dozen ancient Greek modes, were here submerged under modes and scales of inexhaustible variety.'

Khansaheb gave North America its first major recital of Hindustani music at New York's Museum of Modern Art. He featured on Alistair Cooke's television programme *Omnibus*, and recorded the world's first microgroove LP devoted to a

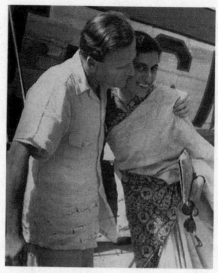

Yehudi Menuhin with Indira Gandhi.

musician from the subcontinent—*Music of India: Morning and Evening Ragas* (1955). Later that year, he gave a recital at London's St Pancras Town Hall, again with Menuhin as the master of ceremonies, who introduced Ali Akbar Khansaheb as a maestro of the sarod. He called him 'an absolute genius . . . perhaps the greatest musician in the world'.[28]

Menuhin made several more visits to India. Once, when he was a guest of Prime Minister Indira Gandhi, as a matter of courtesy, Indiraji asked Menuhin if she could extend any help to him while he was in India. Menuhin told the prime minister that he would like a favour from her, but doubted whether she could fulfil it.

Knowing Indira Gandhi's temperament, it became a prestige issue. She asked Menuhin to spell it out, and he said he wanted to listen to Annapurna Devi's surbahār. It was not as easy a proposition as it seemed.

In Guru Ma's words, 'One day, the doorbell rang. I wasn't expecting any disciple so I didn't answer. However, the person kept ringing and shouting out, saying he had come with a message from the Prime Minister's Office. At first I thought it was a prank. However, when I looked through the peephole, I saw a sepoy-like man wearing an unusual uniform. I gathered my courage and opened the door. He gave me an envelope, which he said contained a message from Prime Minister Indira Gandhi. I requested him to read it out to me. The message conveyed that the state guest, Mr Yehudi Menuhin, wished to listen to my surbahār.

'The messenger didn't leave. He said he was waiting for my reply. He wrote down my reply, "Please convey this to Indiraji, that I am honoured that she hasn't forgotten me after so many years. However, I have taken a vow not to play in front of anyone but to perform my sādhanā in front of the photo of my father-guru and Shārdā Ma." Within a few hours after the messenger departed, Panditji messaged me stating that the prime minister had pressured him, stating marital discord should not be allowed to dishonour the request of a respected state guest, who also happened to be the world's top musician.

'I chose to put the nation before self. I gave him conditional permission. I decided to make an exception and allow him to listen to me when I did my daily sādhanā, which is from about 2.30 a.m. to 4.30 a.m. I agreed to allow him to overhear from outside the door of my bedroom, where I did my sādhanā.'

George Harrison of the Beatles was also in Bombay then. He was with Panditji, and when he came to know about this, he decided to join Yehudi Menuhin. Harrison met Menuhin at the Taj Hotel lobby at about 1 a.m. As they were leaving, Menuhin got a wire message from his family that his father, Moshe Menuhin, had just been hospitalized after a heart attack. Menuhin therefore rushed to the airport to catch the first available flight to New York. However, George Harrison came and heard Guru Ma's sādhanā.

We asked Ma, 'Yehudi Menuhin was very close to both Ali Akbar Khansaheb and Panditji. What was the need to drag Prime Minister Indira Gandhi into this?'

'That was because both Bhaiyā and Panditji had expressed their inability to oblige him,' Ma said. 'Panditji knew that during our Delhi days, I had become quite friendly with Indira Gandhi, so they used Indiraji to pressure me.'

We were shocked to learn this, 'You mean to say you personally knew Indira Gandhi?' we asked Ma. 'How did this happen?'

Ma explained, 'From February 1949 until 1956, Panditji was working as the music director for AIR in New Delhi. Our accommodation was in a guest house adjoining the main bungalow of Bharatramji, the owner of DCM, who was a connoisseur of music. His wife first studied the sitār with Baba, and then from Panditji. His son Vinay learnt vocal music from me.

'Bharatramji used to arrange many baithaks at his house, and so did Karansinghji, the son of Maharaja Hari Singh, the king of Kashmir at the time of Independence.

'Many Indian and some foreign dignitaries attended these baithaks. Indiraji attended a few of them and we became quite friendly. At that time, she was assisting her father, Jawaharlal Nehru, the prime minister. I knew less about politics than she knew about music but, despite us having very little in common, we got along well and ended up meeting a few times.

'In 1968, Yehudi Menuhin came to India to receive the Jawaharlal Nehru Award for International Understanding. Indiraji asked me to suggest a gift our government could give to honour him. I suggested that of all the Indian musical instruments, Shārdā Ma's veena is the one which best symbolizes our ancient Vedic culture. Yehudi Menuhin is a maestro of the violin, which is a stringed instrument, thus the veena would be appropriate. Indiraji therefore gave him a rudra veena.

'Towards the end of 1976, Indira Gandhi visited me here. That was during the Emergency period. One day, to my shock, a large number of policemen appeared out of nowhere and told me that the prime minister was coming up to meet me. They conducted a quick security sweep of the entire building and this apartment. I had no idea what was happening outside, but I later learnt that the area had become a high-alert zone. Within a few minutes, Indiraji came.

'Despite her being so busy, that too during the Emergency, she patiently sat and chatted with me for quite a few minutes. After exchanging some pleasantries and reminiscing about our Delhi days, she asked me if I would agree to allow my surbahār playing to be recorded under the auspices of the NCPA. I politely refused.

'She informed me that she was awarding me the Padma Bhushan. She asked me if I would come to Delhi and attend the ceremony. I apologized, but told her I no longer left the house and these awards meant nothing to me. Amused by my reply, Indiraji laughed.

'She then surprised me by asking my opinion of the Emergency rule. I candidly told her, "I don't have much knowledge about politics, but my personal opinion is that what you have done is very wrong." Indiraji didn't react. After a few minutes of contemplation, she left. Before leaving, she gave me this framed, autographed photograph of her.

'That was the last time I met her and I never heard from her again. Within a month or two, Indiraji withdrew the Emergency rule and declared general elections. The government of India then sent me the certificate of the Padma Bhushan award by registered post.'

Indira Gandhi's photograph with her autograph.

Abhimaan

Around 1971, the famous film director Hrishikesh Mukherjee, with the help of his younger brother, Kashinath, came to meet Ma. Kashinath Mukherjee was a sitārist, and had had a passing acquaintance with Guru Ma during her days in Calcutta.

Hrishida told Ma that he was making a movie based on the theme of marital discord inspired by her real-life story. At that point in time, the film was titled *Raag Ragini*. Amitabh Bachchan and Jaya Bachchan had invested their own money in the project under the banner of Amiya ('Ami' for Amitabh and 'ya' for Jaya).

Hrishida assured Guru Ma he would keep her story discreet by changing the professions of the protagonists, making them singers instead of musicians. Ma gave her consent on the condition that her and Panditji's name would not be used, and it would not be announced by the media that the film was based on their married life.

Ma suggested that unlike the real-life version, the film should have a happy ending, so as to not discourage women aspirants from pursuing a career in music. Hrishida agreed to these conditions. Ma was pleased to know that S.D. Burman was going to be the music director. It is worth reminding readers that Baba Allauddin Khan was S.D. Burman's first music teacher. For a while, Burmanda learnt the bansuri from Baba.

Jaya and Amitabh Bachchan in the film *Abhimaan*.

S.D. Burman, Baba Allauddin Khan and Radhika Mohan Maitra.

Hrishikesh Mukherjee's film *Abhimaan* thus dealt with only the initial part of the actual story—that is, the marital discord resulting from the husband's inability to accept his wife's superiority. The film had a happy ending. Alas, in real life, there is no such thing as 'They lived happily ever after.'

'Music was my refuge. I could crawl into the space between the notes and curl my back to loneliness.'

—Maya Angelou

Destitution

कत बिधि सृजीं नारि जग माहीं। पराधीन सपनेहुँ सुखु नाहीं॥
नहिं दरिद्र सम दुःख जग माहीं। संत मिलन सम सुख कछु नाहीं॥

[Why is it a curse to be a woman in this world
A dependant can't be happy even in her dreams
In this world, there is no sorrow greater than destitution
There is no joy greater than close proximity of a saint]
—*Goswami Tulsidas*

The above lines written by Goswami Tulsidas seem intended for Guru Ma. Shubho was so gullible that he fell prey to his father's green-eyed monster, and ruined his life. After Shubho's exit, Ma was all alone, isolated in her Akashganga flat. She stopped stepping out of her house. It is not possible for any human being to survive in such confinement, that too without funds. She also needed a servant or at least a cohabitant to manage her requirement of groceries, cooking fuel and other myriad essentials. Even the Himalayan yogis come out of their caves to gather food and water. Ma had to depend on the support of her disciples.

Because of their family responsibilities, Ma's female disciples were not as committed to music as her senior male disciples. Ma could never find the kind of commitment Nikhil Banerjee,

Hariprasad Chaurasia, Basant Kabra, Nityanand, etc., had in any of her female disciples. However, for every male disciple who came to Ma, Panditji made it point to slander Ma by alleging promiscuity, regardless of how young he was.[29]

Ma's financial problems got worse when the NCPA shifted from Akashganga to Nariman Point. The meagre salary she received for teaching the pupils at the NCPA stopped. Ma never charged a fee from any disciple coming to Akashganga, and also fed them meals at her expense. She was living beyond her means.

On one occasion, Dhyanesh Khan arrived from Calcutta for his lessons. He rang the bell, but Ma took an unusually long time to respond. Dhyaneshda was surprised at Ma's altered behaviour. She didn't offer him any food, not even a cup of tea. For years, it had been Ma's habit to spend most of her time behind the locked door of her room, but this time she stayed locked in for even longer durations. There was no activity in the kitchen either.

Dhyaneshda was so hungry that he went to the kitchen to help himself. He opened the refrigerator, only to find that it was completely empty. He thought of making himself a cup of tea, only

Ut. Dhyanesh Khan.

to realize that there wasn't a drop of milk in the house. Suspecting the worst, he opened the jars on the shelves to find there was no rice, no flour, no lentils. In short, there was no food in the house.

Dhyaneshda went down to the nearby store and purchased enough rice and lentils for a month. When Ma realized this, she started crying. She said, 'I am your Pishi Ma [father's sister]; I am supposed to feed you, not the other way around.'

Dhayaneshda learnt from Ma that Panditji had reduced the monthly instalments from Rs 3000 to Rs 2000, and even the reduced amount was not reaching in time. Naïve as he was, Dhyaneshda played a prank to solve Ma's financial misery, albeit without her knowledge or approval. After learning that Panditji was in India at the time, he made an anonymous telephone call to him, warning him to stop harassing Annapurna Devi.[30]

Despite his good intentions, the ruse failed. Dhyaneshda had spent many years with Panditji. The young and callow man was not adept at altering his voice. He failed to hide his Bengali accent. Panditji immediately called up one of his toadies to find out who was at Akashganga at that particular time. Within a few hours, it was confirmed that the only person with Annapurna Devi at that time was Dhyanesh, who had come down from Calcutta for his lessons. Later, Dhyaneshda got a serious firing from Panditji.

Thanks to Narayan Menon, the president of the NCPA, Ma's salary was restored. Arrangements were made for her to teach there twice a week. Narayan Menon would send a car to shuttle her from Akashganga to the NCPA and back.

To help solve the financial crisis, Dhyaneshda devised another plan. It was decided that Ma should have paying guests who would pay rent and help provide social support. Dhyaneshda's friend, Mr Vishwas, the director of the NCPA, would rent Shubho's former room.

For a while, this arrangement worked well. However, since Vishwas was Shubho's age and occupying Shubho's room, Ma got

emotionally attached and started treating him like her own son.
She started cooking and feeding him two meals a day, and ended
up spending a lot of money on him; she even stopped charging
him rent. After a few months, Vishwas decided to get married and
moved out. When he was leaving, Ma in an emotional bout, gave
him far more gifts and money than she could reasonably afford.
When he left, her bank balance was just seven rupees.

Soon, the singer Gautam Mukherjee replaced Vishwas.
Gautam wasn't a gifted singer, but as he was living as a paying guest
he started learning from Ma. He hit the jackpot by successfully
wooing Ranu Mukherjee, the daughter of Hemant Kumar, the
famous singer, music director and film producer. Ranu used to
visit Ma for her music lessons. Ranu and Gautam fell in love but
Hemant Kumar didn't approve of their plan to get married, which
prompted them to elope.

Hemant Kumar was a star; successful and opulent. However,
in his anger, instead of welcoming his daughter and son-in-law,
he excommunicated them. Both shifted to Akashganga and lived
with Ma.

After a few days, when his anger subsided, Ma invited Hemant
Kumar to her house and convinced him to accept his daughter and
son-in-law. Once again, Ma was left in solitude.

Gautam, Ranu and Hemant Kumar.

Suresh Vyas.

Suresh Vyas narrates an interesting incident.

'I was going to Ma for my lessons. Those days I used to carry my sarod in a heavy hard case. After disembarking at Grant Road Station, I caught a taxi.

"Warden Road, please," I instructed the taxi driver. The distance of 2 km is too long for us talkative Indians not to strike up a conversation during the trip.

"Which *jantra* are you carrying?" the taxi driver asked.

"You are a Bengali I guess," I said.

"That's right, sir!" he exclaimed. "How did you guess?"

"Jantra is the Bengali term for a musical instrument," I replied in Bengali.

"Oh!" He was thrilled. "You speak Bengali!"

"The instrument inside this case is a sarod."

Thenceforth, our conversation was in Bengali.

"Are you going for a performance?" he asked.

"No, for my lesson," I replied.

"Where at Warden Road?" he asked.

"Akashganga building," I replied.

"Oh! A great music guru lives there," he said. "Her name is Annapurna Devi."

"How do you know about her?" I asked with surprise.

"I've been to her house many times," he proudly replied.

"Really?" I could scarcely believe him.

"Yes, she lives all alone on the sixth floor of Akashganga building," he said.

'I was quite intrigued by all this and asked him to elaborate.

"I too am a lover of music," he told me. "From West Bengal, I came to Bombay in the pursuit of making a career in music. The great Hemant Kumar was kind enough to give me shelter at his home, but he was too busy to teach me. I used to do odd jobs for him. I would escort his daughter Ranu whenever she came to learn from Annapurna Devi. Years passed, but I couldn't excel in music and it was becoming very difficult for me to survive without a source of income.

"Annapurna Devi was the one who suggested that I learn to drive. She even paid my driving school fees. After I got my commercial vehicle driving licence, Annapurna Devi gave me the margin money to pay to the bank to acquire a hypothecated vehicle. Thanks to her, I can now make a living."

'I was astonished to hear his story. He was so pleased when I told him I was Ma's disciple. By now we had reached Akashganga. As I was getting down, I asked him the fare.

"You are Mataji's disciple," he said with a smile. "How can I take money from you?" And he departed with a smile.

'After reaching Ma's house, I shared this story with her, but Ma had selectively forgotten the incident. True to the saying, 'नेकी कर दरिया में डाल [Do good and forget about it].'

Annoyed with Salil Chowdhury

In 1980, to everyone's shock, Ma's interview was published in *Jugantar Patrika*, a Calcutta political weekly.[31]

When Jotin Bhattacharya visited Ma for his lesson, he asked, 'Since you don't meet anyone, how did you end up giving an interview to an unknown journalist?'

'I haven't given any interview,' Ma replied.

'Then how did it get published?' Jotinbabu asked.

'One day, Salil Chaudhury came and rang the doorbell,' Ma said. 'Since Salilda was Panditji's acquaintance and a respected music director, I answered the door and welcomed him in. However, he was not alone. He had a friend named Amitabh Gupta along with him. At that point in time, I didn't know that Amitabh Gupta was a journalist writing for *Jugantar*. Salilda had a long, candid conversation with me, mostly asking about my life.

'After a few days, a female disciple of mine showed me the copy of *Jugantar* which had my interview. I was horrified. I wrote a stern message to Salil Chowdhury to never again visit me. However, Salilda's defence was that he himself was unaware that his friend Amitabh Gupta was going to play such mischief.'

Abandoned

वक़्त की चारागरी यूँ तो मुसल्लम है मगर
ज़ख़्म भी वो है कि ता-उम्र दबाए न बने

[Time is supposed to be a great healer, but
the wounds are such that can't be healed in a lifetime]
—Jamiluddin Aali

After Shubho's departure, Ma seemed to have lost all interest in life. She had nothing to look forward to. One by one, her disciples left her. Aashish emigrated to the USA, Nikhil Banerjee joined Khansaheb, Hariprasad Chaurasia became so busy with his film recordings and stage shows that he visited Ma no more than once or twice a year.

Referring to that period, Ma said, 'I was very happy after marriage, but happiness is so fragile. It is very difficult to predict what would destroy it. Despite having everything, nothing was left with me. My son, my brother and my husband were all alive, but none were with me. Nobody understood me. Jahanara's death, the separation from Panditji, Shubho's leaving, and Baba's death were the major traumas I faced. With advancing age and deteriorating health, staying alone was becoming more and more difficult for me. Life is worthy of living, but only if it has joy and dignity. What is the point of living a disrespectful, melancholic life? Nobody can change what is written in my fate. Only death can liberate me from this torment.'

Ma often said, 'आजकल सिखाने की इच्छा नहीं होती। आजकल के शिष्य थोड़ा सिखते ही प्रोग्राम बजाने की जल्दबाज़ी करते है। कई शिष्यों को सिखाया। जब उन्हें थोड़ा रास्ते पर ले आई, उसी समय चींटी के पर निकल आए [These days, I don't feel like teaching anyone. These days, the disciples with little training are in haste to give public performances and earn quick money. I have taught so many pupils, but no sooner was I able to put them on the right path, they would fly away. What is the point?]'

The most repeated lament we all heard from Ma was, 'कुछ भी अच्छा नहीं लगता [Nothing interests me.] यह जीवन जल्दी ख़त्म हो जाए तो अच्छा [I hope this life ends soon.]'

One of the highlights of my life was that whenever Dadu (grandfather) was out of town, Pishima (father's sister) was in-charge of teaching us.

Once, when Dadu was away for an extended time, Pishima taught me how to play the ālaap. When Dadu returned, he was completely astonished to hear me play it. Thereafter, he started teaching me ālaap as well.

I should also mention that Pishima is the one who made me practise and play 'Da Ra Da Ra', which is not a sarod baaj.

Besides music, Pishima took care of all of us, especially when we were unwell. She would remain awake all night checking our temperature and putting cold towels on our foreheads, cooking and feeding us the right diet.

There are so many fond memories that volumes can be written about her. She was a blessing for all of us. We all miss her very much. My respectful charan sparsh pranam to her feet.

—Aashish Khan

Malnutrition

भाग्यं फलति सर्वत्र न च विद्या न च पौरुषं

[*Nothing can supersede fate*
Neither erudition nor efforts]

Once, Ma's disciples Dr Lalita Rao (who served as the Maharashtra health minister from 1980 to 1985) and Anantramji were visiting Ma by a prior appointment for their lessons. They rang the doorbell, but for a very long time, Ma didn't respond. They were well aware of Ma's reluctance to answer doorbells, but if she gave an appointment, she invariably opened the door.

Though it was forbidden to ring the doorbell more than three times, they persisted, hoping for a response. After a long time, they heard Ma's faint voice from the other side of the door telling them, 'ठहरिए दरवाज़ा खोल रही हूँ [Wait, I am opening the door.]' Before she could, they heard a thud. Suspecting the worst, Dr Rao peered through the letter slot.

Despite the hood on the other side of the letter slot, she could see part of Ma's body on the floor. Ma had somehow managed to open the door, but was semi-conscious. Dr Rao went to her car and brought out her Mercury sphygmomanometer to check Ma's blood pressure, which she realized was the reason for Ma's

212

fall. The fall had fractured Ma's foot. As Ma refused to go to the clinic or a hospital, Dr Rao used her good offices and arranged for an X-ray machine to be brought home, and put a plaster on Ma's foot. Now Ma was both alone and immobilized. The drop in her blood pressure was caused by low intake of food. Her name was Annapurna, the goddess of food and nutrition, and it was ironic that she was suffering from malnutrition. Throughout her life, Ma had cooked and fed numerous disciples, but not a single disciple was there for Ma when she was starving. Wasn't it the moral duty of Hariprasad Chaurasia, Nikhil Banerjee and others to help Ma when she was in this desperate state? But none of them had even bothered to inquire about her.

When the news reached Dhyaneshda, he reported Ma's tragic condition to his father, Ali Akbar Khansaheb, who had emigrated to the US. (In the year 1967, Khansaheb founded the Ali Akbar College of Music in Berkeley, before moving to San Rafael California in 1977.)

Khansaheb strongly proposed Ma to emigrate to the US and teach at the Ali Akbar College of Music. There was nothing unreasonable, illogical or irrational about Khansaheb's proposition as there was a precedent of Ma teaching at the Ali Akbar College of Music in Calcutta. However, perhaps it was xenophobia or some other indecipherable reason for which Ma refused. In hindsight, we now believe that that was the best option for Ma, and she should have accepted Khansaheb's proposal. Alas, that was not to be.

Divorce

When Jotin Bhattacharya arrived for his lessons, he realized Ma was in desperate financial straits. Panditji was concocting various excuses not to pay the society maintenance charges, electricity and telephone bills. Ma eventually had to pay the arrears with interest and penalties.

On his return to Banaras, Jotinda learnt that Panditji was scheduled to visit the next week. Jotinda sent a legal notice to Panditji at his Banaras address that if Annapurna Devi was not paid Rs 5000 on the first of every month, a legal suit would be filed against him.[32]

In Ma's words (translated in English):

'A few days after this legal notice, Panditji's secretary, Mr Dubey, visited me. To my bewilderment, he began inspecting the house and making a list of repairs and renovations needed in the house. When I demanded an explanation, he said that Panditji was going to move in here. Mr Dubey also conveyed Panditji's message that it had been a long time since we had last met, and he was nostalgic about my cooking, so if it wasn't inconvenient to me, he would be coming over for lunch the day after. I was shocked to hear all this. As it was pointless to argue with Mr Dubey, I agreed to meet over lunch so I could hear from Panditji what was happening.

'To my surprise, Panditji came with a gang of eight to ten people. I had cooked, but not for so many people, and had to rush to the kitchen to cook more food. I was well aware of Panditji's food preferences, so I had prepared his favourite dishes. While I was busy cooking for the extra people, Panditji came to the kitchen to have a word with me. We were meeting after almost a decade. Panditji said, "I was told that the amount of Rs 2000 I have been sending you is not enough." I didn't reply.

'"I've heard that you keep feeding pigeons kilos of grains every day. No wonder you run out of money," Panditji said. "Why are you so devoted to them?"

"They are more loyal than humans. They don't betray," I replied.

"Stop feeding them, and they will stop coming to you," he said, as he burst out laughing. He then became serious and said, "You may not believe this, but I swear I didn't know that money was not reaching you on time. Henceforth, I'll send Rs 3000 on the first of every month. But I had never imagined that you would serve me a legal notice. I am deeply hurt by this."

'There was a sense of delight among Panditji and his entourage, who showered praises on my culinary skills. After lunch, Panditji again came to me and said, "Let bygones be bygones. I would like to return to you and begin anew." Without uttering a word, I washed my hands; I took a piece of paper and wrote a note to him. As they were leaving, I handed it over. The note read, "I want a divorce."

'Panditji returned the following day. This time he was alone. He expressed shock about the note I had written. I told him, "I happened to read your interview in the magazine *Desh*. You have brazenly admitted having a series of adulterous affairs. Not only that, I know you have illegitimate children as well. You have been exploiting many women by using bigamy as an excuse for not marrying them, alleging that I am not granting you a divorce.

Also, for years you have been slandering me by alleging I've been having affairs with all my male disciples even if they are half my age. It is better to liberate us both from this meaningless legal bond called marriage."

'This was the time when Panditji had fallen out with Kamala, and one of the options he was considering was coming back to me because we were still legally married. Therefore, he was taken aback by my demand for divorce. After a brief pause, he said, "If this is what you want, I'll ask my lawyer to send you a document. All you'll have to do is sign it. Once the legal formalities are done, I'll stop paying you the monthly Rs 3000. I will no longer pay the society, telephone and electricity bills. Right now, my financial condition is not good, so I'll pay you Rs 1,00,000 now and Rs 1,00,000 later as the final settlement." After saying this, he left.'

When Jotin Bhattacharya visited Ma after this, he asked, 'आपने alimony के बारे में सोचा है? [Have you thought about the alimony?]'

'Alimony?' Ma asked. 'यह alimony क्या होता है? [What is alimony?]'

Jotinda explained, 'Alimony is the compensation given by a husband to his wife at the time of divorce.'

'He has given me Rs 1,00,000,' Ma said. 'He has promised to give me another Rs 1,00,000 after his financial conditions improve. Even if he doesn't give, I am not going to ask for it.'

'Are you serious?' Jotinda jumped. 'With a mere Rs 1,00,000 how are you going to survive?'

In retrospect, it seems Ma was eager to break free from being dependent on the money sent by Panditji and the humiliations it caused.

'People haven't always been there for me but music always has.'

—Taylor Swift

Madina Begum

Madina Begum.

There are some crucial team members working behind the scenes, away from the limelight, who are neither acknowledged nor rewarded. In patriarchal societies, the role of the wife and the mother are invariably taken for granted. With the sole exception of Jotin Bhattacharya, nobody seems to have written much about Baba's wife, Madina Begum.

In his quest to learn music, Baba left home and found his way to Calcutta. His family found him, brought him back to

Brahmanbaria (now in Bangladesh) and got him married to a girl child called Madina Begum. However, Baba again ran away, deserting his wife, and didn't return for almost fifteen years. During this time, there was no news of Baba, and some speculated that he was dead, or perhaps he had remarried. Madina Begum's family wanted her to get remarried to a stable man. However, she refused to succumb to these pressures and attempted to commit suicide.

Her family explained, 'In our family, a girl is not allowed to remain single without a husband. You must marry again.'

However, Madina Begum remained adamant. 'He will come,' she repeatedly said. And Baba did return. After settling in Maihar, Baba remained a family man. He created a raag in her honour and named it 'Madan Manjari'. Also, he named the house 'Madina Bhavan'.

Ma would tell us that her mother didn't want to be the only one in the house who was not pursuing music. She used to play the harmonium and sing a bit. Baba would tease her by saying that her singing was like the howling of a dog. Yet, once in a while he would appreciate her, saying that she was slowly getting it. Madina Ma also tried to learn the sitār. However, as a novice, it was very difficult for her to tune the instrument so she would request Baba, Khansaheb or Ma to do so. However, when she proclaimed that Ma's tuning of the sitār was the best, both Baba and Khansaheb felt offended.

After Baba's death, Ma sent her an airline ticket and brought her to Akashganga with the idea that mother and daughter would stay together. However, what seemed like a perfect arrangement proved to be a disaster.

Life at Akashganga was a culture shock for Madina Begum, who had always lived in a house full of family members and guests, with lots of work to do and many mouths to feed. She was anguished to see her genius of a daughter living a secluded life.

There was nothing for Madina Begum to do at Akashganga. She had nobody to talk to and nobody to take her out. Ma had always been a quiet, introverted person who wouldn't exchange more than a few sentences during the course of an entire day. Madina Begum sunk into depression and began crying profusely over her daughter's dismal fate. Ma therefore had no choice but to send her back to Dhyanesh Khan's overcrowded house in Calcutta.

Few people know that Ma's mother Madina Begum secretly wrote poems. Sharing just one written by her:

न होगी तुम्हारी ज़मींदारी
न होगा तुम्हारा रूपया पैसा
न होगा तुम्हारा नील घोडा
कब्र में होगा सिर्फ घोर अंधेरा

[Your estate won't be with you
Your wealth won't be with you
Your emerald horse won't be with you
In your grave,
Only pitch darkness will be with you]
—*Madina Begum*

'What is the secret of your cooking?' we asked Guru Ma. 'Who taught you?'

'I learnt it from my mother,' Ma said. 'She used to say that the most important ingredients in food are the vibrations of love and benevolence it absorbs from the person preparing it. If the person preparing the food is in a bad mood or of a negative character, the mood will invariably transfer to the food. But if the person preparing it has love and benevolence in his heart, the food will surely be nurturing, satisfying and exude a feeling of well-being in whoever consumes it. It is the same with music.'

Godsent

'Sometimes the gods of adversity
tire of their sport and show mercy.'
—*Charlie Chaplin*

Khansaheb, brilliant as he was, thought of another way to help Ma. During that time, in the mid-1970s, Prof. Rooshi Kumar Pandya, a behavioural scientist, was simultaneously teaching and working on his PhD thesis at John Abbott College in Montreal. During the summer and Christmas vacations, Prof. Pandya used to visit the Ali Akbar College of Music in California for sitār lessons.

'Khansaheb,' Prof. Pandya told Ali Akbar Khansaheb. 'I can no longer visit your college.'

'Why? What happened?'

'I signed a contract with the Indo-American Society to hold training seminars on various subjects like stress management, therapeutic hypnosis, assertiveness, and the like.'

'While you are in Bombay, learn from my sister.' Khansaheb suggested.

On his next visit to India, Prof. Pandya came with a recommendation note from Khansaheb, who had also written a separate letter to Ma requesting her to teach him. Ma was not at all happy to teach Rooshiji. She was rather put off by his looks. In

those days, he looked like an Indian replica of the Beatles's George
Harrison. He gave an impression of being a residue of the dying
hippie culture. However, because of Khansaheb's request, Ma was
duty-bound to accept Rooshiji as her disciple, only to realize that
his aptitude for music was rather low.

Rooshiji came into Ma's life when it was at its lowest ebb.
Panditji had left her. Baba had died. Khansaheb had migrated to
America. Her only son, Shubho, too had left her and migrated to
the US. Ma got a further shock when she learnt that soon after
going there, on the recommendation of Panditji and Kamala,
Shubho had given up music and was trying his luck at commercial
art. The years of labour spent on training Shubho had gone down
the drain.

Prof. Rooshikumar Pandya in the '70s.

Ma had run out of money, and her health was deteriorating.
One day, while taking lessons from Ma, Rooshiji was unable to
grasp what she was repeatedly explaining. Ma got so angry and
agitated that she fainted on her seat. Rooshiji called Dr Nitin
Shah, who put her on medication. Ma refused to be hospitalized.
Dr Nitin Shah warned, 'She cannot be left all alone in this state.'

Rooshiji, who was staying at Dr Ashit Sheth's residence at that time, then took up residence at Akashganga.

Despite the years of separation, Ma remained the subject of slander from the obvious camp. Those people had a field day when Rooshiji shifted to Akashganga. They also sent a couple of fawners to Ma to exaggerate the account of her tarnished image because of Prof. Pandya's presence in her house. Though Rooshiji was thirteen years younger than Ma, he was older than all the other previous male paying guests.

We once asked Rooshiji, how in the world was he able to convince Ma to take such a bizarre step? His exact words were: 'Within a few days, when she had recovered, I pleaded with her, "If you don't take offence, I would like to suggest a logical solution."

"What solution?" she asked.

"First you'll have to promise me that you won't react and think about it for the next few days before responding."

"Okay, tell me."

"For the rest of my life, I am ready to be at your service as your attendant."

"You mean to say you will be living in this house? How is that possible? People are already badmouthing me."

"I have thought about it. With your permission, we can shut their mouths for good."

"How?"

"I'll declare myself your spouse."

"What nonsense?!"

"You promised me that you won't react, didn't you? You promised that you will think about it for the next few days before responding. Please try to understand that if you agree to my proposal, you'll be no more helpless in solitude. I shall remain your disciple the way I have been. Nothing will change between us. The title of spouse is merely a social public status to shut up the slanderers."

"This is just not possible."

"You can make it possible. If you agree, I will resign from my job and leave Canada for good. I am all alone. The money I have made is a decent amount if converted to Indian currency. Just four to five days a month of my lecture seminars will generate enough funds to meet all our expenses and live a comfortable life. You will no longer be helpless; you will no longer struggle for money.'"

Continuing his story, Rooshiji said, 'After giving her a few days to mull over the proposal, I again approached her. She said, "I have lost faith in humanity. I have been failed by my spouse, my son and my best disciples. Baba and I have selflessly taught music without charging a penny to any of our disciples. However, they all have exploited me for their selfish motives. I have cooked and fed my disciples like my sons, but once they became stars they abandoned me. While I suffered in solitude, none came to help me, didn't even bother to inquire about me. After so much suffering, I don't have the capacity for more suffering. All these years, I've managed to live in solitude, but now, when my health is failing, I am finding it very difficult. I don't know what to do. What is the point of having such a wretched life?"

"अकेला तो मैं भी हूँ। क्यूँ न हम एक दूसरे का सहारा बनकर इस अकेलेपन को मात करें? [I too am all alone! Why don't you and I help each other to thwart this solitude?]'

On 8 December 1982, Ma and Rooshiji took this highly unusual step, which was perhaps unprecedented in Indian society and the single biggest risk Ma ever took in her life.

Nothing much changed in her daily routine, but Ma was instantly liberated from her financial and social worries. Rooshiji's constant presence helped manage the household affairs and he ran errands like paying the bills for electricity, the housing society, gas cylinders, groceries, vegetables, medications and the like.

Just three days after they signed the marriage bond, i.e., 11 December 1982, was when I first visited Ma's house and got attached for life. Thenceforth, until the news of Shubho's death on 16 September 1992, there was never a single instance when any of us felt that Ma was suffering from any kind of depression. For Ma, it was a decade full of happiness as she was completely free of social tension and financial woes. However, she continued to remain reclusively confined to her house. The only times she left it were for her cataract surgery and for her dental root canal. Never before or after was she so social, so talkative, so extroverted like she was during this period. She even looked forward to the laughter riot on Saturdays.

There once came some news of encroachment in the land gifted to Ma by the maharaja of Maihar. Rooshiji went to Maihar and disposed of the land. Thanks to Rooshiji, a famous investment banker took the onus of managing Ma's funds and soon her investments showed multifold growth. She was now a rich lady and remained one until her last day, leaving behind quite a fortune.

The Pledge of Renunciation

न मोक्षो नभस: न पाताले न भूतले।
सर्वाशासंक्षये चेत:क्षयो मोक्षं इतीष्यते।।

[Liberation is not found in outer space,
nor in the netherworld, nor on the earth.
The dwindling of mind in which all his
desires have dried up is hailed as liberated]
—*Annapurna Upanishad* (II-23)

Rooshiji's command over the English language was impeccable, but his dexterity was so challenged that his handwriting was just not legible. Therefore, Ma and Rooshiji would request Suresh and me (and later Nityanand) to write letters for them. Around 1984, Rooshiji dictated to me a reply to a letter which Ma had received.

This letter was written by a rich fellow from Calcutta, on behalf of his organization. He had sent a cheque of Rs 2.5 lakh as an advance, together with a promise to pay for two round-trip tickets and two nights in the Oberoi Grand suite for a minimum one hour of a live stage performance of Ma's surbahār rendition.

Of course, the cheque was returned with polite thanks. The letter expressed Ma's gratitude and surprise for not being forgotten despite so many years going by. However, the matter did not end there. The gentleman then flew to Mumbai, arrived at Akashganga and refused to leave without meeting Ma. Rooshiji somehow persuaded Ma to meet the gentleman for a few minutes. Nityanand happened to be present at that time and was a witness to this drama.

In Nityanand's words:

'The suited-booted gentleman started talking in a rather aggressive manner that was comically in contrast with Ma's serene demeanour and simple attire. He was trying to persuade her with a typical corporate-style pep talk, "We'll book the Netaji Indoor Stadium, the biggest indoor stadium of India. It can accommodate 18,000 people with the best available sound system."

'Ma, without even thinking for a second, flatly rejected the proposal. The agitated gentleman then took out his chequebook. Putting a blank cheque in front of Ma he said, "Write whatever amount you want, any amount you can imagine, and I will sign the cheque." Ma laughed at him, got up from her seat and went back to her room, saying, "You may leave now. Please don't bother me again."

'Those were the days when Ma's reclusion was a bother to me. I made several failed attempts to pull Ma out of her reclusion. "Ma, why don't you perform on stage or in the recording studio?" I asked her several times, especially during the mid-eighties. One day I got a bit too agitated and confronted Rooshiji. "In your seminars, you make tall claims about your mastery in the field of psychology," I told him. "Why don't you put it into practice?"

"Could you be more explicit?" Rooshiji asked.

"You managed to convince Ma to sign that marriage bond," I said. "Why can't you convince her to give performances?"

"I did try," Rooshiji explained. "But I failed."

"Why?" I asked.

"She took a vow," Rooshiji explained. 'She gave her word to Panditji that for the rest of her life she would shun the public life and never play in front of anyone except in solitude for her sādhanā.'

"Can't you talk her out of that vow?" I asked.

"As I have taught you in psychology, people operate basically from three levels. Pleasure motives, reality motives and principle motives," Rooshiji explained. "When a person is operating on principle motives it is almost impossible to negotiate with that person. The only person who could have convinced Ma was Baba, who is no more."

'I decided to try. Once, when Ma was in a very jovial mood, I initiated the conversation. "Ma! What was the need of taking this vow?" I asked her.

"To save my marriage for the sake of Shubho and Baba," she explained. "Jealousy ruined our happy married life. Panditji's ambition for stardom was so intense that applause, favourable reviews, being constantly surrounded by accolades and other such frills were of utmost importance to him. His constant preoccupation was to please the audience, to maintain his popular public image, and to expand his fan base. The irony was that without bothering about the audience or critics, I played in adherence to the ancient classical tradition the way Baba had taught me; and surprisingly this pleased the audience more.

"Journalists are always on the hunt for juicy stories. Regardless of their understanding of music, they wrote reviews on our jugalbandis in a manner which made Panditji look inferior. Panditji had some staunch rival sitārists whose partisans never missed an opportunity to humiliate him. All these reasons caused me to give up public performances and made Panditji give up playing the surbahār and focus on the sitār. Panditji's personality and nature was anyway more suitable for the sitār and less suitable for the surbahār. I was never interested in fame and fortune. By nature, I was averse to being surrounded by crowds and journalists asking meaningless questions."

"The whole idea of your taking the vow of renunciation is defeated as Panditji soon deserted you and continued living in his freewheeling wantonness," I argued. "You got married according to Hindu tradition. You and Panditji took seven different vows. However, all your vows became null and void the moment you separated and subsequently divorced him. In the same manner, the vow that you took, the promise that you gave to Panditji to save your marriage, cannot outlast the marriage vows. The way he broke the marriage vows, you may as well break your vow of renunciation."

"Then what would be the difference between him and me?" Ma asked. Her reply had convincingly defeated me, but I persisted. "Ma, like Baba you too worship Lord Krishna, you respect his philosophy. Remember what Krishna preached to Arjun in Mahabharata, 'शठे शाठ्यं समाचरेत् [Measure for measure requital.]"

'Ma got up from her chair and as she went to her room said, "Maybe, but I'd rather be Meera than Arjun."

'I never brought up the topic ever after that.'

> 'He noblest lives and noblest dies who
> makes and keeps his self-made laws.'
> —Sir Richard Francis Burton

Raag Bairaagi

As Ma's disciples, it was improper for us to ask her questions about her marriage and deepest emotions, especially her feelings for Panditji. However, there were some very strong indications.

Indians as a rule are very poor at keeping written, documented historic records. Indian musicians are even worse, as music originated from the Veda, which was *shrawan vidyā* (oral tradition), in practice for many centuries before the Vedas were finally written down. This explains why our music has no standardized form of notation. The ustads were not interested in teaching anyone outside their immediate family. Carnatic musicians were far better in theory and documentation, but nowhere close to the catalogues of documentation produced by Europeans. Therefore, India's collective psyche has always been plagued by controversies. It is very easy to call something 'traditional' or 'ancient' and get away with it as there is no way to prove the authenticity of the claim.

One of the many controversies in north Indian classical music is about Raag Bairaagi. Sometimes in the 1990s, in my presence, Nityanand had sought Ma's verdict on this controversy. Guru Ma categorically told us, 'I was witness to the entire process of Panditji creating this raag. I vividly remember that right in front of me he repeatedly kept playing and trying out different combinations over and over again until he settled upon the one which satisfied him the most. Then there was the brainstorming for naming the raag. Panditji had shortlisted a few names and asked my opinion. Bairaagi was one of the names he had thought of. I told Panditji that I liked the name. It was appropriate as the raag did create a mood of dispassion, detachment and renunciation.'

Nityanand told us, 'Many musicians are performing Raag Bairaagi in public without acknowledging Panditji as the creator of the raag. They shamelessly announce that it is an ancient raag. If it is, why there is no record of Raag Bairaagi in any scriptures of music, nor any record of any ustad or pandit having performed it in any concerts before Pt Ravi Shankar? How is it possible that All India Radio has no record of a single rendition by any artiste ever having performed it before him?'

Once, there was an interview of a sarodist published in the print media. It is difficult to verify whether the sarodist had really said so, or it was the interviewer's shameless adulteration to publish something sensational, but what was published was a sarodist challenging Pt Ravi Shankar to play a duet with him.

We shared this with Ma by reading it to her. As a rule, Ma was always inert and paid no attention to the media, but to our surprise, she was furious at hearing this. In a harsh tone she said, 'यह कम उम्र के लड़कों में ज्ञान कम और घमंड ज़्यादा है। पंडितजी के स्तर पे पहोंचने के लिए इनको अनेक जन्म लेने पड़ेंगे [These young musicians have egos far larger than their achievements. They will need multiple rebirths to reach to Panditji's level.]'

It was not that we had never seen Ma's anger, but getting so very angry at someone who had insulted Panditji didn't fit our logic. We decided not to read the rest of the interview. The sarodist went on to say that Panditji and Khansaheb had escaped to the US because they could not match the prowess of younger musicians like him.

Whenever any of us showed the slightest disrespect towards Panditji, he would get reprimanded by Ma. One Saturday at Ma's house, Rooshiji played a sitār recording on his spool tape recorder. It was a rendition of high calibre, but Rooshiji refused to disclose the name of the artiste and asked us to guess who it was. Some said it was Pt Ravi Shankar, while others said it was Nikhil Banerjee. I said, 'I can't really explain it, but in my opinion Pt Ravi Shankar's elaborations and mood were thematically more consistent, well planned. They are also aesthetically more refined than what we are hearing now.'

From the kitchen, Ma was listening to both the music and our conversation. When the rendition was over, Rooshiji disclosed the name as Nikhil Banerjee. All those who were present started showering praises on Nikhil Banerjee's prowess. One of my gurubhais said, 'Nikhil Banerjee was much better than Pt Ravi Shankar.' Ma immediately countered his statement by saying, 'निखिल को पंडितजी की ऊँचाई तक पहोंचने के लिए बहोत कुछ सिखना बाक़ी था [To reach Panditji's level, there was a lot left for Nikhil to learn.]'

Numerous times, Ma had told us about how sincere and hardworking Panditji was. 'I had to call him repeatedly when dinner was served. Even when he took a break from his practice and came for dinner, Panditji would eat with his right hand and count the *matra* [beats] of the bandish or todā with his left hand, trying to figure out how to render them. His full focus would be on his left hand counting the *taal* [rhythm] cycle and was least bothered about what he was eating with his right hand.'

'Ma, according to you, what was Panditji's single biggest quality?' we asked.

'Panditji had quite a few character issues,' Ma said. 'But the quality that carried him through was his guru-bhakti; his total unconditional surrender and devotion to his guru. He was the epitome of guru-bhakti.'

Batuk Diwanji, the veteran music critic and author, was the first to launch Pt Ravi Shankar in Bombay by arranging a series of his concerts. Diwanji had told me many stories of Panditji and

Khansaheb, and quoted here is one which is in the context of Panditji's guru-bhakti:

'Once, in the early 1940s, when Baba was in Bombay with Ravi Shankar and Ali Akbar, I went to meet them at the place they were lodging at. Panditji and I were conversing in the living room. To my surprise, each time Baba would walk by in the passage opposite, Ravi Shankar would stand up with folded hands until Baba was out of sight.

'During our long conversation, Baba went to and fro quite a few times, and all the time Ravi Shankar would stop talking and stand up with folded hands.

'I have seen many ustads and many disciples, but none to match Ravi Shankar's respect for his guru.'

'Despite what you have gone through,' we asked Ma, 'instead of showing anger or bitterness towards Panditji, why do you always defend him?'

'I don't feel angry with him. I feel pity for him,' Ma said with a serious face. As usual, she went on to quote Baba. 'Baba used to say, we get our pains, sorrows and sufferings because of our *prārabdha* [fate]. And our fate is the result of our karma. The person who gives us pain is just a bearer of the fruit of our karma. Instead of getting angry at him we should pity him because he is just an instrumental medium and not the cause of our suffering. The real cause is our own karma. The only way to exhaust your karma is by living through it. I pray to God that I may bear the suffering for all my karma in this life itself, so that I am saved from rebirth.'

Guru Ma's end was prolonged but not painful. She was bedridden for quite a few years. Mentally, she remained extremely sharp till the very end, but during her last days, she was getting bouts of time distortion. Her mind kept shifting from the 1940s to the 1960s to the 1950s to the 1980s, and again bounce back to the current time.

Sometime in early 2018, during one of her bouts of time distortion, Ma asked Suresh, 'पंडितजी आ गए? [Is Panditji back home?]' The question shocked Suresh as Panditji had died in the year 2012 and the last time he visited Akashganga was way back in the early 1980s. Calm, composed and diplomatic as Suresh has always been, instead of entering into an argument, he gave the shortest possible reply, 'Yes.' However, the conversation didn't end there. Ma further asked, 'प्रोग्राम कैसा हुआ? [How was the concert?]' Again, Suresh played along, saying, 'पंडितजी का प्रोग्राम तो अच्छा ही हुआ होगा [Panditji's concerts are invariably good.]'

Suresh's reply made Ma break into a gentle smile. She asked, 'कौनसा राग बजाया? [Which *raag* did he play?]'

'पता नहीं, मैं तो यहाँ आपके साथ था. प्रोग्राम सुनने नहीं गया [I don't know. I was here with you. I couldn't attend the concert.]' Suresh replied.

'पंडितजी ने खाना खाया? [Did Panditji have dinner?]'

'हाँ खा लिया [Yes, he ate.]'

'ठीक है, अब उनको सोने दो डिस्टर्ब मत करना [Okay, then let him sleep, don't disturb him.]'

Readers may be pleasantly surprised that though I haven't yet met Sukanyaji (Pt Ravi Shankar's last wife and Anoushka's mother) in person, we have a highly amicable equation. We often communicate over phone, email and WhatsApp. Sukanyaji had expressed her desire to meet Guru Ma in her last days, but Ma passed away before Sukanyaji could travel to India. Sukanyaji has been very kind to me, always appreciating the songs I compose, and the songs I produce as a music director. She also introduced me to an extremely high-calibre singer called Indrani Mukherjee, with whom I am hoping to do a project or two.

Matters of Indifference

या निशा सर्वभूतानां तस्यां जागर्ति संयमी।
यस्यां जाग्रति भूतानि सा निशा पश्यतो मुनेः॥

*[What is inconsequential (self-realization) for the worldly beings,
is a matter of importance for the sage; and what is
important (gratification of the senses) for the worldly beings
is a matter of indifference for the introspective sage]*
—*Bhagavad Geeta 2.69*

Ma regularly got letters by post because after the Niloufer incident she had stopped using the phone. The postal mail service was her sole means of communication. Even her local disciples were informed about the date of their next lesson with a postcard. Ma would ask one of us to read out the incoming mails. If she found one worthy of a response, she would dictate her reply, and one of us would write on her behalf and post it. (The post office was in Akashganga itself.) Ma avoided putting her signature unless it was legally required.

Those were the days of landline telephones. Ma did have a phone in her house, but always kept it off the hook. Rooshiji found it extremely frustrating to have a phone but not be allowed to use it. After years of arguments, Ma and Rooshiji reached a compromise which allowed him to use it each day for one hour, between 5 p.m. and 6 p.m. This helped us reduce the tedious task of writing letters, and most of the communication was done over the phone. Rooshiji, however, found one hour insufficient to accommodate all his communication as well as Ma's messages. So we continued writing letters even after the phone restrictions were eased.

Rooshiji had subscribed to a couple of daily newspapers, but Ma wouldn't even bother to glance at the headlines. However, she looked forward to the Bengali magazines Suresh used to bring for her. Over time, her reading activity kept reducing. Rooshiji noticed her vision was deteriorating. This problem made her struggle in the kitchen too, but getting Ma out of the house to see an ophthalmologist was not at all easy. Eventually, he persuaded her to get her eyes checked, and, for the first time in several years, Ma set foot outside the house. The tests confirmed she had developed cataracts in both eyes.

Ma underwent cataract surgery by Dr Ashok Shroff; everything was kept under wraps by Rooshiji. We all learnt about it only after her discharge. I was extra vigilant about her second eye surgery, but learnt about it only a day after it was performed. To be on the safe side, Rooshiji had opted to keep Ma in the clinic for one extra day. I grabbed the opportunity to fetch Ma home in my car.

When I reached Dr Shroff's clinic at Govind Mahal, Ma had already left her room and was seated in the waiting lounge wearing post-surgery sunglasses. The waiting lounge was overcrowded with other patients and their families and it was odd to see Ma among so many people. Fortunately, nobody recognized her. She was sitting there as if the people around her didn't exist, as tranquil and introverted as ever.

Rooshiji was settling the bill. Ma spotted me from a distance and exclaimed, 'अरे! आपने क्यूँ तकलीफ़ ली? [Why did you take the trouble?]'

Ignoring the question, I asked, 'How are you feeling?'

She assured me that she was fine.

I asked about her vision and she said it was much clearer. Just to verify it, I requested her to identify the objects around us, the pictures on the wall, the nearby clock, and more. Indeed, her vision was clear. Then I asked her to read a notice on the board. It was written in English, and, like a schoolgirl, Ma read it out aloud. I expressed my amazement at her knowledge of English and she started laughing.

With Ma in the front seat and Rooshiji in the back seat, I drove the car. It was a Sunday morning, and there was very little traffic. I deliberately took a zigzag route, believing it to be a treat for Ma to be out of the house after so many years and have a drive around the city, but she didn't feel like she had missed anything.

I kept pointing out to her the newly built high-rise buildings, the Arabian Sea, Chowpatty beach, the grand old building of Wilson College, Bharatiya Vidya Bhavan, the Hanging Gardens, etc., but nothing excited her and she kept giving disinterested glances to the places and landmarks. After a while she didn't even bother to look. I switched to automobiles, pointing at the latest models of cars that she had never seen, but she remained indifferent. Realizing the futility, I decided to head home. As we reached Pedder Road, I tested her road sense by asking her, 'Ma, do you remember the way home from here?' To my surprise, she was clueless.

Finally, we reached Akashganga and I stopped the car. As Rooshiji and I got out of the car, Ma asked us, 'कहाँ जा रहे है आप लोग? [Where are you going?]'

'Ma, we have reached,' I said. 'This is Akashganga! This is where you live.'

I was amazed to see her unfamiliarity with the building she had been living in for decades. Standing in the lobby, she wasn't even sure where the elevators were located.

After the surgery, we had to order dinner from a restaurant because Ma was not allowed to enter the kitchen for a few weeks. We were undecided which restaurant to order from. After much deliberation, we chose Punjabi Ghasitaram Kalbadevi. Our Saturday team had once gone there and enjoyed it. Soon, it became the norm to order from there, and Ma always insisted on paying the bill. The only thing we ever asked her to prepare was her signature dāl. But being who she was, she would always prepare something else in addition to it. As a result, there was usually too much food. The biggest advantage of ordering food from a restaurant was that Ma spent less time in the kitchen and more with us. We got to listen to her narrate the stories of a bygone era. She would laugh at our jokes and reciprocate with her witty one-liners.

Rooshiji had an obsession with discussing money. He would tell the sagas of billionaires like Bill Gates, Warren Buffet, Rockefeller and Ambani. However, the one who was least fascinated by such stories was Ma. For example, when he once spoke in detail about some billionaire who had amassed an unimaginable amount of wealth, Ma asked, 'But why?'

I am tempted to quote Ghalib here:

इक खेल है औरंग-ए-सुलेमाँ मेरे नज़दीक
इक बात है एजाज़-ए-मसीहा मिरे आगे

[*Be it the throne of King Solomon,*
Or the miracle of Messiah,
All are mere trivialities for me]

Compassion

ममैवांशो जीवलोके जीवभूतः सनातनः ।

[Every entity in this world is
the fragmental part of the Supreme Self]
—*Bhagavad Geeta 15.7*

Kite-flying is an ancient Indian tradition. Since the Mughal era, it has been a sport. Western India celebrates the kite-flying festival on 14–15 January, signifying the beginning of the harvest season. The sky becomes a battleground full of paper-kites duelling one another. The strings are coated with glass powder to cut opponents' kite-strings; however, they are hazardous for birds, especially pigeons, who get entangled in them.

Dr Sunil Shastri narrates the following incident.

'My sitār lesson with Rooshiji was every Wednesday at 3 p.m. On one occasion, as I reached Ma's house, Rooshiji greeted me by saying, "Ma has been awaiting your arrival for the last thirty minutes."

'I wondered why. I quickly removed my shoes and entered the living room. Ma was sitting with her arms on the dining table, holding a pigeon in her palms. It had become entangled in a kite-string so badly that the poor creature was unable to fly. Ma had a

Dr Sunil Shastri.

pair of scissors and a small knife ready on the table. "For the last half hour, I have been waiting for your arrival," Ma said. "Being a doctor, you'll be able to do this delicate job much better than us."

'It was a well-established fact that Rooshiji's dexterity was challenged, and the string was so tightly wrapped around the pigeon's feet and wing that it was not easy to release the pigeon without injuring it.

'The operation took around forty minutes. The entire time, Ma's face looked just like a mother watching surgery being performed on her child. Finally, when the operation was finished, she took the bird to the balcony and gently placed it on the parapet. It hesitated for a few seconds and then flew to freedom. Ma gave a sigh of relief and thanked me.

'I had gone to Ma's house for a sitār lesson, but ended up learning a valuable life lesson.'

The Spoilt Crow

Ma's generosity was not limited to feeding her disciples and pigeons. She fed crows as well. A bagful of paapadi gaanthia (chips made of deep-fried chickpea flour, a favourite among Gujaratis) was regularly ordered for them. One particular crow was enviably spoilt.

One Sunday afternoon, after Rooshiji's demise, Brijesh and his father, Govindji Bhargav, had come to meet Ma. As I recall, it was just before the annual concert sponsored by Ma under the banner of the Acharya Allauddin Music Circle. Suresh and Nityanand were busy preparing for the event. Out of common courtesy I asked Brijesh and Govindbhai, 'Would you like to have some tea?'

'If it is not much of a bother, I'll have half a cup without sugar,' Govindbhai replied. Brijesh said he would have one as well.

As I headed to the kitchen, Ma stopped me, saying, 'Wait! Let Nityanand handle it.'

'But, Ma, what's the big deal in making a few cups of tea?' I asked. 'I can manage.'

'Okay, but before you pour the milk, keep aside the cream for the crow.' I was puzzled by Ma's instruction. The reference of the crow seemed bizarre. I ran to Nityanand and repeated Ma's exact words. I was surprised that he could fully understand Ma's command. He came to the kitchen and spooned out the cream floating on the milk, collected it in a saucer and then put it in the refrigerator.

'What's the big deal about the cream?' I asked.

'The crow doesn't eat bread unless it has cream on it,' Nityanand explained with a grin. 'Are you guys insane?' I exclaimed. Though I spoke these words in the kitchen, Ma, sitting in the living room, heard me. She came to the kitchen and said, 'You don't believe me?' She asked. 'Watch.'

Ma took a slice of bread and held it outside her window. Within a few seconds, a crow landed a few inches away from her. Ma offered it the bread but the spoilt creature looked away in refusal. Then Ma applied some cream on the bread and the crow immediately took the bread in its beak from Ma's hand.

Nityanand narrates one more incident.

'During her last days, when Ma was bedridden, as per her instructions, I fed the leftovers to the crows. We had installed a large aluminium tray outside the kitchen window just for feeding them. Cleaning it daily was a real chore.

'One day, Ma asked me, "Did you feed the crows today?"

"Yes, I did," I replied.

"But I can hear the crows complaining that you haven't fed them enough," Ma said matter-of-factly.

'She was right. That day, there was hardly any leftover food. Though the window Ma faced was closed, she could discern from the tone of the cawing that the portions were not enough at the crows' favourite joint.

"Give them some more food," she told me.

'I managed to find some more food in the refrigerator and fed the crows. When I returned to Ma's room, she said, "Now they are okay."'

Mysterious Benefactor

Baba was Ma's role model for both music and philosophy. The sole theme of Ma's life-script was total unconditional obedience to Baba. Both Ma's music and behaviour seemed to reproduce the archetype of her father, her guru, to the point where people began calling her an extension of Baba.

'I was about eight years old,' Ma told us as she reminisced about her childhood. 'On his return from the Europe tour, Baba gave me an expensive frock. It was the most expensive piece of clothing of my childhood. As I proudly wore it and walked out in the garden to play, I saw a beggar girl of my age standing on the other side of the gate. The girl was gazing at my gorgeous dress. I asked her, "Do you like it?" She nodded yes, so I took off my dress and gave it to her. The astonished girl grabbed it and sped away. Turning around, I found Baba standing in front of me. I was terrified, thinking Baba would be angry with me for giving away such an expensive dress. On the contrary, he said, "Philanthropy is a good quality, but you ought to be careful. Someone may accuse the poor girl of stealing such an expensive dress. They may even beat her up. Your good deed could put her in trouble."

'Baba used to say, "Philanthropy is more difficult than making money. Few know the art of charity. Your act of charity should not inflate your ego, nor should it diminish the beneficiary's self-esteem.'"

I have witnessed quite a few instances of Ma playing Saint Nicholas. I am narrating just a couple of them here.

Babul's financial condition was far from good. Once, when Babul came from Calcutta to learn from Ma, I happened to be there. Sitting in a corner, I was learning from the lesson Ma was giving him. After giving a phrase, Ma went to the kitchen, saying, 'I'll teach you more once you get this right.'

Babul kept on repeating the phrase. He soon put down his sarod and went to the washroom, which was at the far end of the house in Rooshiji's room. I picked up a magazine from the table and began reading. As Babul went past the kitchen, Ma came out, with stealthy footsteps, approached Babul's seat and hurried back to the kitchen. I paid little attention to what she did, but was a bit surprised by Ma's surreptitious behaviour.

When Babul returned, he noticed an envelope on his sarod case. Curiously, he picked it up and found currency notes inside. 'Atulji, is this yours?' Babul asked, showing me the envelope.

'No,' I replied.

'There are currency notes inside,' Babul told me, showing me the money in the envelope.

'Maybe, but the envelope isn't mine,' I assured him.

'Then whose money could it be?' he asked. 'I didn't even have so much money when I left Calcutta, so it can't be mine. It must be yours as there is no one else here.'

When I refused to take the envelope, Babul turned to Ma, who had just stepped out of the kitchen. 'I found this envelope on my sarod case and I am sure it is not mine,' he told her. 'Atulji too is saying it is not his. So, whose money could it be?'

After making the briefest possible eye contact with me, Ma told Babul, 'शारदा माँ का प्रसाद समझकर ये पैसे आप ही रख लो। जब आप पैसा कमाने लगो तो इतनी रकम किसी ग़रीब की भलाई के लिए ख़र्च करना [Consider this to be a gift to you from Shārdā Ma and take this money. When you start earning well, spend this amount to help someone in need.]'

Another incident involves Aashishda. Those were the days when Aashishda used to frequently visit Mumbai. Love and affection can never be measured, but I believe that as her nephew and disciple, Aashishda had a special place in Ma's heart. Aashishda and Shubhoda were the most promising of Baba's grandchildren. However, Shubhoda's music was finished after he emigrated to the US. Aashishda was all set for stardom, but he too emigrated to the US, where his broken marriage and the lost custody of his son devastated him both emotionally and financially.

All of us revered his knowledge of music, his command over his instrument, and the tone of the pitch-perfect notes which flowed so effortlessly from his fingers. He was an amiable fellow, and treated everyone kindly. He never name-dropped about the illustrious family he belonged to. Whenever he was in Mumbai, we made it a point to spend time with him.

In the mid-1980s, during one of Aashishda's visits to Mumbai, Suresh, Nityanand and I went to Akashganga to be with him and hopefully listen to his lesson with Ma. It was around noon. Ma told Aashishda, 'I'll be cooking dinner for you, but I won't be able to cook lunch. You'll have to go to a restaurant for lunch.'

Around 1 p.m., the four of us left Akashganga. As we debated which restaurant to choose, I instinctively headed towards Churchgate. We ended up at Kamling, a Chinese restaurant, and had a hearty meal. When the waiter came with the cheque, Aashishda grabbed it. We all objected, saying we couldn't let him pay. 'I don't have much Indian currency with me, but let me see how much I have,' Aashishda said with a candid smile. 'If I don't have enough, then you pay.'

As Aashishda opened his travel pouch, he exclaimed in surprise, 'Oh! Who put so much Indian currency here?' Soon, a smile broke on his face as he concluded, 'Pishima [father's sister] must have put this money here. This is an old habit of hers.' We could never have allowed Aashishda to pay the bill, so I snatched the check and paid the bill.

When we returned to Akashganga, Ma asked Nityanand, 'How was lunch?'

'Very good.'

'Who paid the bill?'

'Atul.'

'How much was it?'

'I am not sure, maybe Rs 600 or 700.'

'Call Atul.'

When I went to Ma, she tried to give me Rs 1000. There was no way I could have accepted the money. I just walked away, saying, 'For years you have been feeding us here at your house. Please don't spoil us any more by paying our restaurant bills as well. In this house, it doesn't take long for a precedent to become the norm. Let's not set a wrong precedent.'

Clairvoyance

'Everything in the universe is in a state of vibration.'
—Albert Einstein

Naad yoga is based on the premise that the entire cosmos, and and all that exists within, consists of vibrations called *Naad*. This concept holds that it is the energy of vibrations rather than that of matter and particles that form the building blocks of the cosmos. A limited range of sound frequencies (20 Hz to 20 kHz) is audible to the human ear, and the audible range constantly decreases as we age.

Naad yoga is merging with the superconscious through vibrational harmony. The whole universe hums with its own rhythm and frequency, and when we are able to resonate with the frequency of the universe, we become one with it and are transformed to become naad yogis.

अभि स्वरन्ति बहवो मनीषिणो राजानमस्य भुवनस्य निंसते

[*Many sages pursue the Ultimate with music and succeed*]
—Rigved

It is said that the great sage Yagyavalkya had two wives. Gargi, the first wife, could attain moksha on her own because she was

246

an expert veena player, and Maitreya, his second wife, sought Yagyavalkya's guidance in achieving the same. All three of them were such great musicians that they attained moksha through music.

Naad or sound meditation is the most powerful path to self-realization. Music has been used by most Indian saints as an important and powerful tool in the quest for moksha. Some notable examples of this are Kanakadasa, Thyagaraja, Kabir, Goswami Tulsidas, Surdas, Meerabai, Namdev, Eknath, Purandaradasa, Narsinh Mehta, Dayaram, Chaitanya Mahaprabhu, Guru Nanak, Vallabhacharya, Tukaram and many other saints of India.

Out of the *panchmahaabhuta*, the five fundamental elements which form the microcosm of the body and the macrocosm of the universe, the element of space is the most primal. Space is connected to the ear, the receptor of sound. In that way, sound is the most primal experience, compared to smell, taste, vision and touch. It is also the most accurate and more precise of our senses. Even during the process of dying, our sense of hearing is the last to leave.

The Vedic rishis have classified sound frequencies in four categories: vaikhari, madhyama, pashyanti and para.

Vaikhari is the range of frequencies audible to the human ear, that is, 20 Hz to 20 kHz. Below 20 Hz is infrasound and above 20 kHz is ultrasound. Vaikhari pertains to the Vishuddha Chakra.

Madhyama is the range of frequencies which are not audible but can be felt by human beings. When Ayurveda practitioners check the pulse of their patients, they base their judgement on these vibrations.

Pashyanti is the range of frequencies even lower than madhyama. These vibrations can only be discerned by expert yogis or maestros of music who have done deep sādhanā of music. One who has reached this level experiences clairvoyance, clairaudience and telepathy-like extrasensory perceptions.

Para is the range of frequencies not yet measured by modern science. The most advanced yogis dwell here upon attaining realization.

Why are we discussing this? Because there are several instances of Ma's clairvoyance which we have personally experienced. Here are a few of them.

Lineage album cover.

The auspicious day of Vijayadashami was chosen for the first recording of Nityanand Haldipur under the banner of 'Lineage Maihar Gharana'. With the shoestring budget I had, I booked SL Studio for a day. Those were the days of audio cassettes. Nityanand was to record Raag Yamani Bilawal as Side A, and Raag Desh as Side B. Although Sadanand Naimpalli was Nityanand's preferred tablā player, he had been booked for an outstation concert. The second option was Omkar Gulvady. As luck would have it, Omkar too was travelling. Nityanand opted for his All India Radio colleague Madan Mishra.

Before reaching the studio, we went to Akashganga to seek Ma's blessings. Nityanand was under obvious pressure.

Ma was giving him some last-minute instructions. 'Please ask Sadanand to refrain from using loud aggressive phrases in his tablā playing.'

'But, Ma, Sadanand is out of town,' Nityanand reminded her. 'Madan Mishra is the one who will be playing the tablā.' Despite the reminder, Ma kept referring to Sadanand in her instructions. Nityanand thought it was just another case of a slip of the tongue. When he once again reminded Ma, she asserted, 'No, Sadanand will be playing the tablā.' Nityanand chose not to argue, and I thought Ma was going senile.

As we reached the studio and started preparing for the recording. Madan Mishra was nowhere to be found. He arrived an hour later with the excuse, 'Today being an auspicious day, I went to the Mahalaxmi temple for darshan.'

When the recording started, Madan Mishra's tablā playing was bizarre. When we asked him the reason behind his strange behaviour, he admitted to consuming bhāng, which is an edible form of cannabis—used as early as 1000 BCE in ancient India for intoxication, and even integrated into a traditional custom for certain festivals and occasions.

We had no choice but to ask him to go home. Despite my reluctance, Rooshiji, Pradeep Barot and Nityanand insisted that I pay him his fees. 'Pay him for what?' I angrily asked. 'He should be paying me for the wasted studio charges.' However, I had no choice but to obey my senior gurubhais and let my hard-earned money go down the drain.

Our next problem was where to find a replacement. Because there were no cell phones in those days, Nityanand kept calling different numbers he had in his pocket diary from a landline telephone, but not a single tablā player was available at such short notice. To find other tablā players' numbers, he rang up Sadanand's house, hoping his wife could help, but nobody answered. Nityanand was about to disconnect the call when Sadanand himself answered.

'Sadanand!' Nityanand exclaimed in excitement. 'Weren't you out of town for some concert? When did you arrive?'

'I was,' Sadanand explained. 'But the second concert was cancelled, so I returned a day earlier. Actually, I've just reached home, and as I was opening the door I heard the phone ringing.'

Sadanand came and played for the recording as per Ma's instructions.

The curious case of Anuraag was even more dramatic. Anu, as we used to call him, was a paradoxical character, as if he had emerged out of the satirical novel *Catch-22* by Joseph Heller. Anu was good-looking, smart, educated, polite, soft-spoken, helpful, calm, composed and obedient to his seniors, and yet, for inexplicable reasons, he seemed to be disliked by everyone. Even Guru Ma disliked him. Once the other disciples realized that Ma disliked Anu, in order to gain brownie points, they all made it a point to express their dislike too in front of Ma. Such reinforcements had a spiral effect. Soon, Anu gained the reputation of being the villain of the house.

One afternoon, as I reached the sixth floor of Akashganga, before I could ring the doorbell, the door opened and Anu came out. His face was pale. As he entered the same lift I had come up by, he said, 'You'd better not go inside as Ma is in an exceptionally bad mood.'

Rooshiji was at the door. As I entered, he warned me, 'Atul, my advice to you is avoid meeting Ma today. She is in a bad mood.'

'Why? What is the matter?' I demanded the answer. 'Anu too told me so.'

'Anuraag came to give Ma the good news that his wife is expecting.'

'That is indeed good news; where is the problem?'

'Ma angrily asked him to leave.'

'Is she going crazy?' I exclaimed. 'How can she drive out a disciple coming to give her such good news?'

Rooshiji remained silent. Despite his warning, I went to the kitchen to pay my obeisance to Ma.

'लो आप भी आ गए मेरा भेजा ख़राब करने को? [Now you too have come to irritate me?]' she commented.

'माँ यह भी क्या बात हुई! वह बेचारा आपको ख़ुश ख़बर देने आया, और आपने उसको गुस्सा कर के हकाल दिया? [Ma, what is the matter with you? Anuraag came to share some good news with and you drove him away from the house?]'

'तुम बेवकूफ़ हो, जाओ यहाँ से [You are stupid. Get out of here.]'

'कमाल है माँ! अनु की पत्नी को बच्चा होने वाला है, वह आप को ख़ुशख़बर देने आता है, आप उसे हकाल देती है, इस पूरे मामले में मेरी बेवकूफ़ी कहाँ से आई? [How weird! Ma! Anu's wife is going to have a child, he comes to give you the good news, you drive him away in anger; where does my stupidity show in the whole story?]'

'समझते क्यूँ नहीं कि यह बच्चा अनुराग का है ही नहीं, उसकी पत्नी के बॉस का है [Why don't you people understand that this is her boss's child and not Anuraag's.]'

No other conversation I ever had with Ma was as shocking as this.

'माँ, आप गुरु होने के नाते आपके शिष्य के बारे में ऐसी बात सोच भी कैसे सकती हो? आप कभी अनु की पत्नी को मिली हो? [Ma, as a guru, how can you even think of such an allegation against your disciple's wife! Have you ever met her?]'

'कभी नहीं [Never.]'

'उसके बॉस को मिली हो? [Have you met her boss?]'

'कभी नहीं [Never.]'

'तब तो किसी के बारे में ऐसा सोचना आपको शोभा नहीं देता [Then casting such aspersions is below the dignity of a guru.]'

Never before or after did I speak to Ma in such harsh words. She asked me to get out, and I had no choice but to obey. I went to Rooshiji and continued this conversation.

'On what grounds can she cast such serious aspersions?' I asked. 'From the very beginning, she has been expressing her displeasure regarding Anuraag's marriage. Is she biased against him?'

Rooshiji after a thoughtful pause said, 'There are certain things that defy logic. Her mind operates at a different level.'

We chose to forget the whole incident as if it had never happened. A few months later, we got the news that Anuraag's wife had delivered a baby boy. Anu was as ecstatic as any first-time father would be and treated us with mithai.

When his son was two years old, he arranged a small birthday party at his home. He invited some close relatives as well as us, the gurubhais. Since Aashishda was in town, Anu requested him to come and bless his son. We all decided to attend. Nityanand and I thought we would meet at Akashganga and along with Rooshiji go to Anu's house in my car. However, Nityanand got delayed at All India Radio and by the time he arrived at Akashganga, it was too late.

We remained at Akashganga waiting for Aashishda to return. In those days, Aashishda's command over the sarod was next only to his father, Ali Akbar Khansaheb. An opportunity to witness Aashishda's session with Ma was like witnessing music at its sublime best.

It was Rooshiji's teatime. For a Gujarati, which Rooshiji typically was in his food habits, tea would never be without savouries. Nityanand and I too joined him. Just then, Aashishda and Jaykishore arrived. Ma offered them tea and snacks but they refused, saying they had eaten enough at Anu's house.

'How was the birthday party?' Ma asked Aashishda.

'Well, it was good,' Aashishda replied. 'The way toddlers' birthday parties generally are, with cake and snacks.'

'How is Anu's son?' Ma asked.

'Sweet little boy,' Aashishda replied with a fond smile.

'Whom does he look like?' Ma asked.

'Well, the son doesn't resemble Anuraag,' Aashishda replied, scratching his head. 'Nor does he resemble his mother.'

'Whom does he resemble?' Aashishda asked Jaykishore.

'Yes, it is a bit weird,' he replied. 'The child neither resembles his father nor his mother.'

This was when Ma looked straight in my eyes. I instantly remembered the conversation I had had with her on the day Anu had visited her to give the good news. A cold shiver went down my spine. I looked at Rooshiji. He too was stunned. Ma went to her room and locked herself in. The session was over for Aashishda as well as the rest of us.

A few months later, we got the news that Anuraag's wife and son had left Anuraag and gone to live with her boss. The day the boss's divorce from his wife became final, Anuraag got a divorce notice from his wife.

One day, Anu phoned me to ask, 'Do you know any lawyer?'

'What for?' I asked.

'My estranged wife has sent me divorce papers.'

'For the legal hassles which happened after my father's demise, I was helped by the law firm Bhaishankar Kanga and Girdarlal, but these were civil matters. I will request their partner Tushar Desai to help you, if he can.'

Tushar Desai was kind enough to meet Anuraag and gave him legal guidance without charging any fees. 'Under the Hindu Minority and Guardianship Act, the custody of all children below the age of five years is given to the mother. However, all cases of child custody are treated on a case-by-case basis to ensure that the child is not put in the hands of an unfit parent. In such cases, the court has the discretion to choose what is best for the child. My advice to you is avoid taking the child's custody. As a father with practically no earnings, it could become very difficult for you to raise a child. Considering your financial situation and position as a single parent you should avoid seeking custody of the child. In fact, you should plead accordingly.'

When the matter came up in the divorce court, I warned Anuraag, 'Please be practical. Don't get emotional and ask for custody. Let him go with his mother. Please phone me when the case is settled.' Anuraag agreed.

At around 6 p.m., he called.

'Finally! It's all over,' he said in a subdued tone.

'Good riddance!' I said to comfort him. 'Was the hearing long and complicated?'

'Not at all,' Anu replied. 'As it was by mutual consent, it all went smooth and fast.'

'What about the child's custody?' I eagerly asked.

'I asked my wife, what about our son?' said Anuraag.

'You fool! We had warned you not to even mention it. What was her response?'

'She said, "Don't bother, he is not your son."'

After saying this, Anuraag wept for twenty minutes. The phone line remained connected, but neither of us could speak a word.

I went straight to Ma's house, told her about Anu's divorce and the shocking revelation about his son's paternity. I fell to her feet, begging her pardon for my harsh words when Anu had come to give the news of his wife's pregnancy. Rooshiji was shocked about the revelation, but Ma was unmoved. For her it was just a matter of fact.

Nityanand narrated one of his many experiences as follows:

'Bus No. 81 takes me directly from Akashganga to my house at Santacruz. The last bus leaves at 10 p.m. and if I miss that, I have to either walk all the way to Haji Ali [a distance of 1.7 km] to catch another bus, or spend money on a cab. Therefore, I would get as impatient as Cinderella to leave Ma's house by 9.45 p.m. sharp.

'After my lesson one night, as I was about to leave, Ma insisted that I have a cup of tea. "Ma, if I wait a minute more, I will miss my bus," I explained.

"No, you won't," Ma assured me.

'After a few minutes, she came out of the kitchen and served me tea. "Here, have some," she said, offering me biscuits and snacks.

'It was already 10 p.m., and there was no way I could have caught the last bus. So, I relaxed and sipped my tea, relishing the snacks. Around 10.15, Ma was suddenly alarmed, saying, "Go! Leave at once or you'll miss your bus."

"Ma, it's pointless. It's 10.15 now," I replied. "The last bus passes by here at about 9.55. It can't be delayed by half an hour."

'Ma, however, literally pushed me out. As I reached the building gate, I saw bus No. 81 arrive. The familiar driver stopped it and signalled me to board. I thanked him and said, "God! I never expected you at this time."

"All because of a punctured tyre!" he explained. "We had to replace the tyre as we need to make this bus reach Santacruz Bus Depot. You see, every morning at 7 a.m., this bus is scheduled to start the down journey from Santacruz Depot."

'When I shared this experience with Suresh, he refused to believe me. A few weeks passed. On a Saturday night, we were having dinner at Ma's house. At a few minutes past 11 p.m., Ma instructed Suresh and me, "Leave immediately or you'll miss your bus."

"Ma, it is past 11 p.m.," we argued. "At this time, what bus will we get?"

"I'm telling you," Ma insisted. "If you leave right away, you'll be able to catch the bus."

'We left shortly thereafter, knowing fully well we could not catch any bus at that late hour. As we began leisurely looking for a cab, we saw a bus approaching. It was bus No. 81. The same driver waved at us. "We never expected you at this hour," I exclaimed.

"Our labour union was on a flash strike," he explained. "We just reached a settlement with the management and resumed the service."

What makes music valuable and important is that it leads to introspection and enhances intuition. It leads to deeper insight far exceeding any knowledge that reason alone can impart. Music makes both the performers and the listeners connect with their inner selves.

Baba's routine was jam-packed with activities: his own riyaaz, training numerous disciples, duties as the court musician, a visit to Shārdā Ma temple in the morning, namaaz at the mosque in the evening, going to the market for daily groceries (those were the days when women used to mostly remain indoors and venture out only when a male member wasn't available), gardening, training the Maihar Band, teaching at Maihar Music College and replying to numerous mails he used to receive.

Often, such a busy schedule would be disrupted by the visits of unexpected guests. Baba belonged to the ancient Hindu culture that believed in 'अतिथि देवो भव' [Let the guest be treated like god]. Too many unknown uninvited people would walk in without prior intimation to meet Baba, who would reluctantly but compulsively spend time with them. He would offer them snacks and refreshments, or lunch, or dinner, depending upon the time of their visit.

Most daunting for Baba was the visitors discussing music theories with him despite their lack of knowledge. After hearing their monologue, Baba would say, 'Wow! You are so knowledgeable about music. But enough of शास्त्रार्थ [theory]. अब ज़रा गाके या बजाके सुनाइए [Now please give me a practical demonstration].' Saying this, Baba would ask them to choose from his huge collection of musical instruments. Invariably, the guest would make a beeline out of the house, never to return.

Zero Tolerance

Ma, being an exceptionally honest person, expected the same from her disciples. She hated lies and deception in any form or manner. Here are a couple of incidents from two of her highly promising disciples.

Pradeep Barot.

Coming from a musician family, Pradeep Barot learnt the sarod under Pandit Vasant Rai from 1968 to 1974. Vasant Raiji was Baba's last disciple and a highly respectable name in the music world. Whenever he came to Bombay, he learnt from Ma.

When Vasant Raiji emigrated to the US in 1974, he requested Ma to accept Pradeep Barot as her disciple, to which Ma agreed. This was when the NCPA operated from Akashganga. When it shifted to Nariman Point, Barot, P.G. Parab, Sudhir and Sandhya Phadke all went there to learn from Ma.

Barot had the sweet tone and clarity of his mentor, Vasant Raiji, and was progressing well under Ma. Ma was teaching him the very difficult style of music she had learnt from Baba. For instance, the tempo of the ati-vilambit gat Ma taught was so slow that no other tablā player but Anantramji could handle that tempo. Barot's future was looking promising until a single mistake changed everything.

For years, Barot's parents had arranged his marriage with the daughter of their family acquaintance. Barot succumbed to parental pressure, got engaged and then married. However, he kept this fact concealed from Ma. Once, during a lesson, Ma could discern Barot's mental restlessness manifesting in his playing. When Ma asked the reason behind his state of mind, Barot first went into denial mode, but soon confessed about his matrimony.

From an outsider's point of view, it shouldn't make any difference to Ma whether her disciple was getting married or getting divorced, but what mattered was that he had concealed something vital for so long. Ma there and then decided to no longer teach Barot. 'What I was teaching you was sādhanā, which will no longer be possible for you to do with your altered mindset,' she said. 'Now you are preoccupied with worldly concerns, your earnings, your spouse, your children, etc. Go and play commercial music and make a living.'

Barot then passed the audition test at All India Radio. and got a job in the films division, which was established primarily to 'produce documentaries and news magazines for publicity of government programmes' and keep a cinematic record of Indian history.

'Despite her no longer teaching me,' Barot said, 'I kept visiting her to seek her blessings and keep her updated about my affairs.'

As a true seeker of art, Barot wanted to learn more. He went to the residence of Zarin Daruwala, the best ever sarodist in the domain of film music. However, despite repeated attempts, Zarinji's father didn't allow Barot to meet her. Barot then went to Famous Studio where Zarinji was recording for a film.

'Zarinji was so busy that she was reluctant to teach anyone,' Barot said. 'Nonetheless, she asked me to come to her house with my sarod. I visited and played an ālaap of Raag Bihāg. Zarinji was rather impressed by my proficiency. She said, "You really don't need to learn from a sarodist. Instead, I suggest you go to a vocalist to learn newer raags." Zarinji was preaching something she herself had practised. Despite knowing that she was avoiding me, I once again went to meet her when she was recording at Famous Studio, Tardeo. When she saw me, she rebuked me, saying, "I've already said I can't teach you, so why have you come again?" Ma's disciple Dakshin Mohan Tagore (Taar Shehnai) was also present there at the time and on his next visit to Ma he informed her about my interaction with Zarinji.

'Ut. Zia Mohiuddin Dagar and I were both natives of Udaipur. For some reason, he had a liking for me, so I approached him. After hearing my story, he advised me, "Don't go here and there. Have faith in your Guru Ma; she will teach you."

'The next time I went to meet Ma, she knew of my meeting with Zarinji. As I pleaded with her to teach me, I broke down in tears. Rooshiji intervened and persuaded Ma to forgive me. Ma consented and my lessons resumed after a gap of more than seven years. However, Ma clarified, "The style I used to teach you earlier can't be taught now. Now I will teach you only that which may help you in your commercial pursuits." Ma taught me Purya Kalyan, Sudh Kalyan and a few other raags before her health gave way and she stopped teaching altogether.'

Sandhya and Sudhir Phadke.

Another instance involved Sudhir Phadke, who shot himself in the foot for no apparent reason. The brother and sister duo of Sudhir and Sandhya from Pune had been Ma's disciples since her time at the NCPA. After Ma stopped teaching there, some of her pupils began coming to her house for lessons. After Nikhil Banerjee and Shubhoda, Sudhir and Sandhya were her most promising disciples on the sitār. Sandhya eventually married and could not cope with the dual pressures of family and riyaaz. By contrast, Sudhir did well and began giving concerts, gaining a following and numerous enthusiastic students. The story ended sadly, however, because Sudhir made the cardinal mistake of deceiving Ma.

For years, Ma had stopped using the phone and would communicate only by post. One day, she asked one of us to write to Sudhir, telling him his next lesson would be on Saturday. Sudhir replied promptly, saying this would not be possible because of an important engagement he had in Pune that day, which he could not cancel. Nothing more came of this until Rooshiji happened to visit Bhargava's Music Shop that Saturday. 'You have a long life!' Govindji Bhargava exclaimed when he entered the shop. 'Sudhir Phadke was here for hours, and just left a minute ago.'

'Sudhir Phadke?' Rooshiji asked in disbelief. 'Can't be. Sudhir is in Pune at a very important engagement.'

'We are not kidding. Not only was Sudhir here, he purchased from us two sitārs for his disciples and took them to Pune,' Govindbhai explained. 'We also talked about you and Ma. We asked him to wait a while so he could meet you but he said he was in a hurry and left.'

When Rooshiji recited this to Ma, she was so hurt that she virtually disowned Sudhir. Then we learnt that Sudhir had become an alcoholic. Soon we got the news of his death due to liver cirrhosis.

Forged Letter

'Life is akin to solving a mathematical problem
One wrong step and the solution remains elusive.'
—*Jataayu*

From the eighth century onward, after repeated Islamic invasions, slavery became a major social institution in India, increasing conspicuously after the eleventh century with the systematic plunder and enslavement of infidels and the use of slaves in armies of conquest. Between 1530 and 1740, the Portuguese imported African slaves to their Indian colonies on the Konkan coast. Although slavery was abolished in the territories of the East India Company by the Indian Slavery Act of 1843, the culture and mindset persisted.

For centuries, disciples had to serve their ustads like bonded labourers in the hope that sooner or later, the ustad would share some knowledge with them. Historically, ustads have been reluctant teachers who behave as if they have a legitimate right to exploit their disciples. They would teach and feed the disciples just enough to prevent them from running away. Ustads seldom gave quality training to anyone except their family members. In modern times, I have personally witnessed Bollywood music directors treating aspiring singers in a similar manner.

Baba himself was a bonded labourer to his gurus, especially under Ut. Ahmad Ali Khansaheb. Baba not only worked as a labourer to build a house for Ahmad Ali Khansaheb's parents but ended up spending all his meagre savings towards the cost of building the house. When the building was completed, Ahmad Ali Khan's father candidly told Baba, 'We have nothing more to teach you. You should find a better guru.' Baba then went to learn from Ut. Wazir Khansaheb, a direct descendant of the legendary Tansen, where another long, testing ordeal awaited him before his training finally began.

Babul was a poor boy hailing from a small village in West Bengal. As he was both passionate and talented in music, he started learning from an ustad who was a disciple of Guru Ma. This was the same ustad from whom Anuraag learnt before coming to Ma. The ustad used Babul as his personal servant.

In October 1985, Babul pleaded with his ustad to allow him to accompany him during his visit to Bombay. He expressed his desire for Guru Ma's darshan and said he wanted to pay his obeisance at her feet. The ustad unwittingly allowed Babul to escort him during his ten-day visit to Bombay.

Babul arrived at Akashganga, paid his obeisance to Ma, and quietly witnessed the lessons. Every afternoon after the lessons, ustad and Rooshiji would leave the house for two to three hours, mostly to visit Bhargava's musical shop, where Rooshiji was a partner. They would leave Babul all alone with Ma. This was the routine for all ten days of his visit.

Ma had this amazing trait of instantly transforming from an introvert to an extrovert if the medium of conversation was Bengali, her mother tongue. Those close to Ma have experienced on numerous occasions that the same question asked in Hindi and in Bengali elicited a different response. If a favour was asked in Hindi, Ma's response would routinely be negative; and if the same favour was asked in Bengali, the probability of a favourable response was quite high.

As a Bengali, Babul used this advantage of knowing Bangla to smoothly navigate his interactions with Ma. He managed to sweet-talk Ma into accepting him as her disciple.

A few months went by. Babul's progress in Calcutta was far from satisfactory. In his frustration, he made a visit to Akashganga with his parents, without disclosing the fact to his ustad. Babul's parents pleaded with Ma to accept Babul as her disciple. Ma said she would teach Babul, but only after he sought the permission of his current guru.

But obtaining the ustad's permission was no easy task. When he returned to Calcutta, the ustad was furious. According to him, Babul's act of approaching Guru Ma behind his back was an unpardonable act of transgression. 'How dare you bypass me and approach my guru behind my back?' Saying this, he excommunicated Babul. In his fury, the ustad asked Anuraag to forge a letter which stated that Ma had refused to teach him. Anuraag succumbed to his former guru's pressure. Forging the letter was easy as Ma herself never wrote letters but would dictate her message to one of us, and the letters would be posted without her signature. When Babul received the letter, he was shattered.

Babul gathered the courage and with his parents once again came to Bombay to meet Ma. They showed her the letter. Ma was furious. She made an instant decision to stop teaching both the ustad and Anuraag. Devastated by the developments, Anuraag pleaded with the ustad to save him from this exile. The ustad informed Anuraag that he was being hospitalized for hepatitis and promised that promptly after his discharge, he would come to Mumbai to absolve Anuraag from any blame. However, as luck would have it, he died a few days later, and Anuraag could never prove his innocence. Ma steadfastly refused to teach Anuraag after his forgery, but began teaching Babul.

'During my visits to Bombay,' Babul told me, 'I stayed in a lodge near Marine Lines station. My lunch would be in a nearby restaurant. Post lunch, I would go to Ma for my lessons. She would feed me delicious dinners. Ma never accepted anything in return from her disciples, neither money nor gifts. When I would ask her if she wanted anything from Calcutta, she requested me to bring speciality items from Bengal like a *gamchha* [handloom towel], khejur gur [date jaggery], etc. Ma would forcibly pay me for the things I would bring for her. The amount she paid would invariably be more than what I had actually spent, but she wouldn't allow me to return the balance amount.

'She would tell Rooshiji to treat me to a fancy dinner in some classy restaurant; something I myself could never afford. On the last day before I left, she would give me money and tell me to eat healthy food during my long train journey from Bombay to Calcutta.'

To earn a living, Babul took a job as a music teacher in a school and was soon married. He could no longer visit Mumbai. Meanwhile, Ma asked Anuraag to chart his own course. She suggested he join the Ali Akbar College of Music in California, but he refused. She suggested he move to Jodhpur and learn from Basant Kabra, but he refused. He kept coming to Ma but couldn't convince her to resume teaching him. In her last days, she lamented, 'गुरु होने के नाते, अनुराग की ज़िम्मेदारी मुझपे थी। अफ़सोस, मैं उसका कुछ कर नहीं पाई। मेरी वजह से उसकी ज़िंदगी बरबाद हो गई [As his guru, Anuraag was my responsibility. I regret I could not help him. Because of me his life is ruined.]' In her final days, Ma asked Nityanand to teach him, and Nityanand gave him a crash course of about twenty-five raags.

Outstanding Dues

I am not sure of the date but I guess it was sometime in 1998 when I got the news that the famous music director Kalyanjibhai was bedridden with a lung ailment. I phoned his residence seeking permission to pay him a visit. His daughter-in-law said, 'If you could come during the afternoon time, it would be most convenient as that is the time people are not around and he would be in a mood to converse with you.'

When I reached Kalyanjibhai's residence, I was ushered into the room he was resting in. On seeing me, Kalyanjibhai switched off the portable audio cassette player he was listening to, and greeted me with his typical warmness. Refraining from the ritualistic inquiry about his health, I initiated the conversation on the subject of music.

'What are you listening to?' I asked.

My question lit up his face. With his signature smile, he said, 'Since you are a music buff, give me your opinion about this singer.' Saying this he switched on the cassette player. The played track was of Lata Mangeshkar's hit songs of the sixties, but those were cover versions and not the originals. The singer had rendered the songs excellently well.

'Wow!' I exclaimed. 'This singer has a sweet voice. She is really *surilee* [pitch perfect]. She has both *firat* [flexibility of movement] and *thahrāv* [sustained stability of the notes] which is something so rare these days. She has a terrific range and she is musically well trained too. Who is she?' I asked.

'Your guess?' Teasing me by not revealing the singer's name, Kalyanjibhai kept smiling at me waiting for my reply.

'Well, I have often heard Sadhana Sargam and Sonali Bajpayee's singing at your place. Both are great singers, but I am sure this is not their voice because their timbre is different. And this voice is too young to be of Anuradha Paudwal. So who could this be with a voice resembling Lata Mangeshkar of the fifties?'

'The singer is Shreya Ghoshal. She is only fifteen years old. However, she is dejected that she is not getting a break. Do me a favour, take this cassette to your Guru Ma Annapurna Devi, and request her on my behalf to accept Shreya as her disciple and make her a maestra of classical music.'

I vividly remember that it was a red labelled Sony C60 audio cassette which I took to Guru Ma's house with Kalyanjibhai's message. After hearing Kalyanjibhai's message, Guru Ma said, 'Leave the cassette and come tomorrow.'

The next day when I reached Ma's house, Ma returned the audio cassette saying, 'I heard this girl's singing. She is talented and sings well. However, after reaching this level, it is not advisable to change the genre. Tell her to be patient. श्रेया को कहो शारदामाँ साधकों का उधार लम्बे समय तक नहीं रखती। उसको उसकी साधना का फल आज नहीं तो कल ज़रूर मिलेगा। [Tell Shreya that Shārdā Ma doesn't keep for long her seekers' outstanding dues. Sooner or later she will get the due rewards for her endeavours.]

'My Enemy'

On 27 November 2010, I had some guests for lunch at my house. No sooner did I take the first morsel than my cell phone rang. The screen displayed 'Rooshikumar'. I continued eating while answering the phone.

'Atul! Where are you right now?' Prof. Pandya asked.

'Home.'

'Listen, I am in Baroda conducting a two-day seminar. Ma is all alone and there could be a problem with her.'

'What problem?'

'I don't know. The tiffin delivery boy phoned me to intimate that despite ringing the doorbell repeatedly, Ma is not opening the door.'

'What is so alarming? Ma anyway doesn't like to respond to doorbells.'

'Try to understand. The tiffin delivery boy comes sharp between 12.15 and 12.30 p.m. And Ma always opens the door within a few seconds as she is aware of his timings and is expecting him. However, today he has been ringing the bell for more than fifteen minutes but there is no response.'

'Whoa!'

'Listen to me carefully. You go there and try your luck ringing the doorbell. If she doesn't open the door, just go ahead and break it open. If necessary, hospitalize her, but keep her away from the media. Keep me informed. Though I am in a seminar, I'll keep my cell phone on. Use your discretion and do whatever you think is most appropriate.'

I didn't panic, but I was flooded with emotions because Ma was in crisis. What could have happened? So many thoughts crossed my mind as I drove towards her house at a high speed. I called the fire department on my way there. The fire department said they would not break open the door without permission from the police unless there was a fire or another peril. I kept trying but the Gamdevi Police Station phone was not reachable. My wife was able to get in touch with them, though, and they assured her that a police van would leave shortly for Akashganga to assess the situation.

I reached Akashganga and kept ringing the doorbell frenetically, but there was no response whatsoever. I peered through the narrow opening of the letterbox—all I could see was the floor of the narrow passage but no sign of Ma, nor could I hear any movement. I shouted at the top of my lungs, 'Ma! Ma!' but nothing. Nothing at all. I tried to call Gamdevi Police Station again. This time I was able to connect. A laidback police officer told me a police van was on its way to Akashganga.

I began to panic. I started kicking and punching the door as hard as I could, but despite getting bruised knuckles and swollen feet, I failed to break it open. My loud banging made neighbours and onlookers gather. The security guards came running and asked what was going on. Ambika the liftman brought a big screwdriver. As we were trying to pierce a hole with it in the solid wooden door, a team of policemen arrived.

'What are you doing?' one of them asked me in a stern voice. 'You can't break anyone's door like this. You could be booked for housebreaking.'

I was highly agitated. I said, 'Arrest me if you want, but first let's rescue my Guru Ma locked inside.' The people who had gathered supported me in convincing the police. On his radio device, the police officer called the officer waiting in the van below and asked for a hammer. In a minute, a sledgehammer was produced. I showed the policeman the spot above the lock. One blow, and the door cracked. With a second blow, there was a big hole in it. I inserted my hand to reach the lock and opened the door.

We rushed in past the empty lobby and peeped into the kitchen, but there was no sign of her. We went into the bedroom but Ma was not there either. She wasn't in the living room, nor was she in the balcony. I knew she would never step into Rooshiji's room, nonetheless I checked, but she wasn't there either. Where could she go? We checked the store room but she wasn't there either. Then I remembered to check the bathroom attached to her bedroom.

The bathroom door was shut but not locked. I pushed the door open, but it wouldn't move more than a few inches. Something was obstructing it. As I peered in, I could see Ma lying face down on the bathroom floor. We slowly pushed the door just enough to move Ma's body a few inches further away to allow us to get in.

The first thing we did was roll her body from face down to face up. There were traces of blood around her nose. I tried to feel her pulse by putting my fingertips on her wrist, but I felt nothing. I then tried putting my fingertips on her temple but I could feel nothing. Ma, as always, was wearing a saree and we couldn't perceive any inhale-exhale movement of her diaphragm. It looked like the worst-case scenario. I phoned Breach Candy Hospital for an ambulance and we decided to take Ma out of the bathroom and put her on her bed. As we were struggling to carry her out of the narrow bathroom, she opened her mouth and gasped for air. I breathed a sigh of relief. Ma was alive. Unconscious but alive.

'Let's rush her to the hospital,' I told the police. 'Let's take her down right away to save time.' The policeman called his van for a stretcher. I was surprised to know that police vans are equipped with a stretcher.

Meanwhile, I had phoned Rooshiji, Nityanand and Suresh to give them an update. The irony was that Nityanand too was admitted in Asha Parekh Hospital in Santacruz because of malaria.

We took Ma downstairs, but the ambulance had not yet arrived. There was no way the stretcher could fit in my car, so we decided to take Ma in the police van. I followed in my car. The ambulance arrived as we were leaving. 'Let's not waste time transferring the patient from the police van to the ambulance,' I told the police and the ambulance staff. 'Let's just rush to the hospital.'

As we reached Breach Candy Hospital, Suresh was waiting there.

'Suresh!' I exclaimed in surprise. 'How did you manage to reach so soon?'

'My friend fetched me here in his car. He jumped every signal and broke every speed limit.'

Ma was admitted to the emergency room. Rooshiji caught the first available flight from Baroda and arrived late in the evening.

The doctors told us that Ma was suffering from falciparum malaria and a few other age-related ailments. As she never complained, she never got diagnosed and was never treated.

Despite a warning from doctors to remain in his hospital bed as he recuperated from malaria, Nityanand arrived a few days later.

'Nityanand!' we exclaimed. 'Weren't you in the hospital?'

'I was, but I insisted they discharge me,' Nityanand explained. 'I have recovered. I am just a little weak.'

Suresh was on duty attending to Ma and was waiting outside the ICU when the nurse came and informed him that Ma had regained her senses. Suresh rushed there but Ma was still in a semi-conscious state. She was totally disoriented and saying nonsensical things. Suresh phoned Rooshiji, who told him, as a professor of psychology, 'Worry not, such behaviour is not uncommon for patients in such a situation.'

'What should I do?' Suresh asked.

'Just play along,' Rooshiji advised. 'Keep agreeing with her without argument or confrontation.'

After a few days in the ICU, Ma was moved to a private, sea-facing room. Dozens of pigeons flocked to the windowpane, and were glued to the ledge. It was incredible to see Ma recognize each one individually. From her bed, she spoke to them saying, 'अरे! आप लोग यहाँ आ गए? [Oh! You guys have come here!]' An hour later, she spoke again, 'चले जाओ, यहाँ मैं आप को कुछ नहीं खिला पाऊँगी [Go away, I won't be able to feed you here.]' But the pigeons remained.

When the senior doctor came to see Ma, he asked the nurse, 'Why are there so many pigeons?'

The nurse replied, 'I don't know, they sit here all day. This is the only window they sit at. No other room has this problem.'

'Please ask the maintenance department to remove them,' the doctor ordered.

Ma surprised us by responding to him in fluent English, 'Let them be. Please don't disturb them. They are my friends. They have come to meet me.'

For a long time after her discharge, whenever I met Ma, she would point at me and say, 'यह मेरा दुश्मन है। मैं जा रही थी, इसने रोक दिया [He is my enemy! He didn't allow me to die.]'

Who Played It First?

अयि भुवन मन मोहनी
प्रथम प्रभात उदय तव गगने
प्रथम साम रव तव तपोवने
प्रथम प्रचारित तव नव भुवने
कत वेद काव्य काहिनी।।

[Oh! My beloved motherland!
The knowledge first dawned in thy sky
The music resonated first in thy spiritual retreat
The poetry of wisdom and virtuosity
Was promoted first in thy land]
—*Rabindranath Tagore*

It is unfortunate that both the media and the rising young stars of Indian classical music today are spreading a false history. For example, in a recent video which went viral, a star stated that the entirety of classical music was brought to India by Islamic invaders. Can we therefore infer that there was no structured form of music in India prior to the invasions?

The first clash between a Hindu ruler and the Arab invaders took place as late as 643 CE. Amir Khusrau was born in the year 1253 CE in Patiyali near Etah in modern-day Uttar Pradesh, India, the son of Amir Saif ud-Din Mahmud, a man of Turkic extraction and a native Hindu mother.

Every musician, be it Tansen, Mozart, Beethoven or Lata Mangeshkar, learnt music from someone. Whatever music Amir Khusrau learnt, he learnt it all within India. If most of the music, as claimed by certain ustads, was invented by Amir Khusrau, my question is what kind of music prevailed in the Indian subcontinent between Sām Veda and Amir Khusrau?

Much of ancient Indian culture (including all forms of art, literature and music) has been the result of a long oral tradition, with a wider cultural significance rather than being the result of a solitary composer's work. Vyasa is credited with documenting, compiling, categorizing and writing commentaries on much of this literature. The Mahabharata (the greatest epic), the Vedas, the Puranas (that cover an encyclopaedic range of topics), the Yoga Bhashya, a commentary on the Yoga Sutras of Patanjali, the Brahma Sutras, etc., all are 'symbolically' attributed to Vyasa. That may not mean a single individual did all the work.

In the domain of music, there are far too many dubious credits given to Amir Khusrau such as for the sitār, sarod, tablā, khayāl and various Hindustani raags as well as the qawwali and tarana.

When I was with Ut. Ali Akbar Khansaheb, I asked him about these attributions to Amir Khusrau. Khansaheb told me, 'I know it is wrong, but what can I do? I am a musician, not a historian. Someone like you should write about it.'

The modern astro-scientist Nilesh Oak, with the help of planetarium software, has determined the date of the great Mahabharata War as 16 October 5561 BCE. Another set of scientists have determined King Rama's birthdate as 4 December 7323 BCE. Music originated in the Gandharva Veda (an auxiliary of the Sām Veda), which dates prior to both the Ramayana and Mahabharata. Do they mean to say there was no development in music in India for all these centuries before Amir Khusrau?

As established by Dr Gowri Kuppuswamy and Dr Hariharan, the *tillana* (tarana) has its origins in the Karana Prabandham, which precedes Amir Khusrau.

Ramdev Rao, who ruled Devgiri (modern-day Maharashtra) state, summoned his court musician Gopal Nayak to translate ancient Dhrupad compositions, originally sung in an austere fashion, to match the highly disciplined purity of the scholarly Sanskrit language into a more colloquial dialect. Gopal, a native of Vrindavan (the legendary forest of Lord Krishna), translated the Dhrupads into the Braj language. When Gopal Nayak was captured by the Islamist invader Alauddin Khilji, he used his musical talents to endear himself to his captors. There is evidence he taught Amir Khusrau musical compositions of Karana (or Kaivara) Prabandham.

History is always written by the rulers. In this case, it was written by Khusrau himself, who is perhaps more famous for his writings than for his music. Khusrau wrote *Khaza'in ul-Futuh* (The Treasures of Victories) in 1296 CE with details of Alauddin Khilji's construction works, war chronicles and administrative services.

We do not need Khusrau's word to know that Alauddin Khilji was a religious fanatic and diabolical king who ruthlessly plundered and massacred Hindus. Millions were killed and enslaved and forcefully converted to Islam. Khilji implemented rules and regulations to grind down the Hindus so as to reduce them to abject poverty and deprive them of wealth and any form of possessions more than the bare minimum needed for survival. In 1298, approximately 15,000 to 30,000 people who had recently converted to Islam were butchered near Delhi. They were slaughtered in a single day due to fears of an uprising, showing Khilji's inherent distrust in the converts. Even conversion and submission by betraying their own religion was no escape. How can we expect Khusrau to have any respect for Hindu art and culture?

In one such chronicle, the *Táríkh-i 'Aláí*, Khusrau writes, 'The [Khilji's] army left Delhi in November 1310. After crossing rivers, hills and many depths, the elephants were sent, in order that the inhabitants of Ma'bar might be made aware that the day of resurrection had arrived amongst them; and that all the burnt Hindus would be dispatched by the sword to their brothers in hell, so that fire, the improper object of their worship, might mete out proper punishment to them.' His records betray his beliefs quite candidly here. Let's not foolishly praise Amir Khusrau.

Musical instruments like the lute, very similar to the modern-day sarod, are seen in the sculptures and mural paintings in old caves and temples in various parts of India, dating from at least 200 BCE. During the nineteenth century, the sarod was called *'swarode'* in Bengal. The word is derived from the compound Sanskrit word स्वरोदय (swarodaya), meaning the *uday* (rising) of the swar (musical note). The plectrum used for plucking the strings of the sarod is called the 'java', which is derived from the Sanskrit जीह्वा (*jihva*) or tongue, as it functions like the human organ of speech, and its triangular shape resembles a human tongue as well.

Sharan Rani has done extensive research on this subject and authored the acclaimed book *The Divine Sarod*[33] on the origin, antiquity and development of the sarod since the second century BCE. It was a breakthrough book written on the origin and development of the sarod, which meticulously rubbishes the Islamic claims of its invention.

In Kalidasa's poem *Meghdoot* (The Cloud Messenger), composed in the fourth to fifth century CE, there is a reference to a *'veena'*, the belly of which was covered with skin:

आराध्यैनं शरवणभवं देवमुल्लाङ्घिताध्वा
सिध्दद्वन्द्वैर्जलकणभयाद्द्वीणिभिर्मु कृतमार्गः।

Sculptures from Bharhut and Sanchi (both second century BCE), and carvings in first-century Champa temples depict sarod-like musical instruments. The Bhartiya Vastukala institute has discovered sarod-like instruments portrayed in ancient sculptures and paintings of musical ensembles from Pawaya (the ancient city of Padmavati of Bhavabhuti, fourth century CE), showing a pyriform lute (veena), harp and gandharva with a fretted lute that predates the Afghan *rubab* by more than 200 years. The Ajanta paintings (475 CE) also have gandharvas with sarod-like lutes and harps.

In his book, Pt Jotin Bhattacharya has listed four separate gharanas, claiming that their forefathers invented the sarod or were the first to play it. They are:

1. Gulam Ali, who migrated from Afghanistan and settled in Reva. His descendants finally settled in Gwalior. Hence, they call themselves the Gwalior Sarod Gharana. Radhika Mohan Maitra is from this gharana. Gulam Ali Khan's grandson was Hafizali Khan, the father of the famous Amjad Ali Khan.

2. Niyamatulla is being claimed as the first to use steel strings on the sarod. The claim is that his ancestor Hakeem Sukraat was a visionary who went to Greece via Persia, invented the sarod there, and came and settled down in Shahjahanpur.

3. Inayat Ali's son married Niyamatulla's daughter, but claimed that his father Hussain Ali was the inventor of the sarod.

4. Abid Ali Khan's son was Ahmad Ali Khan, from whom Baba Allauddin Khan learnt the sarod. The sarod used to have only sixteen strings. Baba modified it to twenty-six strings. He used to have five main strings in his sarod. The fifth for Kharaj Pancham (lowest octave) for Dhrupad-style ālaaps. Ali Akbar Khansaheb removed the Kharaj Pancham string and thus made the sarod a twenty-five-string instrument.

Surprisingly, all of the above parties claim that their ancestors learnt from the progeny of Tansen who was a Hindu. The funny part is that though all of them say that their forefathers invented the sarod, there is no record or evidence whatsoever of any of those individuals ever mentioning it anywhere. All the claims are made only by the latter generations.

Some believe that Tansen's son Bilas Khan was the inventor of both the Senia *rabab* and the sarod. However, a fifteenth-century CE record mentions a rabab player accompanying Guru Nanak (1469–1529), long before Bilas Khan was born. The most popular belief is that the sarod is but a modification of an ancient Indian instrument called the shaardiya veena, which bears a striking resemblance to the chitra veena (gottu vadyam) and vichitra veena.

We once asked Ma for her opinion on the various competing claims about who invented the sarod and introduced it to Hindustani classical music.

'Are we musicians or historians?' She asked a question that was loaded enough to shut us up. 'Isn't it amazing that all of them are claiming that their ancestors played it first, but nobody discusses who played it the best. Does any sarodist have the courage to claim that he can play better than Bhaiyā [Ali Akbar Khan], or for that matter is anyone claiming that any of their forefathers played better than Bhaiyā?'

No one can deny the fact that Baba and his disciples elevated the standard of Indian classical instrumental music to a new height.

Queen Elizabeth's Piano

There is a hilarious tale that goes with the absurd claim made by one ustad regarding the invention of the surbahār. This ustad, known for his undisguised lies, floated a story about how his ancestor invented the surbahār. He claimed that when Queen Elizabeth arrived in India, her ship was docked at the Bombay harbour. The piano she had brought with her got badly damaged while it was being unloaded, so they dumped it into the sea.

He claimed his ancestor found this dumped piano on the beach and started playing it, and went on to use its scrap to invent an instrument and named it the surbahār.

Obviously, there are fatal flaws in the story. First and foremost, there were two Queen Elizabeths. Queen Elizabeth I never visited India. Queen Elizabeth II visited India for the very first time as late as 21 January 1961. She arrived by BOAC plane and landed in Delhi, not Bombay. She didn't have a piano or any other musical instrument with her.

If the so-called piano was dumped in the harbour, how come it ended up on the beach? Bombay is an island. The Bombay harbour doesn't have a beach and the Bombay beach doesn't have a harbour as both are on the opposite ends of the island; the harbour is on the eastern side and the beach is on the western side.

There are countless other gaping holes in the story which I need not trouble you with here. Facts matter.

Swar-Samrāt

न भूतो न भविष्यति

*[Before him there was none,
And there will be none after him]*

Ut. Ali Akbar Khan.

Nobody in the history of north Indian classical music learnt and created as many raags as Baba Allauddin Khan did—more than most artistes will ever perform in their entire life.

As the torchbearer of Baba's rich legacy, Ali Akbar Khansaheb's repertoire was the greatest. No artiste performed a greater number of raags than him. What he could do with his sarod was superhuman. Every musician takes a certain amount of risk in his performance, but Khansaheb has been acclaimed for taking the maximum risk. His wondrous creative extemporal phrases, his impossible acrobatics, that too without going off pitch, that too on an instrument as difficult as the sarod, were phenomenal. Every recording and every concert of his has been profound and a lesson. Every minute spent in his proximity has been memorable.

The following anecdote, provided by Suresh Vyas and confirmed by Dhyanesh Khan, illustrates his genius.

Sometime in the mid-1980s, Khansaheb was performing in Calcutta. He had the habit of reaching the concert venue a few hours earlier than the showtime. In the green room, as usual, he was surrounded by many people. A young man came and paid his respects. However, Khansaheb mistook him to be a fan until the young man introduced himself as Sabir Khan, the son of Ut. Karamatullah Khan, the tablā maestro. Sabirji was to accompany Ali Akbar Khansaheb on the tablā for this concert.

'खाँसहेब, आज पहली बार आप के साथ बजाने का मौक़ा मिला है। थोड़ा rehearsal करलें? [Khansaheb, this is the first time I'll be accompanying you. Shall we rehearse a bit?]' Sabirji suggested.

'I don't know how to rehearse, Baba never taught me how to do that,' Khansaheb replied, stifling a laugh.

Sabirji was taken aback by Khansaheb's reply. 'Can we practice the gat you will play?' he asked.

'I haven't yet made the gat.'

Baffled, Sabirji asked, 'Could you tell me what taal you'll be playing? So that I can practise that on my own.'

Realizing Sabir's bewilderment, Khansaheb said, 'Beta, let me explain how I operate. In the next few minutes, I will go to the stage and tune my sarod. During the sound test, I will play all the twelve notes of all the three octaves. Every room, every auditorium, every hall has a specific natural resonant frequency. The musical note which matches that frequency will oscillate with greater amplitude. Therefore, after figuring out which note resonates the most in this auditorium, I'll choose the raag accordingly. For example, if I find that my madhyam [sub-dominant F] is the note that resonates the most in this venue, I will play a madhyam-pradhaan raag [with F as the prominent note]; if I find gandhar [mediant E] resonates the most, then I will choose a gandhar-pradhaan raag [with E as the prominent note]. While playing the ālaap, the phrase that appeals to me the most, I will use the phrase as the mukhda [motif] of the gat. I will tell you the taal of the gat once I figure out the metre of the gat.'

During one of Khansaheb's visits to Mumbai, I had the honour of chauffeuring him around in my car. There were a couple of ideas under consideration. One was my possible role in publishing Khansaheb's recordings in India; the other was writing his biography. However, despite spending hours discussing them, the projects couldn't see the light of day. Some of the anecdotes on Khansaheb included in this book have their origin in those discussions.

Although 8 p.m. was the official starting time of the concert at the Nehru Centre, Khansaheb insisted on reaching by 4 p.m. Reaching the venue an hour before showtime is normal, but four hours earlier seemed strange to me. Suresh placed Khansaheb's sarod and his bag in the boot of my car, but didn't come with us. With Khansaheb in the front seat, I drove away in the direction of Nehru Centre, with an entourage of sorts following. I tend to drive at a higher speed than most, and because of the shortcut I knew, I reached much earlier than the others.

When we arrived, the venue was deserted. There wasn't a soul in sight. All the doors were shut and locked. I couldn't help laughing aloud but fortunately Khansaheb didn't take it as an offence. A solitary security guard appeared out of nowhere and asked us, 'What do you want?'

'We are here for the concert,' I replied.

'But the concert is at 8 p.m. You are way too early.'

'Please try to understand. He is the performing artiste and he wanted to reach early. Could you please open the green room for us?'

'But the duty staff won't arrive before 6 p.m. I am just a security guard.'

After some persuasion, the security guard went to the office, brought keys and opened the green room for us. I switched on the air conditioner as Khansaheb sat on the floor in a corner opposite the door and lit a cigarette. Meanwhile, Suresh Vyas arrived with his father, Madanlalji, who seemed quite friendly with Khansaheb. Khansaheb made Madanlalji sit next to him and offered him a cigarette. They were soon in deep conversation. Suresh and I went out to bring the sarod from my car, but forgot to bring his bag.

In the green room, Khansaheb and Madanlalji seemed to be having a hilarious conversation as both of them were laughing out loud. I tried to join, but I couldn't understand a word because they were speaking in Bengali. Meanwhile, people had started flooding in and soon the green room was jam-packed, every inch of the floor occupied. Suresh was at the door talking to a large group of people waiting outside the green room.

'Has Pradeep Barot arrived?' Khansaheb asked Suresh. Barot was to bring his *tanpuri* which is a smaller version of the tanpurā. Instrumentalists need a quieter, higher octave drone. Khansaheb was very choosy about his tanpurā/tanpuri, and several times in the past, Suresh had accompanied Khansaheb with Barot's tanpuri.

'He'll be here any time.' As if on cue, Pradeep Barot arrived. He quickly removed his tanpuri from the cloth case. Obviously, before leaving his home, Barot had to loosen all the four strings of his tanpuri to prevent them from breaking. As the green room was so crowded, half a dozen people passed the tanpuri along before it could reach Khansaheb.

Khansaheb took the tanpuri in his hands and asked me to give him the pitch-pipe. Suresh and I realized it was in the bag, which we had forgotten to bring from my car. I threw my car keys to him. Like a deft cricketer, Suresh caught the keys and ran to my car parked outside, but didn't return for quite a few minutes.

Before the advent of digital tuners, mechanical pitch-pipes were used to tune stringed instruments and as a reference tone for acapella singers. Pitch-pipes were designed to produce a pure tone (sine wave) of the frequencies of the standard Equal Tempered Scale.

Pitch pipe.

Khansaheb had no patience for inefficient assistants like us. Without the help of a pitch-pipe (reference of the pure tone of standard C = 261.63 Hz), Khansaheb went ahead to tune all the four strings of the tanpuri.

Finally, Suresh arrived with Khansaheb's bag. Khansaheb opened the bag, took out the pitch-pipe, blew the note C, and voila, the frequency of the pitch-pipe and the tanpuri matched most precisely.

The concert started, and Dr Sunil Shastri and I were sitting in the second row. After the ālaap and jod, Khansaheb started an ati-vilambit gat, beautifully accompanied by Ut. Zakir Hussain. Dr Sunil Shastri and I were counting the ati-vilambit teen taal on our fingers. No sooner had Khansaheb started playing the todās when his madhyam string broke. Zakirbhai kept playing, expecting it would be fixed quickly. However, the string broke in such a way that Khansaheb had to remove the whole string, discard it, take out a fresh string from his bag, fix it and re-tune his instrument. As it took longer than expected, Zakirbhai stopped playing, but Khansaheb's right foot continued tapping to the beat. Sunil Shastri and I decided to keep counting the taal along with Khansaheb's foot. It took quite a few minutes for Khansaheb to resume the rendition, but all the while his right foot kept time. When he was ready he resumed on the exact twelfth beat (all masitkhani gats begin on the twelfth beat) and signalled the sum (first beat) to Zakirbhai. If someone else said they witnessed this, we would not have believed them. We were so fortunate to have witnessed this utter mastery for ourselves.

While recording Basant Kabra for the album under the banner of Lineage–Maihar Gharana, we were conversing with Pt Swapan Chaudhuri about Khansaheb's amazing sense of taal. He told us, 'Khansaheb says, "Don't count the taal, feel it." You count with your conscious mind, and feel with your subconscious.'

'The vibrations on the air are the breath of God speaking to man's soul. Music is the language of God. We musicians are as close to God as man can be. We hear his voice, we read his lips, we give birth to the children of God, who sing his praise. That's what musicians are . . . And if we're not that, we're nothing.'

— Stephen J. Rivele (*Copying Beethoven*)

The Rodent and the Pachyderm

Ut. Ali Akbar Khansaheb.

Every moment that we spent with Khansaheb was blissful and memorable. We learnt so much by just listening and watching him. We were amazed by his genius, and laughed uproariously at his one-liners. I felt like I had won the lottery when Khansaheb graced my house for dinner.

One time an interview was printed with a sarodist who was disdainful towards Khansaheb. I asked Khansaheb his view, but he just laughed. Instead, he responded with a little fable he had created:

एक बार, एक वनप्रदेश में बहुत बड़ा तूफ़ान आया। सबकुछ अस्त व्यस्त हो गया। सिर्फ़ दो ही प्राणी बच गए, हाथी और चूहा। हाथी इसलिए बच गया कि वह बलवान था, और चूहा इस लिए बचा की वह ज़मीन के नीचे था।

चूहे ने उसके बिल से ज़ख्मी और उदास हाथी को देखा। चूहे ने इससे पहले कभी किसी हाथी को देखा नहीं था तो समझ नहीं पाया कि यह कौनसा प्राणी है।

चूहे ने सोचा, मैं भी काला हूँ, यह भी काला है। मेरे चार पैर है, उसके भी चार पैर है। मेरी नाक लम्बी है, उसकी भी नाक लम्बी है। मेरी आँखें छोटी है, उसकी भी आँखें छोटी है, मगर क़द में इतना फ़र्क क्यूँ?

चूहे ने चिल्ला कर पूछा, "अबे! कौन है तू?"

हाथी ने विनम्रता से तू का जवाब आप में देते हुए कहा,

"जी, लोग मुझे हाथी कहते है, आप कौन है?"

अब तक हाथी चूहे के काफ़ी नज़दीक आ गया था। चूहे ने जवाब दिया,

"मैं भी वही हूँ जो तुम हो, मगर आजकल मेरी तबीयत ठीक नहीं

[Once upon a time, in a jungle, a destructive storm killed animals and uprooted trees. The only two who survived were an elephant and a mouse. The elephant survived because he was very strong and the mouse survived because he had hidden underground in his little burrow.

Peeping out from his burrow, the mouse saw the sad, injured and lonely elephant passing by. The mouse had never seen an elephant before. The mouse wondered who this animal was, thinking he looked a lot like himself. 'I am dark, so is he. I have four legs, so has he. I have tiny eyes, so has he. I have a long nose, so has he, though his is longer than mine. I have a tail, so has he, but a bit shorter than mine. But why are our sizes so different?'

So, the rodent yelled at the elephant, 'Who in the hell are you?'

The elephant politely replied, 'People call me elephant. May I know who you are?'

By now, the elephant had moved closer to the rodent, who replied, 'I'm the same as you are, but these days, my health isn't at its prime.']

An Early Morning Phone Call

I am an 'early to bed and early to rise' kind of person, and a sports enthusiast too. Each morning I go to the sports club to play badminton or cricket or to work out at the gym. However, I never use an alarm. I wake up when I feel like it and go to sleep when I feel tired.

One morning, the moment I got up from my bed, the phone rang. I was quite used to the phone ringing at odd hours as my younger sister has emigrated to the US, and I had some clients in the far east.

'Hello!' I answered.

'माँ बोल रही हूँ [Ma speaking],' a low-amplitude, hesitant, sonorous feminine voice spoke from the other end. 'Yesterday, all night long, there was no electricity and the supply still hasn't been restored. I didn't want to disturb your sleep, so I've phoned you now. All the ice from the refrigerator has melted, flooding the floor. I don't know what to do . . . if you could please come and do something about it.'

The volume of her voice was just above the audible level. I was so baffled that I couldn't speak a word. Before I could respond, the caller disconnected the phone. The chances of Ma phoning someone, that too at seven in the morning, was a million to one. If Rooshiji was living in the same apartment with Ma, why would she phone me? I was sure it was a prank played by one of my female friends.

My brain started scanning the probabilities at lightning speed. I mentally replayed the telephonic conversation many times over. I used my deductive reasoning to identify whose voice it could be. The quality of the voice made me conclude that the caller was definitely a singer, since singers speak steadily in a consistent pitch with rhythmic diction.

With all probabilities eliminated, Sonali Jalota (now Sonali Rathod) could have been the only one. Sonali was my elder sister's classmate and best friend. Apart from her passion for music, what made Sonali an adorable personality was that she was extremely bubbly, full of life, had a terrific sense of humour and loved to play pranks.

Those were the days of landline telephones without caller ID display. Sonali, for the sake of some harmless fun, had the habit of making calls using a false voice. I distinctly remember her once phoning in an altered voice, faking her identity as Pushpa, asking to speak to my sister. I was the one who answered the phone and failed to guess it was Sonali. It was from Sonali that I had first heard about Annapurna Devi. Sonali's voice was under some trauma once, and she had temporarily stopped singing and had started learning the sitār from Guru Ma. When I asked Guru Ma how Sonali had ended up at her place, she said, 'Sonali had come to me with a letter of recommendation from Lata Mangeshkar.'

To verify the matter, I phoned my friend Sunil Vakil, who lived in Mistry Park, just a few metres away from Akashganga. He confirmed that there was no electricity problem in his building. My doubts about the phone call being a prank became stronger. Then another thought crossed my mind. What if there was really a case of disrupted electricity supply, if not in the entire building but only in Ma's apartment? Since Ma's apartment was in a dilapidated condition with decades-old wiring, it could be a blown fuse.

I decided to drive to Akashganga. As I was changing from my night suit into jeans and a T-shirt, the phone rang again. The same voice said, 'अब आने की ज़रूर नहीं बिजली आ गई [Don't bother to come now. The power has been restored.]'

Indeed, it was Ma. In the evening, I went to Akashganga to make sure all was well. I learnt that Ma was all alone for a few days as Rooshiji was travelling for a seminar. There was a piece of paper with emergency numbers glued to the wall above the telephone set. I was honoured to have my name and number there.

However, after all these years, I am unable to forgive myself for not rushing to Ma's help. I also keep wondering how Ma knew the exact time I woke up.

'Fallen Angel'

There are two kinds of lies people tell—to others, and to themselves. Human beings seldom feel okay about themselves the way they are. It is a compulsive human need to embellish our image with forged attributes to fool not only others but our own selves into believing that we are better than what we actually are.

Maestros make their art look so easy that the audience tends to take their prowess for granted. Too many aspirants of music begin learning music without realizing the difficulties, only to feel disillusioned. Music shops are full of 'as good as new' used musical instruments. I once asked a music shop owner about this, and he explained, 'People buy all sorts of instruments in a fit of excitement, but they soon realize it is far more difficult to play it well. Within a few days or months, they want to return them. Naturally, they lose money, because we buy back these instruments at a deep discount.'

There is no silver bullet for success in Indian classical music, yet so many disciples came to learn from Ma without realizing how difficult the journey would be. Many felt defeated and quit, those with more tenacity persevered, only to feel dejected later. A precious few ever made it to the top. Learning music in the guru–shishya paramparā can never be equated with the time-bound modern academic system in which you can comfortably predict at what age a student will reach graduation.

Like many others, Rooshiji thought 6A Akashganga was a magical machine which converted novices into maestros. I've witnessed many disciples like Rooshiji applying the elementary mathematics 'Rule of Three' formula and begin prematurely planning their performing career. To quote a very talented and gifted sitārist gurubhai of mine, 'Panditji came to Maihar to learn from Baba in 1938, and finished learning in 1944; that is seven years, add about two more years of his lessons from Baba during the Europe tour and Almora. That makes nine years. So, say, in a maximum of ten years from now, I will start giving public performances.' Today after three decades, despite his talent and aptitude, he is nowhere in the music scenario.

People who dream to be like Panditji and Khansaheb have no idea for how many hours a day, for how many years these maestros relentlessly practised, that too under Baba Allauddin Khan, the most able and the most unforgiving taskmaster of all. Music was the sole focus for Ma, Khansaheb, Panditji, Nikhil Banerjee, Panna Babu, Hariji, etc. They kept away from social distractions, nor did they have the burden of an academic career.

Fundamentally, Rooshiji was a combination of a narcissistic and hubristic personality, with the quality of extreme pride or dangerous overconfidence, often in combination with or synonymous with arrogance. His was the case of a traveller who was obsessed with the destination but hated the journey. He didn't love music but he was in it because he thought music was a confirmed ticket to stardom.

In the domain of music, Rooshiji had too many handicaps. To begin with, his musical quotient was very low. Also, forty-two years was too late an age for anyone to start pursuing music. What made things worse for him was that he insisted that Ma teach him the Wazirkhani *beenkaar-ang* (the most difficult style that Baba had taught only to Ma).

When I asked Ma why Rooshiji's progress in music was so disappointing, she said, 'What he wants to learn is very difficult and cannot be achieved with such limited riyaaz. Also, his mind is too restless. A restless mind can't do sādhanā. That is possible only with *kripā* [grace]. There are four types of grace: Ishwara kripā (God's grace), shastra kripā (grace of the scriptures), acharya kripā (grace of one's guide), and swa kripā (your own grace on yourself). However, no sādhanā is wasted. The sādhaks are reborn in a suitable environment and they reawaken the wisdom of their previous lives, resume their sādhanā and strive even harder towards their goal.'

Rooshiji's biggest blunder was that he told Ma, 'Your teaching style is outdated and ineffective. I am an educationist, and I can teach more effectively. I have devised a method by which the process of music learning will become dramatically rapid. You just give me the lessons and I will learn to play it myself.' In order to prove that his teaching technique was effective, Rooshiji obtained Ma's permission to allow him to teach music to a few younger pupils. Ma gave her consent. Rooshiji's first pupil was me, followed by Dr Shastri and Jaykishore. Then came Smarth Bali, followed by Qamar Ali. We all became the subjects of his teaching experiment.

For Ma, it was good riddance. She explained and dictated the notations of Raag Yaman and Raag Jaijaiwanti to Rooshiji and liberated herself from the responsibility and headache of personally teaching him their myriad details and intricacies. The content of Jaijaiwanti given to Rooshiji was something to die for. I had never before heard the Wazirkhani beenkar-ang style ati-vilambit rendition which Ma had taught Rooshiji. Although Rooshiji couldn't render it well, the music was haunting. Years later, Ma taught him Raag Lalit. Before his demise, Rooshiji had learnt just the ālaap and vilambit gat but it had a mesmerizing effect.

Rooshiji adopted Emile Coue's theory of 'If you persuade yourself you can do a certain thing, you will do it, however difficult it may be.' Rooshiji also used the technique of 'fake it till you make it' auto-suggestion (self-hypnosis, by standing in front of the mirror every morning and repeatedly telling yourself you are the best). His self-persuasion was so effective that he began behaving like a star. He started publicly announcing in his seminars, 'There are three pillars of the sitār: Ravi Shankar, Vilayat Khan and Nikhil Banerjee [he never included Abdul Halim Jafferkhan], and soon, the fourth one will be me.'

Rooshiji's euphoria was bound to end. He soon reached a plateau, and then his level of proficiency began to decline. Those of us who were learning from him realized that it was pointless to have him as a teacher. Each and every pupil of his quit. Dr Shastri gave up learning the sitār and started learning the bansuri from Nityanand. In my case, Ma first asked Suresh to take over, and subsequently the onus fell on Nityanand. Jaykishore left India and migrated back to the US. Qamar Ali went back to Abdul Halim Jafferkhan.

Such a situation could be frustrating for anyone, but it was more frustrating for Rooshiji as he was heavily invested in the script, both emotionally and socially. With his dreams shattered to reach stardom through music, Rooshiji was on the lookout for another means to reach the end, which was stardom. With some of his friends, especially Vallabh Bhansali, becoming a billionaire in a short time, he became determined to achieve the same. Suddenly we found him obsessed with the stock market. Music became just a recreational activity for him.

While signing the marriage bond, Rooshiji had promised Ma that he would restrict his leaving the house to five days (from 9 a.m. to 5 p.m.) a month for his seminar within the city. That promise was forgotten, and Rooshiji started going out every single day in pursuit of money and stardom. Although the returns on the money Rooshiji invested in the stock market were handsome, they were nowhere near the level of star players like Vallabh Bhansali or Rakesh Jhunjhunwala.

Rooshiji became a stakeholder and partner in a broad array of businesses, including musical instruments, a dot-com company, catering and event management, jewellery, etc. He also invested in a few real-estate deals. Rooshiji had the gift of the gab. After reading a few dozen management books, he proclaimed himself a management guru and started giving corporate seminars for hefty fees, despite the fact that in his entire life, Rooshiji had never managed any business, not even a roadside mom-and-pop store. The result was that he started suffering from hypertension. But he concealed this fact until the very end.

Baba Allauddin Khan, Ma and Khansaheb never charged money from their disciples. However, Rooshiji used to charge an exorbitant amount for teaching me psychology and subsequently music. There were several other unfair ways he extracted money from me. After losing a considerable amount to him, I had no option but to complain to Ma. She was furious and instructed Rooshiji never again to take a single rupee from me, and she asked me to stop learning from him. She immediately appointed Suresh to teach me in her presence. That was scary for both Suresh and me, but finally I was able to learn an authentic version of Ma's music. With some progress, Ma asked Nityanand to teach me.

All art is at once surface and symbol.
Those who go beneath the surface do so at their peril.
Those who read the symbol do so at their peril.
It is the spectator, and not life, that art really mirrors.

—Oscar Wilde

An Ascetic and a Hedonist

यावज्जीवेत सुखं जीवेद ऋणं कृत्वा घृतं पिवेत।
भस्मीभूतस्य देहस्य पुनरागमनं कुतः ॥

[*For whatever longevity, live joyously;*
Borrow money for bodily pleasures
Once our body turns to dust and ashes,
How shall it ever again return?]
—*Charvaka*

In no time, 6A Akashganga became a clash of cultures. Rooshiji's hedonistic Charvaka philosophy was juxtaposed against Ma's ascetic Vedanta philosophy. Two contrasting pursuits. Ma was always on the path of *shreya* (virtue) and Rooshiji was on the path of *preya* (pleasure). Dr Sunil Shastri, with his command over Sanskrit and a knowledge of Vedanta, often used to give us a brief discourse on Vedanta philosophy. Ma would attentively listen to him, but Rooshiji would counter the Vedic philosophy by quoting Charvaka philosophy.

Once Rooshiji adopted his new avatar of management guru, too many of his business associates started visiting Akashganga. Ma kept herself hidden from them for most of the time, but it was not possible to avoid all of them, especially on Guru Purnima day. Too many of Rooshiji's newfound disciples started coming to seek his blessings. His business partners also started visiting very frequently. Our Saturday rendezvous became history the moment Rooshiji tried to include his business associates. We found their presence rather disturbing as they were the kind of people who had nothing to do with music, art or philosophy. All they could discuss was money and we just couldn't gel with them. They had no idea who Ma was. For them, she was just an eccentric old lady who never stepped out of the house.

Once, a businessman came with his wife and five-year-old son. He said, 'My son is a gifted singer, and you must listen to his singing.' Ma didn't have the heart to discourage a child so she agreed. The child was shy, but the parents pressured him to sing a Bollywood song. Sitting in the very same place where greats like Nikhil Banerjee, Hariprasad Chaurasia, Dakshina Mohan Tagore, etc., had taken their lessons, the child sat and sang 'Chal chaiyya chaiyya chaiyya chaiyya'. The poor child kept singing for a few minutes and Ma had no choice but to sit through the ordeal. When he stopped, his parents looked expectantly at Ma for her reaction. It was impossible for Ma to praise the child's singing, but at the same time she didn't want to discourage him. Ma took a way out by digressing from the topic. She asked the child, 'What is the meaning of this song?' He didn't have the faintest idea, so Ma asked the parents, but they too didn't know the meaning of the song their little son just sang. Ma then asked Rooshiji. Before Rooshiji could reply, Ma got up and locked herself in her room.

After Ma's hospitalization, the topic of discussion during the Saturday rendezvous was often 'After Ma, what?' Rooshiji had already made his plans, including the renovation of the house. There had been so many sudden and premature deaths in my family that I found the whole discussion illogical. Rooshiji was annoyed with me when I asked him, 'What is the guarantee that you are going to outlive Ma? She has inherited Baba's genes in

music, maybe she has also inherited Baba's genes of longevity. She
may outlive you.'

'There is too much negativity in your head,' Rooshiji rebuked
me. 'How can you even think like that?'

'Why not?' I snapped back. 'It is okay for you to discuss Ma's
death, but not for me to discuss your death?'

At 3.15 a.m. on 13 April 2013, Rooshiji suddenly collapsed.
A nurse phoned me to give the news. I rushed to Akashganga.
The ambulance had taken him to Breach Candy Hospital. He was
declared dead on arrival.

Who would break this news to Ma? As usual, my gurubhais
made me the bearer of bad news. I went into Ma's room. She was
bedridden due to the injured spine because of her fall, but wide
awake. Before I could open my mouth, Ma said in a matter-of-fact
way, 'I know he is dead.'

During her last days, Nityanand and I heard Ma lamenting,
'My marriage with Panditji was Baba's biggest mistake. My
marriage with Rooshiji was my biggest mistake.'

As per Rooshiji's will, Ma was the sole inheritor of his entire
estate, with an expressed wish to spend the money on promoting
and propagating Indian classical music. However, Ma was least
bothered about money or material possessions. Rooshiji had his
fingers in so many pies that it was very difficult to track down
all his financial involvements. However, as per his last income tax
return, his estate was valued in crores. A very small portion of it
ever reached Ma.

> 'Odie, let's talk about effort versus return.
> You know, you can still lead a pointless life
> without all that running around.'
> —Garfield

Shravan Kumar

Human life starts with dependency and ends with dependency. Everyone loves to spend time with children, but are rather reluctant to take care of an elderly person, unless they have a handsome estate to leave behind. In such cases, potential inheritors compete with each other to be the caretaker. Precious are the experience and wisdom of elders, but advancing age, senility and loss of memory robs them of that too.

Shravan Kumar is a historical character whose short life is depicted in the Ramayana, an ancient Sanskrit epic dated to 7323 BCE. Shravan Kumar's aged parents wanted him to take them to places of pilgrimage. Transport was scarce and costly in that age, and Shravan Kumar could not afford it. He decided to put each parent in a basket and tie the baskets to the opposite ends of a bamboo pole, which he placed on his shoulders. He carried them and covered a vast geographical distance on foot.

As mentioned earlier, after Rooshiji's demise, Guru Ma was all alone and bedridden in her house. Two nurses were employed in shifts of twelve hours. However, the nurses kept changing and it was impossible to leave Ma with unknown caregivers. We all tried to think of the best possible solution. The investor banker supported by Rooshiji's votaries was of the opinion that the Akashganga apartment should be sold and Ma shifted to Breach Candy Hospital until her last day. However, Ma was horrified by the proposal. In any case, she was getting nothing more than routine oral medication and physiotherapy twice a week.

My father had died in 1979, leaving behind a beautiful house. I was lucky enough to have one extra room in my house, and my wife and mother readily agreed to shift Ma there. Meanwhile, Suresh Vyas too was all alone in his two-bedroom apartment in Bandra. His father had died and his mother had shifted to his elder brother's house. Suresh too was extremely keen to take Ma to his house. However, Ma refused us both.

Then we, her disciples, thought of staying at Ma's house in rotation. During the entire conversation, Nityanand didn't speak a single word. He was quietly waiting for his turn. When we asked him to opine, his one-liner was, 'Ma is going nowhere, I too am going nowhere.'

'Meaning?' we asked in bewilderment.

'I have already informed my wife and daughter. Come what may, I am not leaving Ma alone.'

Suresh too followed suit and both of them stayed put at Akashganga looking after bedridden Ma. However, after a few days, Ma called Suresh and said, 'Listen, your mother too is ailing. She has shifted to your elder brother's residence. You ought to return to your house and bring your mother back to stay with you.'

Fully aware of Ma's clairvoyance, wondering what could be the implication behind the advice, Suresh obediently did what Ma had told him. His mother died within a few days after returning to live with him.

Thus, after Rooshiji's death, Nityanand never went home. He called for his basic belongings and started living in Rooshiji's room, on 24x7 duty as Ma's caretaker. One day, Ma called him and insisted that he should spend at least some time with his wife and daughter. Hence, it was arranged that Suresh would substitute

Nityanand during the weekends (Saturday morning to Sunday evening). However, Nityanand adamantly refused to leave Ma overnight and it was thus settled that Nityanand would leave Akashganga on Sunday morning around 9.30 a.m. and return by 6.30 p.m. With Suresh as the substitute for that period. Nityanand again reduced those timings from 10.30 a.m. to 4.30 p.m.

From 13 April 2013 until 13 October 2018—five and a half years—Nityanand lived in the confinement of Ma's house, never stepping out, except for Sunday lunch. He refused several invitations for live concerts and radio/TV programmes. Ma insisted that he accept at least the important ones, so he agreed to a few stage performances and concert tours, including one in Europe.

Nityanand Haldipur at Akashganga.

After Rooshiji's demise, Nityanand was once cleaning and clearing Ma's wardrobe. He found a folder full of her award certificates, like the Padma Bhushan (India's third highest civilian honour), an award from the Sangeet Natak Akademi (the highest Indian honour in performing arts), Deshikottam (an honorary doctorate degree by Visva-Bharati University), and some other awards.

'Ma, what should I do with all these award certificates?'
Nityanand meant to ask whether he should frame or laminate
them. However, Ma told him, 'फाड़ के फेंक दो [Throw them away in
the garbage bin.]'

Under the aegis of Ma, first Rooshiji, then Suresh and
thenceforth Nityanand have been my gurus. Every lesson I've had
from Nityanand is priceless. Before coming to Ma's house, I used
to hate ālaaps, calling them dull, boring and a pure waste of time.
The way Nityanand has taught me, I am now addicted to the ālaap
and jod, experiencing spiritual bliss in ālaaps and not caring for
anything else.

Despite decades of a harmonious relationship, Nityanand and
I are two very different individuals with extremely contrasting
mindsets. It was impossible for me (or for anyone else) to match
Nityanand's guru bhakti—unconditional devotion towards
Guru Ma. Nityanand's instant relinquishment of his home,
family, personal life and performing career in order to be Ma's
caretaker for several years is perhaps matched by few in the
history of mankind. Yet, it didn't change the fact that his mind,
although amazingly well-endowed for music and devotion, was
ill-equipped for logical, rational, critical and analytical thinking.
As the appointed manager and leader, Nityanand failed to assert
himself, which resulted in the loss of a ridiculously large amount
of Rooshiji's estate and Ma's investments.

When I discussed Guru Ma's health issues with my cousin,
Dr Arun Mullaji, the famous orthopaedic surgeon, he had warned
against both putting Ma in a wheelchair and confining her to the
bed, saying, 'If you don't push her out of the bed, she will never get
out of it, and soon her body will lose the ability to do so.' Though
Ma never used a wheelchair, I failed to convince Nityanand to
pull Ma out of bed periodically and make her stand on her feet
and walk a little, albeit with support and assistance. As feared, the
result was that because of excessive care and spoon-feeding for a

significantly long time, Ma became a complete dependant. Her body lost the ability to walk or even stand on its own. I discussed this with the lady physiotherapist visiting Ma. She fully agreed, but said, 'She is too adamant. Unfortunately, there is nobody who can tell her what to do.'

Old age is the second childhood. Our brains regress to infancy level, as if the lifecycle is returning to its beginning. The way we were dependent on parents during our childhood, in old age we become dependent on our children or caretakers. Prams return in the form of wheelchairs and nannies return in the form of nurses to change our diapers and spoon-feed us.

Senility gradually manifests in us as we age. The way we go through physical changes associated with old age like a stooped posture, wrinkled skin, decreasing muscle strength, brittle bones, stiff joints and hardened arteries, there is constant decline in our mental abilities—impaired judgement, loss of memory, childish behaviour, etc. Our speech becomes more and more unintelligible, and communication is often repetitive and nonsensical. Worse, the affection from our near and dear ones transforms into pity.

As Ma underwent the ageing process, she too had most of the above-mentioned symptoms. However, her mental alertness had its highs and lows. She would suddenly sink, and then bounce back to her normal, sharp and alert frame of mind.

To play the role of Ma's full-time caretaker, Nityanand was in for a Herculean task. We all were aware of Ma's eccentricities, but to face them day in and day out was a whole new ball game. The two biggest problems Nityanand faced were Ma's obsession for precision and her adamant nature. This was when we realized the value of Rooshiji in Ma's life, especially the way he looked after her during her sickness.

For instance, when Ma was mobile enough, and able to walk a short distance with assistance, Nityanand would bring her to the dining table for her meals. After sitting on the dining chair, Ma

would make Nityanand adjust the distance between the chair and
table half a dozen times to arrive at a particularly precise desirable
position. Having an engineering background, Nityanand devised
the solution of using permanent ink. When Ma was fine with the
position of the chair, Nityanand marked the exact positions of
the legs of the chair. The idea worked wonderfully well. Ma was
not aware of the marks on the floor, but if the chair was out of
position even by a few millimetres, she would ask Nityanand to
adjust the position—to his surprise, the legs of the chair would
meet the exact ink marks. To rule out coincidence, a few times
Nityanand deliberately placed the chair a few millimetres off the
mark, but each time Ma could discern the difference and would
ask Nityanand to readjust it.

When Ma became totally bedridden, an automated hospital
bed replaced her age-old narrow single bed. In medical parlance,
'Fowler's position' is a standard patient position in which the bed
is tilted in such a way that the patient is seated in a semi-sitting
position (between 45 to 60 degrees). However, Ma would insist
on precise fixed degrees. After a few days of wrestling with the
remote control, Nityanand ink-marked the position of the tilt, and
it worked. Again, if he missed the mark even by just a few degrees,
Ma could discern the difference and make him readjust the bed.

The next prop we acquired for Ma was an adjustable 'over bed
table' (with casters), like those used in the hospital. It was useful and
convenient, especially during meals, but Nityanand had to undergo
teething troubles there too. Ma insisted on a precise height, but the
hydraulic height adjustment had no markings. Nityanand had to
keep adjusting the level until Ma said it was okay. Again, Nityanand
used permanent ink to mark the exact height of the shaft. Although
Ma was unaware of the mark, she was able to discern even a few
millimetres of difference in the height of the table.

The five and a half years of Nityanand's persistent endeavour
of serving his guru took a toll on his health. Once, the nurse on

duty phoned Suresh and said that Nityanand was running a high fever. Suresh rushed to Akashganga, put Nityanand on complete bed rest and started attending to Ma. Even after a couple days of bed rest and self-medication, Nityanand's temperature kept rising. Suresh kept requesting Nityanand to go home, but he flatly refused. Fortunately, Suresh was assertive enough to prevent Nityanand from going near Ma, thus preventing him from infecting her.

One more day, and Nityanand's symptoms aggravated further. Yet, Nityanand refused to go home or to a hospital. Some aggression was needed, and Suresh phoned me to come and play the stereotypical agonistic role. It was already 10 p.m. when I reached Akashganga. Nityanand was in bad shape. I put the thermometer in his armpit and it showed 106°F. I phoned four hospitals located in the vicinity but all were full. I phoned my doctor friend and managed to get a room in Bhatia Hospital. Nityanand, even in a semi-conscious state, refused to leave Ma and get hospitalized.

By this time Nihar, one of his disciples, reached there. With his help, I literally kidnapped Nityanand, dumped him in the back seat of my car and admitted him to Bhatia Hospital, where he was diagnosed with dengue. It took a month for him to recover and return to Ma. All throughout his stay in the hospital, he felt sorry that he was not attending to her.

One Sunday, in the late afternoon, as Nityanand was teaching me Gaud Sarang, Ma's attendant came running to say, 'Maji feels like throwing up.' Nityanand rushed in; I followed.

Ma was totally bedridden then. There was no time to lift and carry her to the washroom. Nityanand quickly placed his open palms in front of Ma's mouth.

I rushed to the kitchen to bring a plastic tub or some container. But by the time I could find one, Nityanand's palms were full of vomit. When we went back to Ma's room, I realized that he had not allowed a single drop to spill on her clothes or bed.

Eccentricities of a Genius

Genius and eccentricity go hand in hand. Geniuses are difficult to live with. There is a saying in Marathi, 'शिवाजी जन्माला यावा पण शेजारच्या घरात [A genius should be born, but in the neighbour's house, not in mine.]'

An eccentric genius's habits are incomprehensible because they stem from a mind so original that it does not conform to societal norms. Such people invariably find it difficult to live in harmony with society because they are unwilling to compromise what they sense is the truth. They have an enduring and distinct feeling of being different from others. They are entirely unafraid of and uninfluenced by the opinions and vagaries of the crowd.

It is often a curse to be a genius. Society has an overwhelming majority of mediocre people. If you are not mediocre, you are an outsider. A genius is either despised or worshipped, but never accepted by society.

Art is dependent on patronage to thrive and survive. Historically, art has followed affluence. Art patronage has tended to arise wherever a royal, imperial system or aristocracy has dominated society. In other words, whenever and wherever a limited number of people have controlled an abundant share of resources.

European music benefitted tremendously from the patronage of the church and the royal courts. The church from the very beginning practised the ritual of music. Christianity began as a small, persecuted Jewish sect. At first, there was no break with the Jewish faith; Christians still attended synagogues and presumably carried on the same musical traditions in their separate Christian meetings. Subsequently, the ritual of Mass music spawned into the tradition of Mass compositions, to which many famous composers of the standard concert repertory made contributions, including Bach, Haydn, Mozart, Beethoven and Brahms.

'Baba had tremendous respect for Western classical music,' Ma once told us. 'He had a framed photo of Beethoven in his room. When children asked him, "Whose photo is this?" Baba said, "यह बीथोवन है, वहाँ के तानसेन [He is Beethoven, the Tansen of the West."]'

Though music originated in India during the Vedic era, temples failed to patronize, music during the Middle Ages and subsequent periods. If it wasn't for kings, nawabs and rich landlords patronizing courtesans, music wouldn't have survived in India.

Throughout history, genius musicians were left with two options: sycophancy or dupery: 'To crawl and flatter' or 'To dupe and cheat'. Both were repugnant to the sensitive mind. Failing to do either of the two, genius musicians were left to rot in poverty and lost in oblivion. Naming current stars would ruffle too many feathers, so to make my point I'll limit this discussion to historical figures. Great musicians like Amir Khusrau, Tansen, etc., in India, and Bach, Haydn, etc., in Europe opted to 'crawl and flatter', Wagner opted to 'cheat', and Beethoven opted to 'dupe' some aristocrats for financial support. However, Beethoven's arrangement ended in bitter discordance, when Beethoven told

Prince Lichnowsky, 'What you are, you are by accident of birth; what I am, I am by myself. There are and will be a thousand princes; there is only one Beethoven.'

Mozart and his employer, the Archbishop Colloredo, nearly came to fisticuffs, and Mozart was dismissed. For the rest of his life, he remained a freelancer. Others escaped by claiming to work directly for God (Bruckner) or jointly with God (Scriabin). The fortunate ones just married rich and survived (Menuhin, Rachmaninoff, Piatigorsky, Hofmann).

In modern times, especially in socialistic democracies, music has suffered. Corporate sponsors are inconsistent. The rich and powerful may find the talented genius useful for furthering their political ambitions, social positions, prestige, or simply to satiate their narcissistic needs of basking in reflected glory.

The great composer was lonely, but his loneliness was self-inflicted. Beethoven had to abandon the desire of true love. He was all alone with his deafness, which is why he sought a substitute family in his nephew Karl, the son of his brother, who made him the boy's guardian before he died.

Years that could have been spent in creation were eaten up by Beethoven's legal battles for the sole custody of Karl, and his attempts to shape the boy as he would a piece of music. The predictable result was that Karl in his teen years felt suffocated and ran away, leaving Beethoven in tears ('He is ashamed of me!').

Then, he heard that Karl had attempted, but failed, to commit suicide, by trying to shoot himself in the head with not one, but a pair of pistols. Karl confessed to the presiding magistrate, 'I have become worse because my uncle insisted on making me better.' Beethoven's attempts to be a father ended in remorse.[34]

It is extremely difficult for an eccentric genius to be subservient. Baba, Khansaheb and Guru Ma all had a long list of their own set of eccentricities, so many that a volume can be written on the subject.

During the first half of his very long life, Baba, in his quest to learn music, underwent slavery. At Maihar, he resented the subservience and ritualistic pomp and protocols he had to adhere to at the court of His Highness Brijnathsingh. According to Jotin Bhattacharya, Baba's prolonged suppressed resentment manifested in the form of frequent angry outbursts. Khansaheb, too, despite being in dire need of money, was reluctant to cater to the whims and fancies of the maharaja of Jodhpur, who would summon him at any odd hour and command him to entertain with renditions on the sarod. The ordeal would go on for hours, with no empathy for Khansaheb's physical and mental exhaustion.

Ma had her own set of eccentricities. Living a reclusive life in itself was one of them. Reclusion comes as a package deal—reclusive people have unusual eating habits and living arrangements. This made Ma a difficult person to live with. Here are a few of her bizarre behavioural traits.

Diet

After Shubho's migration to the US (1970), and before Rooshiji's entry into 6A Akashganga (1982), Ma was careless about her dietary habits. She used to eat just once a day, that too a little rice with some lentils. Her diet had practically no micronutrients. However, she would cook a proper meal whenever she had to feed any of her disciples. They would bring her sweets, which though expensive, were certainly not healthy.

Cleanliness

From 1970 until 1985. Ma had no servants in her house. She had to clean and mop the floors herself, but the walls and ceilings remained untouched for years. Her house was too big to maintain all by herself. Ma would restrict her sweeping and mopping to her

bedroom, kitchen and living room, and the passage. The rest of
the house, that is, two rooms, two bathrooms, and a storeroom,
remained untouched for decades. Those rooms became worse
than haunted junkyards and would have been a perfect location
for shooting horror movies.

Unable to handle all this, Rooshiji hired a household help,
who would visit them for an hour each day and do the bathrooms,
etc. But only after prolonged negotiations could he convince Ma to
allow the domestic help to clean her room.

Adamant Nature

Ma didn't have opinions, she had verdicts. Right or wrong,
logical or illogical, rational or harmful, they were not negotiable.
Unfortunately, all her disciples were 'over-obedient' and
submissive. They failed to prevent her from committing blunders.
Ma interpreted disagreements as confrontations, and labelled
them as disobedience and disloyalty. Hence, she ended up being
surrounded by 'yes men'. After Rooshiji's demise, her health and
wealth suffered a lot because of this.

Solar Day, Lunar Day

To study the human biorhythm, Western scientists experimented
with a group of people by making them spend a period a month
in a cave with all provisions and resources but without sunlight
and without any kind of watch or clock. The study showed that
the biorhythm cycle of all subjects was twenty-four hours and fifty
minutes. As there is a delay of fifty minutes in moonrise each day,
their biorhythm seemed to be congruent with the moon's synodic
month.

This theory somewhat explains Ma's routine. Though there
was ample daylight pouring into Ma's house, and she was not as

cut off as the subjects in the cave during the above-mentioned experiment, Ma seldom looked out of the window, as if her windows were opaque or the world outside didn't exist. Ma's house had a breathtaking sea view. We all looked forward to gazing at the sky turning crimson as the sun drowned in the shiny waters of the Arabian Sea, but for Ma it just didn't exist.

Ma's daily routine kept getting delayed, gradually but consistently. Visiting her house was like entering a timeless zone. Until the early 1990s, the only timepiece there was a small mechanical table alarm clock next to her bed, the area which none of us had access to. The rest of the house had no wall clocks or table clocks. It was an unwritten law that none of us would look at our wristwatches as Ma would feel offended if we did so. Most of us, while playing our instruments, would remove our watches. There was an inexplicable energy in Ma's house that would take us into a trance-like state and make us lose awareness of time. The phenomenon was more intense than it sounds. There are several instances of people having missed their bus, train, flights, appointments, etc., while they were in her house.

OCD

Ma had dozens of habits that reflected her obsessive-compulsive disorder. For instance, she almost never cared to read the newspapers except once in a while glancing at the headlines on the front page. Yet, she never got rid of old newspapers. She would hoard and make piles of them all around the house. The obsession of cluttering up the house extended beyond old newspapers. As Suresh used to jokingly say, 'Ma's house is like a black hole. Once it's there, it's there.'

And the piles of clutter were not as harmless as they seemed— as they collected dust, Ma got a borderline asthmatic allergy. None of us, including Rooshiji and Dr Nitin, could ever convince her to get rid of the clutter.

However, there was a method in her madness. Nobody argued with Ma more than yours truly. Once, when she was in a good mood, I argued that she should remove the clutter. She explained her logic behind her piling it up, telling me that Khansaheb had multiple marriages and a dozen progeny, some of whom showed their desire to stay at Ma's house during their visits to Mumbai. They wanted to live in and get Maihar-like intensive training. There were also some disciples coming from outstation and overseas who would keep requesting Ma to accommodate them in the small room between Rooshiji's room and the living room. To discourage such guests, Ma had filled up all the empty space in the house with clutter.

Ma also had the weird habit of hiding currency notes inside the piles of old newspapers and other clutter. None of us were aware of this. When Ma was admitted to the hospital, we took the liberty of clearing the newspapers, only to realize later that we had unwittingly thrown away several thousand rupees hidden inside the junk.

Stock of Kerosene

The Nehruvian economic model was disastrous. The Licence Raj (the regulations and accompanying red tape that were required to set up and run businesses in India from 1947 until 1990) was so anti-commerce and anti-industry that it was impossible for the GDP to keep pace with the population burst. Every essential commodity was scarce. Despite her limited needs, Ma suffered a lot. In those days, you needed to bribe the local official to get LPG (cooking gas) cylinders. Every house had to keep a secondary line of the pressurized burner kerosene stove handy. For Ma, the kerosene stove became the sole cooking apparatus, and it emitted so much carbon that all the walls of her house turned smoky grey.

But kerosene too was scarce and black-marketed. Ma kept requesting her disciples to acquire a can for her. In their enthusiasm to please her, the disciples kept getting kerosene cans, and soon there was a roomful of stockpiles of kerosene. This was not only illegal, but also a serious fire hazard. A single spark, and Ma's kerosene stock could have doomed the Akashganga building to be a towering inferno. When Rooshiji learnt about this, he educated Ma about the fire hazard and the illegality of it, and went on to dispose of the stockpile.

Impaired Judgement of the Super-clairvoyant

We experienced and witnessed several instances of Ma's amazing clairvoyance which was indeed super-human. Yet, at times her judgement was foolishly illogical. I ought not to write too much about it, but just enough to explain that there was a series of childish, irrational, illogical decisions Ma took that resulted in her damaging both her health and wealth. Many of her decisions also proved disastrous for many of her disciples' careers.

In her last days, Ma became obsessed with folding tissue paper and arranging it in a certain manner. She was irrationally possessive of the tissue papers and would throw away currency notes.

Too many so-called well-wishers, nurses, Rooshiji's chauffeur, Rooshiji's relatives, Rooshiji's partners and business associates cheated Ma for money. All of them took unfair advantage of her infirmity. Due to senility, she would give away whatever money was demanded. Ma was a sitting-duck for the money hunters. It was painful for me to helplessly witness lakhs and lakhs of rupees going down the drain.

Rooshiji died on 13 April 2013. As per his last income tax returns and accounts ended 31 March, his net capital in a firm he was a partner in amounted to a few crore rupees. However, in fifteen days flat, his surviving partners claimed (without allowing us to verify their accounts) huge losses that ate away his entire capital in that firm.

I wanted to take legal actions against those surviving partners. I met the topmost lawyer of the Bombay High Court and he and his firm were ready to fight Ma's case free of charge, but Nityanand failed to get Ma's signature on the *vakalatnama* (the document empowering a lawyer to act for and on behalf of his client). Despite my highest respect for Nityanand for selflessly teaching me so much music and for being Ma's most devoted disciple, I dare to say that Nityanand, despite being at the helm, failed in his duty to prevent such a huge loss of Ma's funds. His argument was that Ma had declared, 'I don't want anything from Rooshiji's estate.' My argument was that despite guru bhakti, we couldn't be so blindly obedient to Ma, especially when she had gone senile. It was our duty to safeguard her interests, and we failed miserably.

In her will, Ma wanted to donate her entire estate for teaching, promoting and propagating Indian classical music. However, the investor banker who was in possession of Ma's investments had nothing to do with music and was so obsessed with Buddhism that he suggested to Ma, 'उससे तो अच्छा है एक पेगोड़ा बना दो [Better to erect a pagoda instead.]'

Ma had nothing to do with Buddhism, nor she had ever heard the word 'pagoda'. After the gentleman left, Ma asked us, 'यह पकोडा क्या होता है [What is this pakora?]' We laughed at her question and explained, 'माँ, पकोडा नहीं पगोड़ा। बुद्ध भगवान के मंदिर को पगोड़ा कहते है [Ma, he said pagoda, not pakora. A pagoda is a Buddhist temple.]'

Ma was aghast. She exclaimed, 'मैं क्या संगीत को न देते, पगोड़ा बनाने पैसे दूँगी? [Why would I donate my estate to a pagoda instead of music?]'

I am not doubting the integrity of this gentleman of high repute; however, his arguments made us think. To begin with, he had no respect for Nityanand, believing he had neither the skill, nor the mindset, nor the experience to handle the funds. Well, there were several others who were of the same opinion, but they all said so only behind Ma's and Nityanand's backs.

What was most shocking was when we asked the investor about Ma's and Rooshiji's portfolio, he said, 'I am not answerable to any of you. I am answerable only to Rooshiji and Ma.' He was right, but with Rooshiji dead, and Ma suffering from senile dementia, it only meant that he was not answerable to anyone alive on this planet.

Inconsistent Behaviour

Rooshiji, with his acute narcissism, had several ridiculously flashy tailor-made diamond-studded gold rings, diamond buttons, pure gold Rolex watches and other valuables. When he died, these items were sent for valuation. Ma became a bit agitated and kept asking us, 'Why haven't they returned Rooshiji's jewellery? Their intentions seem doubtful.' I phoned the gentleman and gave him the hint. The gentleman came to return all the valuables, but Ma said, 'What am I going to do with all these? You keep it.' The gentleman went back with all the jewellery and watches.

The biggest victim of Ma's inconsistent behaviour was Nityanand. Many disciples and relatives, and even journalists and artistes, kept visiting Ma to meet her for darshan. Ma as a rule would refuse them all. However, at times, she would allow them to meet her with a conditional instruction to Nityanand, 'In two minutes flat they should leave my room.' However, after a few minutes when Nityanand would request them to leave the room, Ma would contradict Nityanand by saying, 'Let them sit, they have come from such a long distance to meet me.'

Linguistic Bias

There were numerous instances of Ma's bias in favour of those who spoke Bengali. A case in point was Tathagata Ray Chowdhury. When he approached, Ma refused to give him an appointment, but eventually agreed after a lot of pleading. She instructed Nityanand to allow him to see her just for a few minutes but insisted that she wouldn't give an interview. However, she ended up giving a very long one. The entire conversation was in Bengali, so Nityanand could not verify whether Ma had said what Tathagata published.

She never allowed any of her disciples to photograph her. I could have easily taken her photograph without her knowledge, but, as her disciple, I had no choice but to respect her wish. However, she ended up giving a video interview to Shekhar Sen. I am one of his biggest fans for both his talent and his nature, but the film Sangeet Natak Akademi made on Ma is unpardonably poor.

'The Last Man In' Syndrome

In her last years, because of her mental infirmity, Ma suffered from what we call 'The Last Man In' syndrome. She would agree with each person interacting with her, regardless of how contradictory their versions would be. In such a case, the obvious winner would be the person who had met her the last.

Fanaticism of Precision

As Nityanand was working with All India Radio, he once happened to tell us the precise time broadcast on the radio. We considered it to be useless trivia for Ma, but she wanted to learn about it as if it was a question of life and death.

'On the odd hours the Bombay A station, and on the even hours Bombay B station of All India Radio announces the precise time,' Nityanand explained. 'There are four short pips followed by a long pip indicating the precise stroke of the hour.'

Ma was quite well-versed with radio, yet she brought a pen and paper to write down the frequency of the radio stations 'Bombay A' and 'Bombay B'.

'Bombay A is 1044 kHz, and Bombay B is 558 kHz,' Nityanand informed.

Thenceforth, every day, Ma would eagerly wait for the fifth peep of the hour on the radio to adjust her clock with engineering precision to the fifth long pip. Mechanical clocks are not as precise as electronic clocks, but there was absolutely no need to do this exercise every day. Even if the arm of her table clock was a millimetre off, Ma would correct it, as if she was tuning the main string of her surbahār, and the fifth pip was the most important rhythm beat of her life.

Nityanand tried to reason with her, 'Ma, you don't have to reach anywhere, you have no flight or train to catch. You are not expecting anyone. Even your disciples are not given a fixed time to arrive at your place. You just ask them to come on Monday evening or Thursday evening. Then what is the point of fretting so much over the precise setting of your alarm clock?'

Ma had no explanation to give.

A Psychiatrist's Perspective

Dr Ashit Sheth.

I once interviewed Dr Ashit Sheth, a world-renowned professor of psychiatry.

How did you get acquainted with Guru Ma?

My acquaintance with Annapurnaji was because of Rooshibhai. I attended his seminar on hypnosis and learnt that he hailed from Ahmedabad and knew my uncle's family. He had emigrated to

North America and annually visited India to hold training seminars. For seven years, during all his visits to Bombay, he used to stay at my residence. When he finally came back to stay in India, he resided with us till he got married to Annapurnaji. Vallabh Bhansali and I were the two legal witnesses to their civil marriage.

What was your assessment of her mindset at that time?

The incidents of Annapurnaji's playing music with Ravi Shankar and the subsequent drama of his jealousy is well known. I came to know her very late in her life. I could perceive that face was hiding years of agony behind a sweet smile. Her eyes conveyed deep melancholy. I could sense that she was a simple woman with no high aspirations.

With the help of Rooshibhai, I gained some more insight about her past. Ma was born and brought up in Maihar. Her father, Guru Ut. Allauddin Khan, was orthodox, and she had a very conservative and traditional upbringing. Around the early and middle of the twentieth century, women did not get much opportunity to get educated and pursue a career. It was a male-dominated society. A woman's role revolved around her husband and children. Every woman was expected to give in to the demands of her husband and in-laws. Her mother, Madina Begum, had personally gone through a challenging period in her marriage. Her elder sister too had died after being tortured by her in-laws. All these incidents must have left a deep impression on Annapurnaji's mind.

Most musicians and performing artistes face difficulties in coping with the problems of reality. They do not get an opportunity to learn survival skills to face the complexities of the world. Right from childhood, they spend their time and energy rigorously practising their art. This requires total devotion. Annapurnaji was cheated by many but that did not affect her. Her vow not to give any public performances kept her away from the negativity of the music world.

She could laugh at people who fell prey to money and publicity. Her focus was on teaching and it remained on teaching only.

Artistes are highly emotional people, and creativity involves converting these unstructured emotions into a structured piece of art. A proficient artiste, through music, conveys their feelings to the heart of the audience. Annapurnaji was a true artiste, and she had mastered putting her emotion into the strings of her surbahār.

What would you say about her failed marriage with Panditji?

From early childhood, she showed brilliance in learning music. She was fortunate that her father was a great maestro. Her very first performance proved her superior competence. Unfortunately, she was victimized for her excellent abilities by her jealous husband.

Before marriage, a traditional Indian woman is dependent on her parents. After marriage, she is dependent on her husband and expects him to treat her with respect and dignity. Her upbringing taught her to sacrifice her privileges for the comfort of her husband and children.

Annapurnaji had a similar expectation from her marriage to Ravi Shankar. She knew her future husband well as he had spent many years at her house for training. She was a simple woman with simple expectations. She just wanted to value her marriage, her son and her music. She didn't anticipate that Ravi Shankar would turn out to be the dominating, ruthless, promiscuous and jealous husband to push his way on to a newly married unassuming mild wife. This scenario is an oft-repeated theme in Indian marriages. Generally, Indian women tend to view their husbands' infidelity as a reflection of something that is wrong in them. They feel responsible for their husbands' interest in other women. Ravi Shankar's extramarital affairs and his lack of compassion on the family front is a well-publicized fact. Annapurnaji's life became a series of unhappy incidents, and with every crisis, coping became difficult for her.

Annapurnaji just gave in to Ravi Shankar's demands to keep him happy and preserve their marriage. Under pressure, she took a vow not to give any public performance, but despite that, the marriage couldn't be saved. Her husband walked out on her and left her alone with an infant son. Later, her beloved son, Shubho, was snatched away from her. She had no skills to assert and protect her interest against Ravi Shankar.

In my experience, women bound by tradition live by one rule, and that is to buy 'peace' by accepting whatever the husband desires. Many women falsely believe that wisdom will dawn upon him and he would realize her value and return. I think that she understood quite early in life that her husband was never going to stand by her side.

How do you explain jealousy among artistes?

It is not easy to be an artiste. No matter how deserving they may be, a performing artiste does not get the deserved recognition until they give public performances. When they start getting recognition for their hard work, many musicians become victims of insecurity, jealousy and rivalry. There is perpetual fear of losing their success. Very few are capable of dealing with this fear. This emotional turmoil influences their personal and artistic life. Even at the height of success, these negative emotions interfere with their life. Many become victims of sleep problems, alcohol abuse, extramarital affairs and inferior respect for close relationships.

Why did she become a recluse?

As a psychiatrist, I wondered how she coped with her life, staying alone in this vast flat. After her disciples left in the evening, she would be in total isolation till the next evening or the next few days. I asked myself whether it was by choice or by compulsion. I soon realized that she had selected this solitude calculatedly.

Anthony Storr, a psychoanalyst, mentions in his book *Solitude* the advantages of being away from the world's intrusive noise. Solitude is different from loneliness. Loneliness is involuntary, destructive and painful. People fear loneliness and avoid it. Isolation too is known to be stressful. Solitude is removing the self voluntarily from social humdrum. It promotes self-understanding and allows a person to remain in contact with the inner depth. German poet Goethe very aptly has said, 'One can be instructed in society, one is inspired only in solitude.' Being alone allows one to contact the inner depths of being, enhancing one's mental freedom from worldly bondages.

Was she suffering from depression?

The records of her medical history don't show a single instance of antidepressants prescribed to her. What may seem like depression to a layperson like you is actually prolonged grief, which was handled very well by Rooshibhai without any medications. Rooshibhai's presence in her life was instrumental in reducing her grief and her insecurities. She felt more secure; her life gradually regained normalcy. She resumed teaching. She regained her sharp wit and sense of humour.

Could you help us understand her psychological make-up?

Anna Freud, daughter of Sigmund Freud, and George Valliant, Harvard professor of psychiatry, describe various adaptive defence mechanisms. They are normal and natural. Whenever the mind is stressed, it unconsciously resorts to a specific set pattern of behaviour, depending on adaptive capacity. Freud and Valliant divide mental mechanisms into 'immature' or 'mature'. Immature mental mechanisms are 'projections'—where a person feels that others are responsible for their problems—or 'displacement'—

where a wife displaces anger against her mother-in-law on her children or husband.

Mature mental mechanisms help individuals actualize their potential. Annapurnaji personally suffered from a series of traumatic situations in her life. How could she have the strength to face so many problems? She had two important mechanisms to protect her against the long-term effects of stress. First, her devotion to music. It is a well-known fact that music, especially classical music, has healing powers. Second, she selflessly taught music. Her personal pains would be resolved by practising and teaching music. This mature mental mechanism is called sublimation. Her sorrows, pains and sufferings were unconsciously converted into her musical prowess.

Another factor in her life that was glaringly apparent was her aversion to any temptation. Neither money nor glory distracted her from her chosen path; she was devoted to teaching without any expectation from her disciples. Anna Freud and Valliant call this attribute 'altruism' which they describe as the ability of an individual to give without expectation.[35]

How would you explain her irrational attitude towards money?

Money was never important to her. She willingly or unwillingly allowed greedy people to take advantage of her. When told, 'This is your money, why don't you demand it?', her simple answer was, 'What will I do with this money?' I would leave it to readers to decide whether this was a virtue or a weakness.

Her character's strongest point was her conscience and her ability to stick to what she believed in without compromise. It helped her in two ways. It made her stronger to protect her music from getting corrupted by money while she witnessed the contamination of traditional Indian classical music for the same. And it gave her the strength to look down on those who ran after

cash. She also refrained from publicity as she thought it to be
cheap and frivolous. All those who were trained by her fell prey
to those superficial temptations; she was the only one who did not
succumb. She always taunted Rooshibhai in front of me about his
tendency to run after material gains.

What made her so rigid?

What happens to people who go through emotional trauma is
their personality develops a certain rigidity in thinking, feeling and
behaviour. This rigidity was apparent in Annapurnaji. In a normal
individual, values go through modification as you grow older. Your
conscience develops flexibility and adapts to evolving situations. In
her case, her conscience took a different form. The rigidity of her
values dominated her behaviour. Many wanted to learn under her,
but only devoted candidates were eligible. Her demands were high,
difficult to fulfil, and she would not compromise. Many would leave
halfway as they couldn't cope. She never bowed down to anybody,
at the same time she never asked any favours from anyone. She
generously gave the only things she had: music and love.

Anything else you would like to share?

Annapurnaji regularly visited the NCPA to teach music. They
insisted on recording her recital for their archives but she
persistently refused to do so. The matter went to the then prime
minister, Indira Gandhi, who requested Annapurnaji to record her
recital for the NCPA archives, which she declined. She requested
the PMO to make her two doctor friends life members of the
NCPA. Immediately her request was granted, and my wife and I
got the life membership. I always remember her whenever I attend
any performances at the NCPA.

Leenta Vaze

Leenta Vaze

I requested Leenta, Ma's student from Pune, to write her experiences with Ma. Her narrative follows.

I hail from Pune and am married into a family of musicians. I was already a musician playing the sitār at AIR Pune and the Films Institute, but it was all light music. I didn't know much about Indian classical music. Sometime in 1977–78, during his visit to Pune, my father-in-law's friend, Pt Anant Kunte, the sarangi player, on realizing my quest for a guru, gave me the address of Annapurna Devi.

I immediately went to the Pune railway station and caught the first available train to Bombay. It was quite an adventure for me, a girl in her twenties, to go to a city like Bombay all alone, that too for the first time—I had never been to Bombay.

When I reached the sixth floor of Akashganga, Annapurna Devi was on her way out. I paid my obeisance by touching her feet and told her that I had come to learn from her. She said, 'Look, I have stopped teaching girls. In order to learn, one needs to come to me uninterrupted for twelve years. But the girls get married, have kids and give up music. All my time and efforts are wasted.'

'I am already married and my kids are grown up enough to be autonomous. So, there is no likelihood of interruption in the tālim.'

'Right now, I have to leave as pupils are waiting for me at the NCPA. You may come tomorrow.'

'But I am from Pune. I came to Bombay just to meet you. I have nowhere to spend the night.'

On hearing this, she took me along with her to the NCPA. There she asked me to play the sitār, with Anantramji accompanying me on the tablā.

After gauging my proficiency, Ma made me sit beside her and said, 'I will teach you, but first you have to train yourself to develop control over your instrument. Until then you won't be allowed to give a public performance of solo renditions.'

I readily agreed.

She then took my address and said that she would intimate me by post when to come for the lessons. I was moved by her caring gesture of asking an elderly male disciple of hers to escort me to

VT station. I couldn't really see his face as he sat in the front seat next to the driver and I sat in the backseat right behind him.

I was so excited that I was going to learn from Annapurna Devi that my impatience got the better of me. Without waiting for Guru Ma's intimation, I went to her for my lessons uninvited; not once but thrice, only to be sent away each time with a stern rebuke. The fourth time, I took my mother along.

Guru Ma politely welcomed my mother, with me hiding behind her. On a chosen Thursday, my training began. She explained to me that by sending me away with stern rebukes, she was testing my tenacity; something she had been doing with all her disciples.

As time went by, the duration of the lessons increased. The result was that I kept missing my return train to Pune. I therefore had to spend the night in the waiting room of VT station. This happened about two or three times. Except my husband, nobody knew about this, but to my utter surprise, Ma came to know. Till date it has remained an unsolved mystery for me how Ma found out. When I shared this with my gurubhais Nityanand, Suresh and Atul, they were not surprised at all, as they have experienced numerous such instances of Ma's clairvoyance. With the help of someone, Ma found a hostel accommodation for me, but the hostel fees were so high that I couldn't afford it. Ma then arranged for me to stay with my *gurubhagini* [a female fellow disciple] Nanda Sardesai who stayed at a distance of about 2 km from Akashganga.

Once, during Diwali, I came to Bombay for eight days and requested her, 'Maji, I haven't clearly understood how to play the jod. If you could allow me to come to you and learn the jod for the next eight days.'

'Crazy girl!' Ma exclaimed. 'In these festival days, you left your family and came to Bombay to learn music!'

Ma taught me the jod for eight consecutive days, and those eight days were the most blissful days of my life.

I was in dire financial straits when I got a contract offer from the Blue Diamond Hotel, the only five-star hotel in Pune then. They were offering to pay me a decent amount of money to play in their restaurant six days a week. However, when I sought Ma's permission, she expressed her displeasure, saying, 'You'll be playing in the restaurant where people will be busy eating, drinking, chatting, laughing. Playing Baba's music in such an environment, that too a decent girl like you, doesn't seem appropriate to me. I know you are in need of money, but you don't need to do all this. With Shārdā Ma and Baba's blessings, your difficult time shall soon pass.'

Miraculously, within a few days after she said this, I started getting many tuitions and invitations to play in musical programmes. I ended up making more money than I would have playing in the restaurant.

My learning from Guru Ma came to a sudden stop when I met with a road accident, followed by hip replacement surgery, followed by other health issues. Ma too was ailing with age-related issues and was bedridden. She consoled me, saying, 'Music is a constant sādhanā. It takes the persistent endeavour of many lifetimes to attain moksha. Sādhaks are reborn in a suitable environment where they reawaken the wisdom of their previous lives, and resume their sādhanā. With the accumulated efforts of past births, these sādhaks engage in a sincere endeavour to progress further to attain moksha.'

These words had a profound impact on me. I underwent a transformation. My attitude towards life changed dramatically. It liberated me from my anxieties and regrets.

Finale

एष सर्वेश्वर एष सर्वज्ञ एषोऽन्तर्याम्येष ।
योनिः सर्वस्य प्रभवाप्ययौ हि भूतानाम् ।।

*[The world outside and the world within
rise up from the pure Consciousness,
exist in this Consciousness, and when
the Consciousness is withdrawn,
merge back into the Consciousness Itself]*
—*Mandukya Upanishad* (1.1.6)

The Annapurna Mountain: the Himalayas.

Dr Nitin Shah was Ma and Rooshiji's physician for decades, and Ma was rather comfortable with him. However, Dr Nitin himself got admitted in the hospital and couldn't visit Ma for quite some time. After his recovery when he visited Ma, he apologized for his absence and, in the same breath, lamented that he was not sure how long he would survive.

Ma as usual told Dr Nitin that she had no interest in living and asked if he could give her some injection to end the ordeal. He laughed and said, 'Ma, if I do so, Nityanand will take me to the cops and I will be hanged on charges of murder. I'd rather take the exit before you do.' His words proved prophetic. Dr Nitin Shah died a year before Ma did.

When Ma was taken for an MRI scan, she repeated the same dialogue to the consultant doctor there who readily prescribed anti-depressant pills. These pills didn't make any difference to Ma's mindset. I guess Western medical science is unable to differentiate between vairagya and depression simply because the concept of vairagya is not there in their culture. They vaguely translate it with the words like 'dispassion', 'detachment', which are unable to explain the concept. Vairagya is the realization that all that we perceive through our senses as the physical world and the world that we create in our minds are actually illusionary, impermanent and devoid of essence, which doesn't merit importance.

Nityanand was in search of a suitable general physician who would visit Ma. Mumbai city had more and more clinics and hospitals coming up each day. As all new doctors aim to become specialists, general physicians had become an endangered species.

Once, in the dead of the night, my telephone rang. Such phone calls invariably bring bad news, and after the one that informed of Rooshiji's sudden demise, the phone ringing at such an hour invariably makes me panicky. The phone screen showed · 'Nityanand'.

'Ma's health has deteriorated, but she is refusing to get hospitalized,' Nityanand said in a worried tone. 'Do you know of any doctor who can visit her at this hour?'

I thought for a moment. Geographically, the nearest was Dr Mahesh Balsekar, who was also a cousin of Nityanand's wife. So, I gave Nityanand Dr Balsekar's number.

'Hello, Mahesh?' Nityanand spoke in a hesitant voice.

'Speaking.' Dr Balsekar replied.

'This is Nityanand Haldipur. Sorry to bother you at such an odd hour, but Ma's health has deteriorated. After Dr Nitin Shah's demise, we don't have any general physician who could visit her at this hour. If you could suggest any.'

'Why don't we hospitalize her?' Dr Balsekar suggested.

'No! Ma is adamant against hospitalization.'

'Look, I am actually a paediatrician, but it would be an honour to be of any service to such a great lady,' Dr Balsekar replied. 'If you allow me, I can reach there in a few minutes.'

Mahesh Balsekar is a doctor and a healer. He is not only my schoolmate, but he, his wife and daughter are like extended family to us, especially to my elder sister. As a rule, children are scared of doctors, but all the children of our family look forward to visiting their favourite Mahesh Uncle. He is an ardent lover of Indian classical music, and as music is the ultimate bond, Ma was extremely comfortable with him. Dr Balsekar kept visiting her and kept refusing to accept any fees.

In the early hours of 12 October 2018, Ma sank into a semi-conscious state. Dr Balsekar said that Ma was suffering from hypostatic pneumonia and was sinking. Nityanand was in a dilemma. It was indeed a catch-22 situation—if he took Ma to the hospital it would be going against her wish; if he didn't, he would be blamed for not giving her due medical treatment. It was decided that she would be taken to the hospital. According to Dr Balsekar, the attempt was more to give her a smoother exit and less on delaying the inevitable by artificial means. On the morning of 13 October, Ma was declared dead.

> Tiny droplets from the ocean of eternity evaporated to form a cloud, soared to unprecedented altitude, travelled northeast to condense on the highest summit of the mighty Himalayas, dwelled there as shiny-white snow away from humanity, gradually melting downhill as the Ganges, quenching the thirst of a lucky few to finally remerge with the ocean of eternity.

Epilogue

भ्रमभृतमिदं सर्वं किंचिन्नास्तीति निश्चयी।
अलक्ष्यस्फुरणः शुद्धः स्वभावेनैव शाम्यति॥

*[The Pure One knows with certitude that this universe is
the product of illusion, and that nothing really exists
The Imperceptible Self is revealed to him
and he naturally becomes tranquil]*
—*Ashtavakra Geeta* (xviii-70)

In the early 1980s, when I was new to Ma and her world, I used to think her renunciation was a mental disorder. My persistent attempt was to pull her out of her reclusion and make her give public performances or a series of studio recordings. Did I succeed? Of course not.

At the time of my father's sudden untimely death and the subsequent reversal of fortunes, I was a college student. For the rest of my life, I have always pondered about death. Each day, en route to work, I used to pass by Marine Lines where a graveyard and two crematoriums (electric and conventional) are located. Corpses being taken for burial or cremation was a common sight on that route, serving a repeated reminder about the inevitability of death, which could strike anyone at any time—in the end, we are nothing but ashes and dust.

The thought of death invariably leads us to the fundamental questions which have haunted humankind since time immemorial. Who am I? Where did I come from? Where will I go? Why am I here? What is the meaning of life? What is the purpose of existence? The answers to these questions remain elusive.

In the pursuit of making a living, I used to spend my weekdays in the gem and jewellery industry, full of greedy, unscrupulous scamsters frittering away their existence in the rat race, each on their own hamster wheel of futility. Visiting Ma's house on Saturday nights was like entering an altogether different world. The more I came to know Ma, the more I was influenced by her way of looking at things, and the worse off I became in my worldly pursuits. I was torn between the two worlds, unable to adjust to either one.

न मिला ख़ुदा न हुआ विसाल-ए-सनम, न इधर के हुए न उधर के

I didn't have the courage to follow Ma's footsteps by renouncing everything to pursue music as a sādhanā. To focus on my career, I decided to quit music, but I couldn't stop visiting Ma's house. There was something that kept pulling me there and kept transforming me. A stage came when the futility of my existence started bothering me. It led me to contemplate that there had to be more to life than struggling to earn, striving to possess, labouring to hoard and hurrying to spend with the instinct of exhibitionism. I started losing interest in worldly pursuits and was drawn deeper into music and Vedanta philosophy.

I am now in a state where people taunt that I am becoming a bit of a recluse, like Ma. For the last two decades, I've stopped visiting restaurants, cinemas, public concerts and public events. Being a person who advocates teetotalism, I hate pubs, loathe parties, and just can't tolerate crowds. High-decibel sounds make me sick. My annual family holidays are invariably at secluded, forested mountain destinations. For years, I haven't visited a shopping mall. I've lost all business ambitions. Nothing satiates me more than practising the ālaap on my sarod. My eccentricities have proliferated. My solace is that I am not the only one showing such traits. Most of Ma's disciples, like Suresh Vyas, Nityanand, Basant Kabra and his daughter Devyani, Hemant Desai, Sandhya, Amit Bhattacharya, are even more reclusive than I am.

We live in a नाशवंत ephemeral world. Even the longest life is too short. Baba, Ma, Khansaheb, Panditji, Panna Babu, Nikhilda, Bahadur Khan, Sharan Rani and others are all dead and gone. The way our culture is changing, future generations seem quite likely to shun Hindustani classical music. These great maestros and their works will sink into oblivion. Whenever we think about it, the question keeps haunting us: What is the meaning of all this?

Metaphorically, life is a perpetual cellular confinement. All beings are incarcerated in solitary cells; each cell having blank white walls without a window or a door. Each inmate is given a magical set of colours and a brush. Whatever image each inmate paints on his wall becomes a reality for him.

Some use their brush and paints to create an image of cornucopia of exotic food and wine, and they end up having a grand feast. And the moment they exhaust their bounty, they paint more. Some seek comfort and create images of objects of luxury. Some paint flora–fauna and exotic landscapes and bask in their beauty. Some paint erotica, some paint horror. Some write poems on their walls and some paint portraits of their folks to have a bash of frolic and fun with them. Those who paint trophies get awards and accolades and those who paint money have their cell full of currency notes.

Sooner or later, every inmate wears his brush out, runs out of paints or wall space. Such inmates are taken out of their cell and thrown into another cell with fresh white blank walls and a new set of paints and brush. They resume their fancies all over again in their new cell. It is a never-ending story.

However, those who paint an image of a window get to peer outside their cells. They are the ones who realize there exists an infinite world beyond the walls of the cell they are incarcerated in. The wise inmate who creates an image of a door, for him the door become his reality. He gets to exit the confinement.

Ma and Baba were among the rare few who used every ounce of their share of paints and brushes to create a door. They were not interested in the wine-and-dine or fun and frolic. They sought an exit from perpetual incarceration.

The last photograph taken a few days before her demise.

बज़्म से दूर वो गाता रहा तन्हा तन्हा
सो गया साज़ पे सर रख के सहर से पहले

[Away from Humanity,
She kept playing her music in seclusion
Resting her forehead on her instrument,
She passed out before the break of dawn]
—*Makhdoom Mohihuddin*

Acknowledgements

I am grateful to my gurubhais: Nityanand Haldipur, Hemant Desai, Basant Kabra, Suresh Vyas, Pradeep Barot, Sunil Shastri, Sashwati, Sandhya, Leenata and Meena for their help and contribution, due to which I have been able to compile and write this book.

To my gurubhai Amit Bhattacharya, who was kind enough to allow me to borrow the contents from his father Pt Jotin Bhattacharya's book *Ustad Allauddin Khan Aur Hum Sab*. Since the book is written in Bengali, a language I don't understand, Amit Bhattacharya sent me copies of the magazine *Sangeet* published by Sangeet Karyalay, Hathras where the Hindi translation has been published in parts in their monthly editions.

I am grateful to Pt Hariprasad Chaurasia for his kind gesture in writing the foreword, and Ms Kasturi and Rajiv Chaurasia for their kindness and help, especially by introducing me to Ms Sathya Saran, my guardian angel.

I thank Ashishda for his blessings, and for the stories he contributed.

I am grateful to Sagarika Biswas. There has to be a celestial plan, as Sagarika lives in Sydney and I live in Mumbai. We've never met and yet she has been of tremendous help and encouragement in writing this book. Sagarika introduced me to Munmun Mittra, who again is godsent in the fullest sense of the term. Purely out of love and respect for Baba and Guru Ma, and with no self-interest whatsoever, Munmun, in record time, edited and transformed all the angularities and idiosyncrasies in my language and made it a sublime read. I am yet to meet Munmun in person.

I am grateful for Matt Dubuque from San Francisco, a lawyer by profession, a true sādhak and a philanthropist whose heroic deeds have saved numerous lives. Matt is someone I've never met or spoken to even over the phone as all our communications have been through email. Music is the only bond between us. Matt encouraged me to write this book. He has not only extended his invaluable help in editing the language, but with his educated guidance, he has helped me raise the book to an altogether different level. I shall forever remain indebted to Matt.

I thank my friend Pavan Lall for his valuable guidance and help.

I am grateful to Kishore Merchant for his selfless guidance and encouragement in all my pursuits, especially this one. People in music circles believe he is my elder brother. How I wish he was.

Manisha Doctor is another godsent person who has been kind enough to be my partner in many music projects. I am grateful for her interest and valuable feedback in writing this book.

Right from nursery school, my classmate Sonal Vora has always encouraged me in all my creative and spiritual pursuits, especially this one. I am grateful for her help and guidance in writing this book.

I am thankful to Bina Shah and Amisha Adatia for their deep interest in this project and for their encouragement and valuable suggestions.

Dr Ashit Sheth was the first one who suggested that I write such a book. I am grateful for his detailed interview which is a valuable inclusion in this book.

I am fortunate to have a family that allows me to 'waste' my time and money in the pursuit of things 'beyond the horizon' that don't bring home a single dime.

My last salutations are to my wife, Jalpa, who knows my imperfections, yet loves me. I am fortunate to have a spouse who respects my daydreaming as she understands that when I am lost in my prolonged pensive spells of deep contemplations, something creative in music or writing could be brewing.

Notes

1   Henry Wadsworth Longfellow, 'The Ladder of St Augustine'.

2   *Jawab-e-Shikwa* (The Answer) was written by Allama Iqbal in 1912, which is a response to the book *Shikwa* written by Allama Iqbal in 1909. In *Shikwa*, he had complained to Allah about the condition of Muslims and asked many questions about its cause. In *Jawab-e-Shikwa*, he has tried to answer these questions.

3   Jotin Bhattacharya, *Ustad Allauddin Khan Aur Hum Sab* (Hathras: Sangeet Karyalaya, 2007), p. 31.

4   Ibid.

5   https://www.biography.com/musician/ravi-shankar; https://www.lifepositive.com/the-highest-form-in-music-is-sprituality/

6   Bhattacharya, *Ustad Allauddin Khan Aur Hum Sab*.

7   https://rec.music.indian.classical.narkive.com/FWUPPdRA/the-emperor-of-sitar

8   *The Hindu*, 'No Compromise in His Art: An Interview with Vilayat Khan', 28 March 2004. Retrieved 12 October 2020.

9   We the disciples have together written this as narrated to us by Annapurna Devi first-hand. Also published in Bhattacharya, *Ustad Allauddin Khan Aur Hum Sab*, p. 31.

10 Swapn Kumar Bondyopadhyay, *An Unheard Melody: The Authorised Biography* (Delhi: Roli Books), pp. 83–84.

11 http://archive.indianexpress.com/news/notes-from-behind-a-locked-door/619877/6.

12 https://lookingfromsolitude.tumblr.com/post/37918648438/ annapurna-devi-ravi-shankar-the-tragedy-of-a-relationship; https://www.kuaf.com/post/she-was-poised-be-star-instead-she-spent-60-years-her-apartment#stream/0

13 https://www.kuaf.com/post/she-was-poised-be-star-instead-she-spent-60-years-her-apartment#stream/0; https://mumbaimirror.indiatimes.com/entertainment/ music/legendary-loss/articleshow/66192717.cms

14 https://mumbaimirror.indiatimes.com/entertainment/music/ legendary-loss/articleshow/66192717.cms

15 https://mumbaimirror.indiatimes.com/entertainment/music/ legendary-loss/articleshow/66192717.cms

16 Bhattacharya, *Ustad Allauddin Khan Aur Hum Sab*, p. 29.

17 https://dhvaniohio.org/wp-content/uploads/2018/12/ Annapurna-Devi.pdf.

18 Bondyopadhyay, *An Unheard Melody: The Authorised Biography*.

19 Bhattacharya, *Ustad Allauddin Khan Aur Hum Sab*.

20 Ibid.

21 Ibid.

22 Ibid., p. 25.

23 Ibid., p. 20.

24 Sandy Hotchkiss, *Why Is It Always About You?: The Seven Deadly Sins of Narcissism.*

25 Bhattacharya, *Ustad Allauddin Khan Aur Hum Sab*, p. 21.

26 Ibid.

27 Ibid., p. 28.

28 https://www.nationalheraldindia.com/people/ali-akbar-khan-maestro-who-displayed-technical-finesse-and-stirring-intensity.

29 Bhattacharya, *Ustad Allauddin Khan Aur Hum Sab.*

30 Ibid., p. 33.

31 Ibid.

32 Ibid.

33 Sharan Rani, *The Divine Sarod: An Ancient Indian Musical Instrument (Antiquity, Origin and Development from Circa 200 BC)* (Sangeet Kala Bhawan, 1992).

34 Jane Swafford, *Beethoven: Anguish and Triumph* (Faber and Faber).

35 G.E. Vaillant, *International Encyclopedia of the Social & Behavioral Sciences* (2001).